R. J. Hanavan

worship:

initiation
and the
churches

worship:

initiation
and the
churches

Leonel L. **mitchell**

The Pastoral Press
Washington, DC

ISBN: 0-912405-84-8

The Pastoral Press
225 Sheridan Street, N.W.
Washington, D.C. 20011
(202) 723-1254

The Pastoral Press is the publications division of the National Association of Pastoral Musicians, a membership organization of musicians and clergy dedicated to fostering the art of musical liturgy.

Printed in the United States of America

Contents

Introduction

THIRTY YEARS AGO, IN 1961, MY FIRST ARTICLE ON CHRISTIAN INITIA-
tion appeared in print, a study of the then newly discovered
baptismal homilies of John Chrysostom.[1] The following year
my study of the Ambrosian baptismal liturgy, chapter 4 of this
volume, appeared in the first volume of the new journal *Studia
Liturgica*. By then I was writing my doctoral dissertation,
"Baptismal Anointing,"[2] under the direction of H. Boone Porter, Jr. It was he who started me on the study of Christian initiation. I do not claim that Dr. Porter taught me everything I
know about liturgics, but he did teach me something much
more useful: how to find out most of what I know, and for
that I am profoundly grateful and deeply in his debt.

In 1964 I was appointed a consultant to the Standing Liturgical Commission of the Episcopal Church and began the pre-
paratory work for the revision of the baptismal liturgy in The
Book of Common Prayer.[3] In 1971 Aidan Kavanagh invited me
to join the faculty of the Graduate Program in Liturgical Studies at the University of Notre Dame. So, while working on the
revision of the Episcopal baptismal liturgy, I was introducing
the brand new study edition of the RCIA to graduate liturgy
students. Since 1978 I have been Professor of Liturgics at Seabury-Western Theological Seminary, attempting to teach ordi-
nands the theology and practice of the revised rites.

In one way or another the study of Christian initiation has
been a primary element in my work since 1961, and is an area

in which I continue to speak and write. My principal scholarly and pastoral interest has been the relationship of confirmation to baptism, and of chrismation to the laying on of hands. The essays in this volume were written at various times over the past thirty years and present a fairly balanced picture of my work in the area. I have attempted to revise and update them, especially where significant new developments have occurred since their original publication, but they still bear the marks of their varied origins.

Chapter 1, "The 'Shape' of the Baptismal Liturgy," was originally a position paper for the opening meeting of the Drafting Committee on Christian Initiation of the Episcopal Church.[4] In it I drew practical conclusions about the traditional "shape" of the initiation rites from the research I had done for my book *Baptismal Anointing*. For the present volume, I thoroughly revised the paper in the light of the actual revisions made since 1965.

Chapter 2, "Baptismal Catechesis from Hippolytus to Augustine," was my contribution to a book on issues in the history of catechesis.[5] It provides a good introduction to the content of the classical catechumenate, and a background for the study both of its subsequent decline and its contemporary revival.

Chapter 3 was originally published in India as part of a volume on the baptismal rites of the Syrian Church,[6] to which Indian Christians look as the source of their tradition. It gives us a glimpse of four Syrian theologians of the fourth and fifth centuries expounding the meaning of Chistian initiation in that tradition.

Chapter 4 and Chapter 5 present the baptismal rites of two major non-Roman liturgies of the Latin West, Milan and Spain.[7] Both have always been of particular interest to me because they did not separate baptism and confirmation, as the Roman rite did. There is, unfortunately, no comparable treatment of the medieval Roman rite in this volume, but its history is at least outlined in Chapter 11.

Chapter 6, on the Reformation, was originally a presentation at a 1974 conference sponsored by the Murphy Center for Liturgical Research, now the Notre Dame Center for Pastoral Liturgy.[8] It shows the effect of the loss of catechesis during the Middle Ages manifested in the separation of word and sacrament and the rejection by the Reformers of what they considered, not unreasonably in the light of the practice which they observed, to be mere ceremonies without theological content or grounding in God's word.

Chapters 7 through 9 discuss the contemporary revisions of initiation rites. Chapters 7 and 9 were written for this volume and have never appeared in print before. Chapter 8, on the American Episcopal Church, was published in *Studia Liturgica* in 1974, two years before the final text of the Episcopal revision was approved.[9] It retains much of its original substance but has been substantially revised in the light of the changes made since then.

Chapter 10, written for a *Festschrift* honoring the English liturgist Arthur Couritan,[10] is a study of Western prayers for the blessing of baptismal water, a study which includes my translations of the classic medieval texts. Chapter 11, a 1977 presentation to the Canadian Liturgical Society,[11] is a brief history of confirmation in the Western Church, one of my particular concerns. Finally, Chapter 12 was written in 1988 at the request of the editors of *Liturgy* for their issue on the Lord's Day.[12]

I wish to thank the various publishers and others for extending permission to use again this material.

I hope it will appear from these essays that I consider the historical study of liturgy to be a theological discipline with heavy pastoral implications, not at all a matter of aesthetics or antiquarianism. Why I believe the study of Chistian initiation to be important was well expressed by Aidan Kavanagh in the introduction to *Made, Not Born*, and with his vivid words I conclude this introduction:

> Who does not know initiation does not know the Church. And who does not know the Church does not know the Lord. And who knows neither the Church nor the Lord does not know the world as God meant it to be from before always.[13]

Notes

1. "The Baptismal Rite in Chrysostom," *Anglican Theological Review* 43 (1961) 364-368.

2. A revision of this was published as *Baptismal Anointing*, Alcuin Club Collections, vol. 48 (London: SPCK, 1966); 2nd edition (Notre Dame: University of Notre Dame Press, 1978).

3. Initially I worked with Bonnell Spencer, O.H.C., a member of the commission. In 1967 we became part of a larger drafting committee.

4. "The 'Shape' of the Baptismal Liturgy," *Anglican Theological Review* 47 (1965) 410-419.

5. "The Development of Catechesis in the Third and Fourth Centuries: From Hippolytus to Augustine," in *A Faithful Church*, eds., John Westerhoff and O.C. Edwards (Wilton, CT: Morehouse-Barlow, 1981) 49-78.

6. "Four Fathers on Baptism," in *Studies in the Syrian Baptismal Rite*, ed., Jacob Vellian (Kerala, India: Catholic Mission Press, 1973) 37-56.

7. "Ambrosian Baptismal Rites," *Studia Liturgica* 1 (1962) 241-253. "Mozarabic Baptismal Rites," *Studia Liturgica* 3 (1964) 78-87.

8. "Christian Initiation: The Reformation Period," in *Made, Not Born* (Notre Dame: University of Notre Dame Press, 1976) 83-98.

9. "Revision of the Rites of Christian Initiation in the American Episcopal Church," *Studia Liturgica* 10 (1974) 25-47.

10. "Christian Initiation in the Western Church," in *Initiation Theology*, ed., James Schmeiser (Toronto: Anglican Book Centre, 1978) 58-71.

11. "The Thanksgiving over the Water in the Baptismal Rite of the Western Church," in *The Sacrifice of Praise and Thanksgiving*, ed., Bryan D. Spinks (Rome: CLV-Editioni Liturgiche, 1981) 229-244.

12. "Sunday as a Baptismal Day," *Liturgy* 9:1 (1989) 25-29.

13. *Made, Not Born* 6.

TRADITION

1

The "Shape"
of the Baptismal Liturgy

THE PERIOD FOLLOWING THE PUBLICATION OF THE CONSTITUTION ON
the Sacred Liturgy in December 1963 gave birth to a vast mul-
titude of revised, reformed, and renewed liturgies, not only in
the Roman Catholic Church, but throughout the Christian
West. In the revision of the eucharistic rites a restoration of the
primitive "shape of the liturgy," to use Gregory Dix's apt
phrase, has been almost universal. When we turn to the rites
of Christian initiation, however, there has been less general
agreement as to what the primitive "shape" of the baptismal
liturgy was, and even less as to how to adapt it to contemporary use. In the nearly thirty years which separate us from the
constitution, a great deal of convergence has developed, but
little convergence was evident in 1964.

The intention of this chapter is to examine the "shape" of
the ancient baptismal liturgy and to look, in the light of classical patterns, at the revisions made since 1964.

HIPPOLYTUS AND TERTULLIAN

The earliest text of an actual baptismal rite which we possess is that of the *Apostolic Tradition* of Hippolytus.[1] Without
entering into the technical problems concerning the text of
Hippolytus, we may claim that the *Apostolic Tradition* reflects

Roman usage of the early third century.[2] Even the most cursory examination of this rite will reveal the aptness of the phrase Christian initiation as a description of it.

Baptism, according to this document, was normally preceded by a catechumenate of three years, during which the candidates were not allowed to pray with the faithful, eat with them, or exchange the kiss of peace with them.[3] Those in the final stage of preparation were separated from the other catechumens and permitted to hear the reading of the Gospel. During this time they received daily exorcism, with the laying on of hands.[4] The actual baptism took place at cockcrow on Easter, and so the period of final preparation corresponded to Lent.

The candidates for baptism prepared themselves by fasting on (Good) Friday, and on Saturday they received their final exorcism, at the hands of the bishop. Saturday night was spent in vigil "listening to reading and instruction."[5] At cockcrow the bishop blessed the water and oil, and the candidates prepared for baptism by removing their clothes. First each catechumen renounced the devil, and all his servants, and all his works, and was anointed by a presbyter with the "oil of exorcism."[6] Each was then led down into the water by a deacon and asked: "Dost thou believe in God, the Father Almighty?" When they replied, "I believe," a hand was placed on the head of the candidate, and each was dipped into the water. They were then asked:

> Dost thou believe in Christ Jesus, the Son of God, who was born of the Holy Ghost of the Virgin Mary, and was crucified under Pontius Pilate, and was dead and buried, and rose again the third day, alive from the dead, and ascended into heaven, and sat on the right hand of the Father, and will come to judge the quick and the dead?"

Again each replied "I believe" and was baptized, and again was asked: "Dost thou believe in the Holy Ghost, and the holy church, and the resurrection of the flesh?"

A third response and immersion followed. The neophyte was then led up from the water and anointed by the presbyter with the "oil of thanksgiving," and was then immediately dried, clothed, and brought into the church.[7] The bishop at once laid hands upon the newly baptized, praying:

O Lord God, who hast made them worthy to obtain remission of sins through the laver of regeneration of the Holy Spirit, send them thy grace, that they may serve thee according to thy will; for thine is the glory, to the Father and the Son, with the Holy Spirit in the holy church, both now and without end.

The bishop, pouring the "oil of thanksgiving" from his hand onto the forehead of each neophyte, then signed each with the cross and extended the kiss of peace.[8] The initiation was then considered to be complete and the neophytes to be members of the community of the faithful.

The new Christians then exercised their privileges and responsibilities by joining in the prayer of the faithful and exchanging the kiss of peace, and by offering at the eucharist and receiving holy communion. On this occasion they received also chalices of water, and of milk and honey, symbolizing their entry into the promised land and their new birth in Christ.[9]

Although some details of this rite are unique, the pattern or shape of the baptismal liturgy which it embodies may well be called the ancient pattern. From the writings of Tertullian, for example, we can reconstruct a basically similiar liturgy.[10] The baptismal washing, the anointing with chrism, as the "oil of thanksgiving" was normally called, the laying on of hands, and the reception of the eucharist were considered to be a single action by which the neophyte participated in the death and resurrection of Jesus Christ, was incorporated into his Mystical Body, and received the indwelling of the Holy Spirit. The three central liturgical actions of the sacrament—the washing, the anointing, and the laying on of hands—were identified with the events in the baptism of Jesus: the baptism by John, the descent of the Holy Spirit "like a dove," and the voice of the Father proclaiming his Sonship.[11] The signing with the cross was similarly identified with the marking of the foreheads of the faithful with a *tau* in Ezekiel 9:4 and the sealing of the servants of God on their foreheads in Revelation 7:3.[12]

Of the ceremonies described in the *Apostolic Tradition*, the anointing with oil is undoubtedly the least familiar to those outside the Roman Catholic tradition. It is certainly the ceremony which has been most consistently ignored even in proposed revisions of the baptismal rite prior to 1967.[13] A survey of the ancient and medieval rites of Christian initiation will reveal, however, that, although the laying on of hands was frequently omitted, the anointing with chrism formed a regular part of the rite.[14] Its restoration should therefore receive much more serious consideration than it has as yet in most revisions.

Tertullian reminds us that the title Christ means Anointed, and that it is by our baptismal anointing that we are made Christ-ians and partakers of Christ's royal priesthood. It is the glory of Christians that, while under the Old Covenant only the king and priest were anointed, under the New, the whole Christian people is anointed at baptism as a "royal priesthood," members of the Great High Priest and King of Kings. We read in 1 Samuel 13:16 that the gift of "the Spirit of the Lord" was one of the effects of the anointing of kings; Acts 10:38 tells us: "God anointed Jesus of Nazareth with the Holy Spirit and with power"; and Jesus spoke of himself as anointed with the Spirit in Luke 4:18. It is not surprising, therefore, that Christians began to speak of the baptismal anointing as "the unction of the Holy Spirit." This identification of unction with the Holy Spirit may also be seen in 1 John 2:20-27 which speaks of the anointing from the Holy One which abides in us and teaches us all things, in terms parallel to those in which John 16:13ff speaks of the "Spirit of truth."

We cannot, of course, in this brief study, trace the development of the baptismal rite throughout the Eastern and Western branches of the church, but we can look briefly at two representative Western rites, so that we may see the persistence of this classical pattern into the developed rites of the Middle Ages.

THE GELASIAN SACRAMENTARY

The Gelasian Sacramentary is an eighth-century manuscript believed to represent Roman practice at the end of the sixth century.[15] In it the baptismal rite is integrated into the church year, the daily instruction taking place during Lent, and the baptismal rites forming a part of the Easter Vigil. As in Hippolytus, candidates received a final exorcism on Holy Saturday. At this time they renounced the devil and were anointed with the "oil of exorcism."[16] Specific provisions were made for a vigil of prayer and bible reading, after which the font was solemnly blessed. The candidates then replied to the three creedal questions, as in the *Apostolic Tradition*, and were immersed at each affirmative reply. They then came up out of the font and were signed on the head with chrism by a presbyter, who prayed:

> The Almighty God, the Father of our Lord Jesus Christ, who has made thee to be regenerated of water and the Holy Spirit and has given thee remission of all thy sins, himself anoints thee with the chrism of salvation in Christ Jesus unto eternal life.

The bishop then bestowed "the sevenfold Spirit," laying on hands and saying:

> Almighty God, Father of our Lord Jesus Christ, who hast made thy servants to be regenerated of water and the Holy Spirit, and hast given them the remission of all their sins, do thou, Lord, pour upon them thy Holy Spirit the Paraclete, and give them the spirit of wisdom and understanding, the spirit of counsel and might, the spirit of knowledge and godliness, and fill them with the spirit of fear of God, in the Name of our Lord Jesus Christ, with whom thou livest and reignest ever God with the Holy Spirit, throughout all ages of ages.

We believe that this prayer was normally said by the bishop with hands extended over all the neophytes. After this he signed them individually on the forehead with chrism.[17] At the Mass which concluded the vigil they received the eucharist.

We may note the persistence of the same "shape" as in Hippolytus. The candidates renounce the devil, are baptized affirming their faith, are anointed, receive the laying on of hands, and participate for the first time in the eucharist. The prayer used by the bishop is, of course, the source of that in the traditional Anglican and Roman Catholic confirmation offices. It is equally an expansion of that in the *Apostolic Tradition*.

We must realize that in actual use the episcopal laying on of hands must frequently have been omitted from the Roman rite and supplied at a later time when, and if, the bishop visited the local church. The Roman *ordines* direct that the bishop, if not present for the baptism, supply the episcopal rite as speedily as possible.[18]

THE MOZARABIC RITE

Among the non-Roman rites, the Mozarabic baptismal rite, used in Spain before the introduction of the Roman rite in the eleventh century, provides an excellent example of the retention of the classical "shape." As at Rome, the rites of initiation were integrated into the church year. On Palm Sunday the final exorcism and pre-baptismal anointing of the candidates, together with the solemn delivery to them of the text of the creed (the *traditio symboli*) took place.[19] The baptism itself was part of the Easter Vigil. Our surviving texts expect that the candidates will be infants, and so we are assured that these ceremonies were performed for those baptized in infancy, as well as for adult converts.

The baptismal rite began with the blessing of the font. This was followed by the presentation of the naked infant to the priest, who called upon the child to renounce the devil. The answers were made, as in present practice, in the infant's name. The infant was then asked the traditional three questions:

N., do you believe in the Lord, the Father Almighty?
And in Jesus Christ his only Son our God and Lord?
And in the Holy Spirit?

The baptism, however, did not accompany the affirmative replies, but followed the third *Credo*, and was accompanied by a declarative formula:

And I baptize you in the Name of the Father, and of the Son, and of the Holy Spirit, that you may have eternal life.[20]

The child was at once clothed, and the priest marked the sign of the cross on the newly baptized's forehead with chrism, saying:

The sign of eternal life, which God, the Father Almighty, gave through Jesus Christ his Son to those who believe to salvation. Amen.

The priest then lays on hands, with a prayer for the bestowal of the sevenfold gift of the Spirit, concluding:

And so grant that being strengthed in the name of the Trinity, they may by this chrism be accounted worthy to become Christ's, and by the power of Christ to become Christians.[21]

The communion of the infants concluded the baptismal rite. Even when the baptism was removed from its place in the Easter Vigil, the entire rite, including communion, albeit from the reserved sacrament, was maintained as a unit.

We can see from this description that the Spanish Church, rather than break up the unity of the baptismal rite, permitted bishops to delegate the laying on of hands to presbyters. Spanish theologians contended that the bishop was the normal minister of baptism, as of the eucharist, but that he might delegate the administration of baptism to a presbyter, and if the sacrament were performed with the permission of the bishop, and with the use of chrism consecrated by him, it was considered as done *quasi de manu episcopi.*[22]

PRESENT REVISIONS

We are now ready to consider our present round of revisions. It is not possible, even if we believed it desirable, to roll back the centuries and adopt the liturgy of the *Apostolic Tradition*, or even that of the Gelasian Sacamentary or the Mozarabic rite. This was clearly recognized by the 1549 Anglican Prayer Book, which spoke of the impossibility of returning to the custom of administering baptism only at Easter and Pentecost. What is required of revisers is to remain loyal to the principles of the classical rites, adapting them to the present age.

The two principal revisions of the initiatory rites are those of the Roman Catholic Church and the American Episcopal Church. The Roman Catholic *Ordo Baptismi Parvulorum* appeared in both Latin and English in 1969, the new rite of confirmation in 1971, and the *Ordo Initiationis Christianae Adultorum* (almost universally called the RCIA from its English title) in Latin in 1972, with ICEL's draft English translation in 1974. The Anglican *Prayer Book Studies 18* appeared in 1970, *Prayer Book Studies 26*, an almost total revision of it, in 1973, and the final text in 1976.

The first point which had to be considered in any revision of the baptismal liturgy was the unity of the initiatory rite. As the Church of South India so clearly stated in the preface to its Order for Holy Baptism: "With us, those baptized in infancy are confirmed . . . several years after; but we must remember that the two rites are part of one process of entry into the Church." The Rite of Christian Initiation of Adults dealt with this problem by providing a normative rite for the baptism of adults, while maintaining the two-stage process for children. The Episcopal Church attempted a different solution: the inclusion of all of the initiatory elements in the baptismal rite, much like the Mozarabic liturgy and treating confirmation as a renewal and reaffirmation of baptism.

The elements of the classic "shape" include:

1. The blessing of the font. Traditionally this is a thanksgiving similar to the eucharistic prayer, thanking God for creation and redemption, including the Lord's commission to baptize (i.e., the words of institution of baptism) and the invocation of the Holy Spirit.

2. Renunication of the devil, accompanied by a confession of the candidate's sinfulness, namely, an acknowledgment that one has been under Satan's tyranny.

3. Acceptance of Jesus Christ as Lord and Savior and assent to the Apostles' Creed. Both the RCIA and the Roman rite for the baptism of children do this in the traditional form, using the interrogative form of the creed to which the candidate (or the parents and godparents) reply: "I believe." The Episcopal rite includes a threefold acceptance of Christ and has the candidates actually recite the creed, in response to a triple questioning.

4. Baptism with water in the name of the Trinity. The traditional declarative formula has too long a history to be discarded. It also serves a practical purpose in providing a short form for individual administration, permitting the longer questions to be asked of the entire group of candidates.

5. The anointing with chrism and signing with the cross. This is retained in the Roman rite for children, but is omitted in the RCIA when the anointing of confirmation follows. The signing with the permissive use of chrism introduced by the Episcopal and (following it) the Lutheran rite is almost certainly related to the single anointing of the Mozarabic and other classic non-Roman Western rites.

6. Presentation to the bishop with the laying on of hands. The RCIA has followed the precedent of the classic non-Roman rites and permits the presbyter to confirm adults in the absence of the bishop. Episcopalians require the presiding

bishop or priest to recite the Gelasian prayer for "the seven-fold Spirit," sign with the cross, and impose hands, but do not describe the rite as confirmation.

7. The welcoming of new members into the Christian fellowship. Anciently this was done with the kiss of peace, and its modern form has become part of the revised rites.

8. Participation in the eucharist and the reception of communion.

The Great Vigil of Easter is, of course, the best possible time for the celebration, but it can be held on other Sundays. Pentecost and Baptism of Christ are traditional alternative days, and as necessity frequently requires, it can be performed at other times, such as the bishop's visitation.

This has become not only the normative but the normal "shape" of adult baptism for Roman Catholics, Episcopalians, and Lutherans, and for other Christians basing their liturgy on theirs, or on that of the Consultation on Church Union. The one sticking point appears to be the refusal of Episcopalians to call the post-baptismal rites confirmation when they are not administered by a bishop.

Regarding the baptism of infants, there are two possible procedures, both of which have been followed to some extent. The more radical is to maintain the unity of the rite and to admit infants to communion, as in the Mozarabic and medieval Roman rites. This was advocated by Massey Shepherd in 1964[23] and has become increasingly the practice of the Episcopal Church.

The Roman rite has not admitted infants or young children to confirmation and communion, causing Aidan Kavanagh to wonder theologically why not.[24] In this the Roman Church is by no means alone, and admission to the eucharist, and some sort of confirmation rite, are deferred to "catechetical age" or "years of discretion" in many churches. This is clearly an area in which greater convergence is desirable.

Except in cases of genuine necessity, the celebration of baptism, including infant baptism, should be part of the church's regular worship, namely, the Sunday liturgy. The reformed Roman rite of baptism for children states:

> To bring out the paschal character of baptism, it is recommended that the sacrament be celebrated during the Easter Vigil or

on Sunday, when the Church commemorates the Lord's resurrection. On Sunday, baptism may be celebrated even during Mass, so that the entire community may be present and the necessary relationship between baptism and eucharist may be clearly seen, but this should not be done too often.[25]

The theological principle is excellently stated, but the fear of doing this "too often" seems overdrawn. Obviously it is easier for smaller congregations to arrange to hold all baptisms at the chief parish eucharist, as The Book of Common Prayer directs, but if baptism is indeed what the church claims it to be, it almost demands being celebrated at the eucharist, and for the reasons given in the Roman rite. The question needs also to be raised in all the churches of whether it is proper or not to communicate the newly baptized, of whatever age, at their baptismal eucharist.

Those baptized in infancy can appropriately be confirmed in the context of adult baptism. They renew their vows in the company with those taking them for the first time, and are brought to the bishop for the laying on of hands. The Roman rite, going back to the time of the *Apostolic Tradition*, has had a double post-baptismal chrismation: that of the head by the presbyter which is considered a part of baptism, and the signing of the forehead by the bishop which has been identified with confirmation. This was not usually a part of the classic rites outside of Rome, and there seems little reason why those who do not follow the Roman baptismal rite should repeat the anointing and signing of those so anointed and signed at baptism. It is interesting that the post-conciliar reform of the Roman rite has given up, in the case of those baptized as adults, both the double chrismation and the restriction of the rite to bishops. G.W.H. Lampe has pointed out that the anointing and signing with the cross refer to what is done at baptism, not confirmation.[26] The theological problems really result from attempting to define confirmation as an initiatory sacrament apart from baptism, without attributing the proper effects of baptism to confirmation.[27]

A great deal of progress has been made since 1964. To a large extent the unity of the fragmented initiation rite has been restored, at least for adult baptism. The paschal link between baptism and eucharist is seen not only by theologians but by those celebrating the rites, especially when they are publicly celebrated together as parish liturgy. As we have seen, more needs to be done. Much of this is pastoral work and the development of new attitudes not only among priests and bishops, but among lay people who participate in baptismal liturgies and present their children to be baptized. Rubrics alone cannot overcome the attitude that "my child's baptism" is a private and personal event involving only God, the family, and the priest. As long as this attitude persists, real public baptisms will be exceptional.

Largely through the influence of the RCIA, the theological primacy of adult baptism is widely recognized, and the Easter Vigil is restored as the baptismal day *par excellence*. Baptism has begun to find its place again within the mystery of the liturgical year. Certainly one important aspect of this which we have not mentioned is the emergence of the entire catechumenal process for the preparation of adults. The effect of this on the renewal of the baptismal spirituality of the church has been profound. It places the rites of Christian initiation within an even larger "shape" of Christian conversion and formation, which necessarily takes place at the principal parish liturgies over a substantial portion of the year. Here the RCIA stands alone. It is the source and inspiration of the introduction of the catechumenate in other churches, which are only now beginning to catch up.

In one sense the success of the RCIA has made infant baptism seem less important. This is unfortunate. There is only one baptism, whatever the age of the candidates, and infant baptism remains numerically the most significant. Its relationship to the celebration of the eucharist and to the admission of baptized children to reception of communion needs more thought and greater clarity.

The classic "shape" of the baptismal liturgy is reflected in the rites which have been adopted since Vatican Council II in a way that they were not in the earlier rites. Confirmation remains a source of confusion, if not of division. The restoration (at least optionally) of chrismation, with its rich biblical and patristic symbolism, to the post-baptismal consignation in American Anglican and Lutheran rites, and the introduction of the post-baptismal imposition of hands in other liturgies does a great deal to restore the "shape" more widely.

Notes

1. Burton Scott Easton, ed. (Cambridge: Cambridge University Press, 1934); reprint (New Haven, CT: Archon Books, 1962); Gregory Dix (London: SPCK, 1937; revised ed., Henry Chadwick, 1968); Bernard Botte, *La Tradition apostolique de Saint Hippolyte* (Münster: Aschendorff, 1963). Quotations from the *Apostolic Tradition* are from the edition of Easton.

2. "But to date no significant doubt has been raised respecting the relative date of composition of the *Apostolic Tradition*—i.e., within a few years before or after A.D. 200—nor has there been any disposition to contest the fact that its place of origin was the church in Rome." Massey H. Shepherd, *The Paschal Liturgy and the Apocalypse*, Ecumenical Studies in Worship, no. 6 (Richmond, VA: John Knox Press, 1960) 48f. But see J.M. Hanssens, *La Liturgie d'Hippolyte* (Rome: Pontifical Oriental Institute, 1959) for a dissenting view.

3. *Apostolic Tradition* 17-18, 26.

4. Ibid. 20.

5. Ibid.

6. Ibid. 21

7. Ibid.

8. Ibid. 22.

9. Ibid. 23.

10. *De Baptismo* 7, 8; *De Corona* 3; *De Resurrectione Carnis* 8.

11. Optatus of Milevis, *De Schismate Donatistorum* 4:7; Augustine, *Sermo* 324; Pacien of Barcelona, *Sermo de Baptismo* 6.

12. See Shepherd, *Paschal Liturgy* 63, 90.

13. Among Anglicans, the Church of India, Pakistan, Burma and Ceylon, and the Church of the Province of South Africa had adopted permissive anointing at confirmation, but not at baptism. Developments since 1967 are discussed below and in the following chapters.

14. The present writer has made such a survey in *Baptismal Anointing* (London: SPCK, 1966); 2nd ed. (Notre Dame: University of Notre Dame Press, 1978).

15. Ed. H.A. Wilson (Oxford, 1894) and L.C. Mohlberg (Rome: Herder, 1960. Critical discussion by Antoine Chavasse, *Le Sacramentaire Gélasien* (Tournai: Desclée, 1958). The translations of prayers from this sacramentary are from E.C. Whitaker, *Documents of the Baptismal Liturgy* (London: SPCK, 1960) 178.

16. Gelasian Sacramentary, sec. 42.

17. Ibid., sec. 44.

18. For example, *Ordo Romanus XV* 119.

19. Marius Férotin, ed., *Liber Ordinum* (Paris, 1912), col. 27, 184-187. Translations of the Mozarabic forms are my own.

20. Ibid., col. 32-37, 217-219.

21. Ibid., col. 34.

22. Braulion of Saragoso, *Epistola ad Eugenum Toletanum* 4.

23. "There is no good reason why we should not reintegrate in one single rite Baptism, Confirmation, and admission to the Eucharist—whether this is done for infants or for adults, depending upon the pastoral needs in these respective cases. A Christian should be fully initiated once for all, for at whatever age he undergoes this experience, he will need Christian nurture for the rest of his life." From a lecture entitled "The Reconstruction of the Liturgy" delivered at General Theological Seminary, 14 February 1964, and subsequently printed in Massey H. Shepherd, Jr., *Liturgy and Education* (New York: Seabury, 1965) 85-112; the passage cited is on pp. 106f.

24. "The theological point made here is of such consequence that one feels compelled to wonder why it can be construed as applying only to adults and children of catechetical age but not to infants and young children. Unless the theological point is dismissed as mere rhetoric it seems inescapable that all who are deemed fit for baptism, no matter what their chronological age, should also be confirmed within the same liturgical event." Aidan Kavanagh, *The Shape of Baptism* (New York: Pueblo Publishing Co., 1978) 138ff.

25. Introduction 9.

26. G.W.H. Lampe, *The Seal of the Spirit* (London: Longmans, Green and Co., 1951) 321.

27. An excellent treatment of this question is Nathan D. Mitchell, "The Dissolution of the Rite of Christian Initiation," in *Made, Not Born* (Notre Dame: University of Notre Dame Press, 1976) 50-82.

2

Baptismal Catechesis:
From Hippolytus to Augustine

HINTS PROVIDED IN EARLIER AUTHORS OF A CATECHUMENAL IN-
struction of adult candidates for baptism develop and flower
into a full catechetical system in the writers of the third and
fourth centuries. The catechetical works of Ambrose in the
West, and of Cyril of Jerusalem, Theodore of Mopsuestia, and
John Chrysostom in the East remain the classics in the field,
and the work of Cyril in particular became a model for such
instruction. The necessity of producing behavioral and cultural change in those converted in increasing numbers from paganism demanded more than an intellectual exposition. It required an environment suitable for conversion and growth
into Christ.

HIPPOLYTUS

The *Apostolic Tradition* of Hippolytus, usually dated about
215, is frequently put forward justifiably as a model of the liturgy of the ancient church. The late Burton S. Easton, professor of New Testament at General Theological Seminary and an
early editor of the text, said of its directives:

> [They] represent the normal practices at Rome in Hippolytus'
> younger days, and he is quite sincere in believing that they are
> truly apostolic and therefore unalterable. And that they actual-

ly are rules of real antiquity is shown by the corroboration they receive from other early Christian writers, among whom Tertullian in particular describes usages extraordinarily like those expounded by his Roman contemporary. *The Apostolic Tradition*, consequently, is more than a source for Roman customs at the beginning of the third century; it may with equal safety be invoked for the practices of even fifty years earlier.[1]

The study of this work, nevertheless, is a labyrinth of pitfalls for the unwary, since neither the text nor the context is secure. Only a few fragments of the original Greek text survive, none dealing with the catechumenate. The most reliable witness is a single sixth-century manuscript containing a Latin translation of the major part of the work. The second best witness is an eleventh-century manuscript of a Coptic (Egyptian) translation, also incomplete. The reconstruction and identification of the text has been a sort of scholarly jigsaw puzzle and is the work of the present century. One scholar has even raised the possibility that the work represents nothing but the author's "ideal" church, and reflects actual practices nowhere.

Even with these reservations, the work is too important to ignore, and even if it could be proved, which is far from the case, that it does not represent late second-century Roman usage, it still describes something very like what must lie behind the practice of the third and fourth centuries.

The principal section on the catechumens, chapters 15 to 20 in the edition of Dom Bernard Botte, is missing in the Latin and therefore depends on the Coptic. Newcomers to the faith, it tells us, are brought to the teachers before the people arrive and are examined as to their manner of life. Are they married? Are they slaves? If they are slaves of Christians, do their masters recommend them? The primary considerations seem to be ethical:

> If his master is a heathen, teach him to please his master, that there be no scandal. If any man has a wife, or a woman a husband, they shall be taught to be contented, the man with his wife and the woman with her husband. But if any man is not living with a wife, he shall be instructed not to fornicate, but to take a wife lawfully or remain as he is.[2]

There is also an initial inquiry about trades and professions, and those engaged in occupations considered unsuitable for Christians are told to desist. Most forbidden are those considered immoral or which involve any sort of participation in formal pagan worship, such as the making of statues of the pagan gods, or the teaching of classical literature (!).

The expectation is that catechumens will spend three years as hearers of the word, but it is not *kronos* (time) but *tropos* (conduct) which is to be judged. During this time they receive instruction and pray, not yet with the faithful but by themselves. They are also forbidden to exchange the peace or to eat with the faithful *in cena dominica*, which probably means at the *agape* since there would have been no question of their participation in the eucharist. They are not given blessed bread as the faithful are, but exorcised bread and an individual cup.

No description is given of the instruction which the catechumens receive, but the teacher, at the end of the instruction, lays hands upon them, prays for them, and dismisses them. Finally the catechumens are told they need not fear arrest, for if they make their witness before the magistrate, they are considered as baptized in their own blood.

The picture which emerges from the *Apostolic Tradition* is of catechumens forming a separate class in the church, distinct from the baptized faithful. They are Christians *in fieri*. Their participation in the life of the community, although restricted, is not optional. They are treated much the same as contemporary fraternities treat "pledges." They are excluded from the privileges of membership as uninitiated, but to those in the outside world they are members with a real place in the life and concern of the church.

At the end of the three-year catechumenate, those who are to receive baptism are chosen. This group of *electi* (chosen) are called by later Latin authors *competentes* (seekers), as opposed to the simple *audientes* (hearers). In Greek they are called *photizomenoi* (those being enlightened). In the fourth century the seekers are those actually preparing for baptism, in contrast to those who remain catechumens for some time, like Augustine, or until the approach of death, like Constantine.

The *Apostolic Tradition* asks of the seekers:

Have they lived good lives when they were catechumens?

Have they honored the widows? Have they visited the sick?
Have they done every kind of good work?[3]

If their sponsors bear witness that they have, they are admitted
"to hear the Gospel." It is not certain what that means, and
there are a number of scholarly theories which need not detain
us. What is clear is that the examination is on the manner of life
of the candidates. No questions are asked concerning their understanding of Christian doctrine, or even of their acceptance
of Jesus Christ, although presumably some form of rudimentary belief must have been responsible for their initial approach to the church. This confirms our view that the instruction which they received was primarily in Christian living and
was to enable them to adopt what we would call a Christian
lifestyle, not to make them theologians.

The period of actual preparation for baptism is marked by
daily imposition of hands and exorcism, and presumably by
instruction as well, although nothing is said of that. If they
have "heard the word in faith," it will be manifest in the puri-
ty of their lives.

References to instruction in the baptismal rites themselves
are few but significant. Immediately before the reception of
communion by the newly-baptized, "the bishop shall give a
reason for all these things to those who receive," and at the
end of the rites:

> We have handed over to you in brief these things about holy
> baptism and the holy offering, for you have already been in-
> structed about the resurrection of the flesh and the other things
> as it is written. But if there is anything else which ought to be
> said, the bishop shall say it privately to those who have re-
> ceived baptism. Unbelievers must not get to know it, unless
> they first receive baptism.[4]

Sacramental instruction, at least according to the Coptic
translator, was not to be given to the unbaptized, but the bishop was to explain the meaning of what was done to the newly-
baptized, and if there were more to be imparted, it was to be
done privately later. On the other hand, scriptural instruction,
at least as it concerns the resurrection, had already been given,
apparently as part of the catechumenate.

In the *Apostolic Tradition* we find three stages of catechesis at least in outline. There is general instruction in Christian living for those who come to hear the word. "Hearing the word" also implies some biblical instruction. There is more intensive instruction, described as hearing the Gospel, in the period of immediate baptismal preparation. Finally, at the time of baptism, and immediately thereafter, there is sacramental instruction, or mystagogy. This is the same pattern we find in the classic writers of the fourth century.

THE CATECHETICAL SCHOOL OF ALEXANDRIA

The work of the catechetical school of Alexandria and its famous masters, Clement and Origen, is, strangely enough, only peripherally related to our study. Although we are told by Eusebius that Origen engaged in the instruction of catechumens, the Christian school at Alexandria was really a type of higher education on the model of the pagan philosophical schools. Its object was to provide for orthodox Christianity the sort of intellectual respectability which Greek philosophy or Gnostic speculation provided. It was to lead the Christian Gnostic to true knowledge and initiation into the holy mystery of God and Christ. As Clement rhapsodizes:

> Then thou shalt have the vision of my God, and shalt be initiated into those holy mysteries, and shalt taste the joys that are hidden away in heaven, preserved for me "which neither ear hath heard, nor have they entered into the heart" of any man.[5]

Yet when, in the opening chapter of his *Paedagogus* (Instructor), he expounds what we might call his educational theory, it sounds much like the traditional Christian catechetical system. His first phase of instruction he calls exhortation. His work by that title, *Protrepticus*, is, for the circumstances of its composition, a work of evangelism. It seeks to draw the educated student of Greek philosophy to Christ. The *Paedagogus*, his second volume, is what he considered elementary instruction. It is largely of a moral nature. *Didascalicus* (Teacher) should properly have been the third section of Clement's work, since he considered intellectual education to be the third stage of the education of the Christian Gnostic, but, from what he says in the opening chapter of *Stromateis* (Miscellanies), he chose instead to write in riddles, making his meaning clear only to those who understood. The parallel to the *disciplina arcani*, the concealing of the rites of the church from the unbaptized, is too strong to be ignored. Intellectual education, Clement believes, is not for everyone, but only for those who were not content with what Origen calls an "unreasoned and common faith."

Clement's school was apparently a personal enterprise which was destroyed in the persecution of 202. When it was restored by Origen, it was with the support of the bishop. In 215 Origen divided the school curriculum, bringing in a new teacher to instruct the beginners, while he himself taught the more advanced students.

With the work of Origen we have moved well beyond the instruction of catechumens to the establishment of a theological academy, which has nonetheless taken the basic plan of catechetical instruction as the outline of its curriculum, as many of Origen's exegetical and theological works clearly reflect. He wrote in the *Peri Archon:*

> The holy apostles, when preaching the faith of Christ, took certain doctrines, those namely which they believed to be necessary ones, and delivered them in plainest terms to all believers, even to such as appeared to be somewhat dull in the investigation of divine knowledge. The grounds of their statements they left to be investigated by such as should merit the higher gifts of the Spirit . . . There were other doctrines, however, about which the apostles simply said that things were so, keeping silence as to how or why; their intention undoubtedly being to supply the more diligent of those who came after them, such as should prove to be lovers of wisdom (i.e. Philosophers) with an exercise to display the fruit of their ability.[6]

Origen himself was obviously concerned with the Christian philosophers who had received the gifts of language, wisdom, and knowledge, but he does provide us with a somewhat idiosyncratic listing of the doctrines which the apostles taught in plain terms. Presumably these are the doctrines which were to be imparted to all Christians, while the other, more advanced material, was for the lovers of wisdom.

The first such doctrine is the unity of God, "who created and set in order all things, and who, when nothing existed, caused the universe to be." In next place comes the doctrine of Christ:

> He who came to earth, was begotten of the Father before every created thing. And after he had ministered to the Father in the foundation of all things, for all things were made through him, in these last times he emptied himself and was made man, was made flesh, although he was God; and being made man, he still remained what he was, namely God. He took to himself a body like our body, differing in this alone, that it was born of a virgin and of the Holy Spirit. And this Jesus Christ was born and suffered in truth and not merely in appearance, and truly died our common death. Moreover he truly rose from the dead, and after the resurrection companied with his disciples and was taken up into heaven.[7]

Certainly, Origen here is rehearsing the preaching of the apostolic church, the *kerygma*, which he says is preserved unaltered and handed down in unbroken succession from the apostles to the churches of his own day. It must have been something like this which Origen taught his catechumens, some of whom, Eusebius tells us, went to martyrdom.

The third doctrine Origen mentions is "that the Holy Spirit is united in honor and dignity to the Father and the Son," and inspired the saints, prophets, and apostles.

He also states as apostolic doctrine the temporal creation of the world and therefore the necessity of its end, the reward and punishment of the human soul after death, the resurrection of the body, the freedom of the human will and the reality of the moral struggle, and the existence of good angels and of the devil and his angels.

This, of course, reflects Origen's own interests and controversies in which he was engaged, but it does give a clue to the content of basic catechetical education. I think we can also assume that much of the instruction was biblically based, and that its goal was to produce a holy person, not a theologian.

CATECHESIS IN JERUSALEM

A more fertile field for our investigation of catechesis in the ancient church is fourth-century Jerusalem. We are fortunate in possessing two major overlapping sources for the practice of the Jerusalem Church in this period. The first is the complete set of catechetical lectures thought to have been delivered by Cyril of Jerusalem in 348, along with a complete set of mystagogical lectures given to the baptized. The mystagogical lectures were not given in the same year as the pre-baptismal lectures and are thought by many scholars to be the work of John, Cyril's successor as bishop of Jerusalem. This question of authorship is not of great importance for our purposes, since the lectures do represent the Jerusalem Church, and in any case they must have been quite similar from year to year. It is, in fact, likely that Cyril's lectures were substantially copied for over a century. The second source we possess is the journal of the pilgrim Egeria, or Etheria, usually described as a Spanish nun, who visited Jerusalem in the 380s.

Fourth-century Jerusalem was a place of pilgrimage. The new buildings of Constantine on Golgotha and other sacred spots, and the opportunity to walk in the holy places where the Savior taught and died and rose again, were a powerful magnet for pilgrims, or perhaps simply for tourists. Piety after the conversion of Constantine was more historical and less eschatological than it had been in earlier centuries, and there was an increased desire to celebrate sacred anniversaries, to visit sacred sites, and to venerate the relics of the martyrs. The *Martyrium* in Jerusalem, the great church Constantine had built on the site of the death of the King of Martyrs, with the adjacent shrine of the *Anastasis*, or Resurrection, containing the empty tomb, was the natural focus of this piety. Fourth-century Jerusalem was no longer the obscure city of Aelia Capitolina; it was now the Holy City. What was done in Jerusalem was reported and copied throughout the Christian world.

There is no mention in our sources of the long period of "hearing the word" which the *Apostolic Tradition* describes, except for Cyril's instruction that his hearers are not to divulge what is taught them to catechumens. Apparently there were still many catechumens who were not candidates for baptism. By the middle of the fourth century there were probably a substantial number who had identified themselves with Christianity, not necessarily for political advantage, but who were not yet ready to "take the plunge" in the baptismal waters.

The time set apart for the catechizing of those preparing to be baptized at Easter was *quadragesima*, our forty-day Lent. Egeria tells us that Lent in Jerusalem was eight weeks, since they did not fast on Saturday or Sunday (except on Holy Saturday), and that they called it *Heortae* (The Feasts). Before Lent the names of those wishing to be baptized were turned in and written down by a presbyter. At the beginning of Lent a solemn ceremony took place, which she describes in detail.

The bishop's throne is set up in the great nave of the *Martyrium*. The presbyters sit with him, in chairs on either side, with the deacons and other clergy standing behind. The effect is certainly that of a formal act of the hierarchically ordered church. Those seeking baptism (*competentes*) are brought up with their sponsors and questioned by the bishop. The questions concern the manner of life of the candidate. Neighbors as well as sponsors are asked to respond, and Egeria says: "It is not too easy for a visitor to come to baptism if he has no witnesses who are acquainted with him."

Those who were well reported were enrolled by the bishop, and others were told to amend their ways before coming to the font. Each male candidate was accompanied by a godfather and each female candidate by a godmother. After their enrollment they were seated in a semi-circle facing the bishop and clergy, all together forming a complete circle. The sponsors and such other of the faithful as wished were permitted to attend the lectures, but the ordinary catechumens were excluded.

The Procatechesis, the address delivered on this occasion, is the first of the lectures of Cyril that is preserved. It gives us a picture of what sort of thing was said.

The candidates are addressed as *photizomenoi* (those who have come to be enlightened) who have been enrolled for baptism. Then two negative examples are given them: that of Simon Magus, who "while his body went under the water, his heart let not in the light of the Spirit," and that of the man who came to the feast without a wedding garment. Cyril's comment is: "There has been nothing to stop you coming here with your soul covered in the mire of your sins." He tells them that they have forty days in which to put off the covering of sin and clothe themselves in the proper wedding garment, otherwise, he warns them, they will receive only the water and not the Holy Spirit. Clearly conversion, not theological education, is the goal. Even, he suggests to his audience, if you have come from an ulterior motive,

> now you are inside the ecclesiastical fishnets. Let yourself be taken. Jesus is angling for you, not to make you die, but by his having died, to make you live.[8]

Cyril goes on to urge the candidate to participate eagerly in the preparations for baptism. "Let your feet hasten to these times of instruction. Submit yourself to be exorcized with all eagerness." They are urged to persevere through these cate-chizings, to learn the things they are taught, and to hide them from catechumens. Cyril's reason for this concealment is that the catechumen cannot comprehend the material. This is the *disciplina arcani* to which we have already made reference. Although the reason given here is sufficient, we must realize that the practice of concealing the "mysteries" from those not yet initiated was common in the pagan mystery cults to which many of the converts to Christianity had formerly belonged. To some extent the revelation of hidden mysteries was part of their expectations, and the catechists appear to have built upon these expectations.

According to Egeria, the daily exorcism of the *competentes* took place first thing in the morning, after what we would call morning prayer. Although exorcism is not congenial to most twentieth-century American Christians, it was an integral part of the ancient preparation for baptism. The comment of William Telfer is most significant:

> The most important thing about the pre-baptismal exorcism was that, in those days of increased numbers, it supplied the surviving element of individual and personal ministry in the preparation for the candidates.[9]

His point is that no great intellectual demands were made of the exorcist, only piety and the ability to say the exorcisms. It was therefore possible to have a large corpus of exorcists, so that each candidate might be in the charge of an individual exorcist. This was certainly true in Jerusalem, if anywhere, as the *Martyrium*, where the catechesis took place, was particularly mentioned by Jerome as a place of exorcism.

Following the exorcisms, the candidates sat in a circle in the nave of the *Martyrium*, where the bishop's chair had again been placed, while the bishop gave his instructions. According to Egeria, the instructions took three hours and were held every day for seven weeks. Contrary to the custom of other churches, there were no instructions in Jerusalem during what we call Holy Week. This was presumably because of the special observances connected with that week in Jerusalem, which Cyril is believed to have introduced. The instructions were attended by the sponsors, and by as many of the faithful as wished, but were closed to catechumens. Egeria's description of the content of the lectures is instructive:

> His subject is God's Law: during the forty days he goes through the whole Bible, beginning with Genesis, and first relating the literal meaning of each passage, then interpreting its spiritual meaning. He also teaches them at this time all about the resurrection and the faith. And this is called *Catechesis*. After five weeks' teaching they receive the Creed, whose content he explains article by article in the same way as he explained the Scriptures, first literally and then spiritually.[10]

Cyril, in his Procatechesis, said that as catechumens they had heard the Scriptures without understanding, but now that the Holy Spirit was fashioning their minds into mansions for God, when they heard the Scripture in the future they would understand its mysteries. Egeria was, in fact, impressed by the ability of the people to follow the Scripture in Jerusalem, an ability which she ascribed to the three hours of daily instruction during Lent.

If we turn from Egeria to Cyril's lectures, we shall see that they follow the general pattern which the Western pilgrim expounded. There is, however, one significant problem. All the evidence indicates that the instructions were held daily, but there are only twenty lectures, counting the Procatechesis. This is apparently not simply a peculiarity of the set of lectures we happen to possess, but the way it was normally done. Perhaps the best explanation is Telfer's suggestion that in the bilingual Church of Jerusalem twenty lectures were given in cultural Greek, the ones we possess, while twenty more were given in the vernacular *Syriste* (Palestinian Aramaic), but this cannot be considered more than a convenient hypothesis.

Cyril, in the Procatechesis, mentions the reading of Scripture as a part of the instruction of the candidates, and in the lectures scriptural texts are given for all but the Procatechesis. These texts correspond to the citations given in the Armenian lectionary which reflects fifth-century Jerusalem usage. Nineteen readings are assigned by the Armenian lectionary to pre-baptismal instruction and four to post-baptismal lectures.[11] There are, in fact, only eighteen lectures in the suviving series, but the eighteenth is a double lecture broken by the *redditio symboli*, the recitation of the creed by the candidates for baptism, and the passage assigned by the Armenian lectionary for lecture 19 is quoted twice in the second part of Cyril's final lecture.

It appears that a standard series of catechetical lectures was given each year on fixed scriptural texts, and that having missed one for some reason in the year from which the lectures are preserved, Cyril combined the final two, like many other lecturers before and since. We may assume, then, that the topics of Cyril's catechetical lectures were traditional for over a century, at least in the Jerusalem Church.

The outline of Cyril's lectures is clearly the baptismal creed of the Jerusalem Church, which is taught to the candidates in the *traditio symboli* in the fifth lecture.

The first two lectures, on Isaiah 1:16 and Ezekiel 18:20, deal with the need for moral integrity, and for repentence and confession of sins in preparation for baptism. The third lecture, on Romans 6:3, deals with the meaning of baptism. The three together might be taken as dealing with "one baptism of repentance unto the remission of sins," although the creedal statement has not yet been introduced. The rites themselves are not discussed until the mystagogical lectures, and by comparing the third lecture with them we can see the different type of sacramental instruction which Cyril felt it appropriate to give to those preparing for baptism and to those already baptized.

The approach here is through biblical narrative, recounting the preaching of John and the baptism of Christ, thereby tying baptism to the call to repentance and confession in the first two lectures. Cyril tells the candidates that Jesus by his own baptism has broken the heads of the dragons who dwell in the water and bound them so that the baptized have "power to tread upon serpents and scorpions."

For you descend into the water laden with your sins. But the invocation of the grace causes your soul to receive the seal, and after that it does not let you be swallowed up by the dread dragon. You go down "dead indeed in sin," and you come up "alive unto righteousness."[12]

The reference is, of course, to Romans 6, the appointed lesson. Cyril's sacramental premise is simple: "The water washes the body and the Spirit seals the soul." The emphasis is on the joint action of water and Spirit to raise us to newness of life. "The seal of the Spirit" is what we would call the inward part of the sacrament, whereas the water is the outward part.

In the fouth lecture Cyril turns to doctrine, for he tells the *photizemonoi* that the way to godliness lies in both good works and pious dogmas. He then gives what he calls a brief recapitulation of the indispensable dogmas. He implies that this recapitulation will be the basis of the remainder of his lectures, but, in fact, they follow the outlines of the baptismal creed which he presents in the next lecture. This arrangement of material appears to be Cyril's own, probably based on that in Origen's *Peri Archon*. The lecture is entitled "The Ten Doctrines" in the manuscript, but it is not clear exactly what the ten are. The text is Colossians 2:8f, which certainly lends itself to the kind of exposition Cyril gives, combining Platonic philosophy with a concern for practical moral action by the candidate. It includes a section on Holy Scriptures which spells out which books are canonical and warns against others. The sermon contains a sort of apology to "the more advanced" of his hearers for giving them instructions more fitting for children and for spoonfeeding them. His list of doctrines includes the "monarchy" of God, Christology, the Virgin birth, cucifixion, burial, resurrection, ascension, the coming judgment, Holy Spirit, soul, body, and our resurrection. This may well have been Cyril's preferred organization of material, but, as we have said, he follows the traditional outline of the creed, which is introduced in the fifth lecture.

For Cyril, the *traditio symboli*, the teaching of the text of the creed to the candidates, is the moment when they pass from being catechumens to believers. The basis of this homily is Hebrews 11, and it deals with faith. Cyril, following tradition, is quite specific:

> Now the one and only faith that you are to take and preserve in the way of learning and professing it is that which is now being committed to you by the Church as confirmed throughout the Scriptures . . . This doctrine I want you to commit to memory word for word and say it over to one another as much as you can, not writing it on paper but using memory to engrave it on your heart.[13]

The text of the creed was repeated phrase-by-phrase for them to commit to memory. They were warned not to let any catechumen overhear them repeating it, but to memorize it as a guarantee of fidelity to the Gospel, for "this creed embraces in a few phrases all the religious knowledge contained in the Old and New Testaments together." The creed is the real core of his instructions and the homilies which follow are a phrase-by-phrase commentary on it. Cyril calls the creed *Pistis* (Faith) and tells the *photizomenoi* that they are to preserve and maintain the Faith which he has delivered to them.

The creed itself is to be memorized, both for what it is in itself as a summary of scriptural teaching and the professsion which will be made at baptism, and also, clearly, because it is the outline of the instruction, and its repetition will call to mind the entire content of the instruction given on it. The creed was not recited in worship in the early church, except in connection with baptism, and it is from this use that the creeds developed.

The actual topics covered by the remaining lectures are (6) the unity of God, (7) the fatherhood of God, (8) the omnipotence of God, (9) God the creator, (10) one Lord, Jesus Christ, (11) "the only begotten Son of God, born of the Father before all ages, true God, through whom all things were made," (12) the incarnation, (13) the crucifixion and burial of Christ, (14) the resurrection of Christ, his ascension, and his sitting at the right hand of the Father, (15) "And he will come in glory to judge the living and the dead, whose kingdom shall have no end" and the Anti-Christ, (16 and 17) the Holy Spirit, and (18) the resurrection of the flesh, the Catholic Church, and eternal life. The reconstructed text of the Jerusalem creed (which, of course, is not printed out in the manuscripts) is this:

> We believe in one God the Father Almighty, Maker of heaven and earth, and of all things visible and invisible. And in one Lord Jesus Christ, the only-begotten Son of God, true God be-

gotten of the Father before all worlds, by whom all things were made; who was made flesh and was incarnate, crucified and entombed, who rose again on the third day and ascended into the heavens, and sat down on the right hand of the Father; who is coming in glory to judge the living and the dead, whose kingdom shall have no end. And in one Holy Spirit, the Paraclete, that spake in the prophets. And in one baptism of repentance for the remission of sins, and in one holy catholic Church, and in the resurrection of the flesh and the life of the world to come.[14]

In the middle of the last lecture Cyril refers again to the creed, repeating it once again and urging the candidates for baptism to repeat it with him. He then gives the candidates an opportunity to recite the creed individually, a ceremony called the *redditio symboli*.

Egeria says that it took place on the Saturday before the beginning of Holy Week. The bishop's chair, she says, was placed at the back of the apse behind the altar, and the candidates went up to him one by one and recited the creed, after which the bishop addressed them:

During these seven weeks you have received instruction in the whole biblical Law. You have heard about the faith and the resurrection of the body. You have also learned all you can as catechumens of the content of the Creed. But the teaching about baptism itself is a deeper mystery, and you have not the right to hear it while you remain catechumens. Do not think it will never be explained; you will hear it all during the eight days of Easter after you have been baptized. But so long as you are catechumens you cannot be told God's deep mysteries.[15]

Cyril, at the conclusion of his final lecture, describes his purpose as preparing their souls to receive the heavenly gifts. He says that he has given them as many lectures as possible during the forty days "concerning the holy and apostolic faith it was given to you to profess," and that further lectures concerning the meaning of baptism and the spiritual and heavenly mysteries of the altar will be given them after Easter in the *Anastasis*, the holy place of the resurrection:

In these you will be instructed again in the reasons for each of the things that took place. You will be given proofs from the Old and New Testaments, first, of course, for the things that

were done before your baptism, and next how you have been
made clean from your sins by the Lord with the washing of water by the Word, then how that you have entered into the right
to be called "Christ" in virtue of your "priesthood," then how
you have been given the "sealing" of fellowship with the Holy
Spirit, then about the mysteries of the altar of the new covenant
. . . and finally, how for the rest of your life you must walk
worthily of the grace you have received . . .[16]

There are, of course, minor differences between the two accounts, but the overall picture of what was done in the Jerusalem Church is clear enough. The Lenten instructions were doctrinal and practical, heavily laced with references to the Bible.
Cyril certainly does not, in the lectures we have, undertake a
systematic exegesis of the Old and New Testaments, as Egeria
implies was customary, but the pattern of instruction on the
creed is sufficiently clear. Detailed sacramental instruction
was postponed until after baptism. Cyril suggests that the candidates received only basic instruction in what to do before
the event itself.

THE JERUSALEM MYSTAGOGUE

The scholarly debate over the authorship of the post-
baptismal lectures, or mystagogical catecheses, need not concern us, since the lectures are certainly from Jerusalem in the
fourth century, whether they were written by Cyril or his successor John.[17] As we have seen, Egeria and Cyril agree that
these lectures were given in the week after Easter in the *Anastasis* itself, the site of the empty tomb:

The newly-baptized come into the Anastasis, and any of the
faithful who wish to hear the Mysteries; but, while the bishop
is teaching, no catechumen comes in, and the doors are kept
shut in case any try to enter. The bishop relates what has been
done, and interprets it, and, as he does so, the applause is so
loud that it can be heard outside the church.[18]

The bishop of Jerusalem has, indeed, almost the ideal setting for impressing his hearers. Coming as the mystagogy
does at the climax of the intensive period of catechesis and following hard on the administration of the rites themselves in

the night of the Easter Vigil, the imparting of this knowledge, which had previously been withheld at, so to speak, the very place where their redemption was accomplished, must have moved the neophytes deeply.

Both Egeria and Cyril, in the final catechetical lecture, speak of lectures every day in the Easter week, but the series we possess has only five lectures, and the Armenian lectionary provides for only four. Current scholarly opinion is that the lectures were given only when the bishop could be present at the *Anastasis*.

The first lecture is on the rites before baptism, chiefly the renunciation of the devil. The text is 1 Peter 5:8-14, and the lecture is an explanation in straightforward terms of the meaning of what is said and done. The anointing of the door-posts of the ancient Hebrews with the blood of the paschal lamb against the angel of death is put forward as a type of our salvation from the tyranny of Satan by the blood of the unblemished Lamb Jesus Christ.

The second lecture, on Romans 6:3-14, discusses the rites of baptism itself, and Cyril explains his sacramental theology:

> We did not really die, we were not really buried, we were not really crucified and raised again, but our imitation was in a figure, while our salvation is in reality.[19]

By our celebration of the rites, we perform in a figure (or icon) those things which Christ suffered in reality, and by this imitation we obtain salvation, not in a figure but in truth.

The third lecture is on the holy chrism. Its text is 1 John 2:20-28: "As He was anointed with the spiritual oil of gladness, the Holy Ghost . . . so ye were anointed with ointment (*myron*), having been made partakers and fellows with Christ." Cyril's theme is that we are imitators of Christ, being anointed as he was, and from this anointing (*chrism*) we are called Christians. These things, he says, happened to the priests of the Old Testament figuratively, "but to you not in a figure; because ye were truly anointed by the Holy Ghost."[20] Cyril's sacramental understanding of the anointing is clear:

> While thy body is anointed with visible ointment (*myron*), thy soul is sanctified by the Holy and life-giving Spirit.[21]

The fourth lecture is on the eucharist, with the text 1 Corinthians 11:23ff. Here Cyril departs from his pattern of the first three lectures and discusses not the rite but the theology of the eucharist. On the analogy of the changing of water into wine at the wedding in Cana, he asks:

> Since then He Himself has declared and said of the Bread, *This is my body*, who shall dare to doubt any longer?[22]

The lecture makes clear that the neophytes, dressed in white baptismal robes, go directly from the anointing described in the previous lecture to the eucharist, indicating that baptism, chrismation, and first communion were integrally the rites administered to the candidates at the Easter Vigil.

The fifth lecture, on 1 Peter 2:1ff, deals again with the eucharist, and this time returns to the pattern of exegeting the rite:

> We call upon the merciful God to send forth His Holy Spirit upon the gifts lying before Him; that He may make the Bread the Body of Chist, and the Wine the Blood of Christ; for whatsoever the Holy Ghost has touched, is sanctified and changed.[23]

This corresponds to his statement in the third lecture:

> For as the Bread of the Eucharist, after the invocation of the Holy Ghost, is mere bread no longer, but the Body of Christ, so also this holy ointment (*myron*) is no more simple ointment, nor (so to say) common, after the invocation, but the gift of Christ, and by the presence of His Godhead, it causes in us the Holy Ghost.[24]

Our intention is not to examine the sacramental theology of the Jerusalem mystagogue in detail, but rather to see how he presents that theology to those who have just been baptized. As the creed was the framework of his exposition to the candidates for baptism, so the text of the rite itself is the framework for his explanation of the sacraments. The neophytes are reminded of what was done, and the theological explanation is then given. There is, of course, a certain artificiality in this, since the tendency of the mystagogue is to attribute one effect to each ritual act and to avoid ambiguity in the interests of clarity of presentation.

Cyril does not seem to have been able to follow his own method in the fourth lecture, and instead speaks directly from the Pauline account of the Last Supper of the meaning of the eucharistic food, but the tendency in both the mystagogical and catechetical lectures is to be practical and to tell the new Christians what they need to know and believe in order to live as Christians. It is not surprising, then, that the final lecture contains a phrase-by-phrase commentary on the Lord's Prayer. Other catechists provide a *traditio* of the Lord's Prayer as well as the creed in the final lectures before baptism, but Cyril includes it here, in its place in the eucharistic liturgy. In either case the use of the Lord's Prayer with an understanding of its meaning is expected to be part of the new life of the baptized.

The combination of our sources provides us with a detailed picture of the catechetical instruction given in fourth-century Jerusalem. The candidates were given first biblical and then creedal instruction, with a heavy emphasis on practical morality, and after baptism instruction in the meaning of the sacraments and the Lord's Prayer was given, with the goal of enabling the new Christians to live the life in Christ.

JOHN CHRYSOSTOM

This same emphasis on practical morality is found in the baptismal instruction of St. John Chrysostom. We do not have a complete course of instruction from him, but we do have what might be called the key addresses from two series of instructions given in Antioch, probably in the years 388 and 390. The more extensive series contains a sermon on the occasion of the enrollment of the candidates for baptism, another at the conclusion of their instructions which describes what will happen to them in the baptismal rites (a sermon apparently delivered at the Easter Vigil itself), and his sermons to the newly baptized during Easter week. These last are not about the meaning of the rites but are moral exhortations to them to live the Christian life. These homilies were discovered in 1955 by Fr. Antoine Wenger, A.A. in a manuscript in the Stavronikita monastery on Mt. Athos.[25]

Wegner's discovery called attention to the other series of homilies thought to have been preached in 388, which had been published in 1909 as part of an obscure volume from the University of St. Petersburg.[26] This contained four homilies: one given thirty days before Easter to the candidates, one given ten

days later, one preached on Maunday Thursday describing the
rites, and the same Easter sermon found in the other series. It
has been suggested, not unreasonably, that these sermons were
preached the same year as Chrysostom's homilies on Genesis
and his Easter week sermons on Acts.[27]

Chrysostom was a priest of the Church of Antioch and not
its bishop when these homilies were given, and his role may
have been somewhat different from that of Cyril in Jerusalem.
These series appear to be complete and interrelated, and presumably represent Chrysostom's contribution to the preparation of the candidates. They are in many ways typical of the
sermons of Chrysostom and show his activities as a catechist
and mystagogue. Chrysostom greets those enrolling for Easter
baptism as being betrothed for spiritual marriage and enlisted
for military service in spiritual warfare. The catechumens, in
their sinfulness, are described as "deformed and ugly, thoroughly and shamefully sordid." Seeing his bride in such a
state, the heavenly Bridegroom has come to her,

> that by his own blood He might sanctify her; that, having
> cleansed her by the bath of baptism, He might present her to
> Himself a Church in all her glory. To this end He poured forth
> His blood and endured the cross that through this He might
> freely give sanctification to us too, and might cleanse us through
> the bath of regeneration, and might present to Himself those
> who before were in dishonor and unable to speak with confi-
> dence, but now are glorious without spot or wrinkle, or any
> such thing.[28]

The force of Chrysostom's argument is somewhat lost on us
in our different cultural context, but he likens baptism to the
coming of the bridegroom at night to claim his bride. He takes
the girl, who had sometimes never even seen him before, from
her father's house and brings her to his own, producing an in-
stantaneous change in both environment and lifestyle. The
change expected in the catechumens at baptism is, Chrysostom tells them, this dramatic. The marriage contract is simply
to renounce their former life of service to the Evil One and to
accept the service of Christ. This involves right belief in the
Trinity and a new life in the power of Christ:

> Even if one is a fornicator, or an adulterer, or effeminate, or un-
> natural in his lust, or has consorted with prostitutes, or is a

thief, or has defrauded others, or is a drunkard, or an idolater, the power of the gift and the love of the Master are great enough to make all these sins disappear and to make the sinner shine more brightly than the rays of the sun, if he will only give evidence of good resolution.[29]

Chrysostom likens the training of the catechumenate to the practice sessions of a wrestling school. They are not fraught with spiritual dangers for the candidate, but after baptism, he warns them, the real contest against the power of the Evil One begins:

> Let us learn, during this time of training, the grips he uses, the source of his wickedness, and how he can easily hurt us. Then, when the contest comes, we will not be caught unaware nor be frightened, as we would be if we were to see new wrestling tricks; because we have practiced among ourselves and have learned all his artifices, we will confidently join grips with him in combat.[30]

Chrysostom couples this teaching with practical warnings: against expensive clothes, omens, oaths, performances in hippodrome and theater, and especially against sins of speech. We may take these as typical of Chrysostom's moral concerns and a commentary on his own culture.

In the lecture which he gave to the candidates who had begun their preparation ten days previously, Chrysostom reiterated his moral exhortations, but also talked about the significance of the season of Christ's triumph over death and the devil as the time of baptism. Exegeting Romans 6, he explains:

> In baptism there are both burial and resurrection together at the same time. He who is baptized puts off the old man, takes up the new, and rises up, just as Christ has arisen through the glory of the Father.[31]

He describes the catechumens as taken captive by Christ in his victory over the devil, but captives being transformed from slaves into free citizens. He refers all of this to the exorcism which the catechumens must undergo, at which they stand naked and barefoot "to remind you by your appearance that the devil held sway over you." His picture of what is happening is most striking:

> The catechumen is a sheep without a seal; he is a deserted inn and a hostel without a door, which lies open to all without distinction; he is a lair for robbers, a refuge for wild beasts, a dwelling place for demons. Yet, our Master decreed that through His loving-kindness this deserted, doorless inn, this robbers' refuge should become a royal palace. On this account He sent us, your teachers, and those exorcists to prepare the inn beforehand. And by our instruction, we who teach you are making strong and secure the walls of the inn which were weak and unsound.[32]

The importance of the catechetical task in preparing candidates to receive the baptismal gifts has seldom been so forcefully stated.

The final pre-baptismal address in both series is chiefly devoted to a description of the baptismal rites. This differs from the practice of Jerusalem, and other fourth-century evidence, where this information was delayed until the post-baptismal lectures.

Chrysostom explains that the true actor in the sacraments is not the priest, but the Triune God.

> [The priest] is only the minister of gace and merely offers his hand because he has been ordained to this end by the Spirit. The one fulfilling all things is the Father and the Son and the Holy Spirit, the undivided Trinity. It is faith in this Trinity which gives the grace of remission from sin; it is this confession which gives to us the gift of filial adoption.[33]

Chrysostom explains that he has described these events before they take place so that when the candidates come to the event itself they may set their minds on the things above and "see the objects of bodily sight more clearly with the eyes of the spirit."

His Easter sermon commends the example of St. Paul to the neophytes. Chrysostom's attitude is well summarized in this passage:

> Since we have become Christ's and have put him on, since we are judged deserving of His spiritual food and drink, let us train ourselves to live as men who have nothing in common with the affairs of this present life. For we have been enrolled as citizens of another state, the heavenly Jerusalem. Therefore, let us show forth works worthy of that state . . .[34]

In a real sense, Chrysostom's post-baptismal instruction is not catechesis but moral exhortation, the pupose of which is to assure that the lessons of the catechumenate and the rites of initiation are not forgotten by the neophytes. The final sermon, preached not only to those baptized in the city but to those who have come in fom the countryside for the final day of the Easter octave, concludes:

> And especially do I exhort you who have recently put on Christ and received the descent of the Spirit. Each day look to the luster of your garment, that it may never receive any spot or wrinkle, either by untimely words, or idle listening, or by evil thoughts, or by eyes which rush foolishly and without reason to see whatever goes on. Let us build a rampart about ourselves on every side and keep constantly before our minds that dread day, so that we may abide in our shining brightness, keep our garment of immortality unspotted and unstained and deserve those ineffable gifts.[35]

In many ways, Chrysostom's catecheses are too personal and too culturally conditioned to be helpful models for the present. I believe their chief value is to show us one of the great Christian preachers fulfilling this role and speaking to the adult converts of his day about real issues in their lives and about the power of Christ to change those lives through the sacraments of baptism and eucharist.

THEODORE OF MOPSUESTIA

Theodore was a friend and contemporary of Chrysostom. His baptismal homilies, written in Greek, are preserved only in Syriac. It is believed that they were at one time used as a textbook for catechesis in the Church of Antioch. In their Syriac form they became classics of the Syriac-speaking Nestorian Church, centered in Edessa and later in the Persian Empire.

Theodore's addresses are much more traditional in structure than Chrysostom's. There are ten homilies on the creed, one on the Lord's Prayer, and five on baptism and the eucharist. It appears that, like Chrysostom, Theodore explained baptism before the candidates received the sacrament, but his last three lectures on the eucharist appear to have been given after baptism. His style is exceedingly diffuse and repetitive, and his homilies are more often quarried for information about the rites than read as sermons. If Chrysostom is moralistic, Theodore is doctrinal.

Theodore tells those preparing for Easter baptism that his topic is "the New Testament which God established for the human race through the economy of our Lord Jesus Christ, when he abolished all old things and showed new things in their place."

> Because of this covenant we receive the knowledge of these mysteries so that we should put off the old man and put on the new man who is renewed after the image of Him who created him where there is neither Jew nor Greek, bond nor free, but Christ is all and in all. This will take place in reality in the next world when we shall have become immortal and incorruptible . . . While still on earth we have been inscribed in that awe-inspiring glory of the future world through these mysteries.[36]

This participation, Theodore assures his listeners, requires faith, and faith is expressed in the "profession of faith which we make before Christ the Lord at the time of our baptism." The fist ten lectures consist of a careful exposition of Trinitarian faith expounded in the creed. In the tenth lecture, having completed his discussion of the doctrine of the Holy Spirit, Theodore returns to the Matthean commission to baptize in the name of the Trinity and explains that baptism into the name of the Father, Son, and Holy Spirit follows upon the doctrinal exposition of the catechumenate. He then moves from that to the One Catholic Church into which we are baptized.

> He [Christ] calls the Church all the congregation of the faithful who worship God in the right way and those who after the coming of Christ believed in Him from all countries till the end of the world and the second coming of our Savior from heaven, which we are expecting.[37]

The lecture concludes with a discussion of the notes of the church and the resurrection of the body.

The sermon on the Lord's Prayer was given the day after the final sermon on the creed. Theodore explains that after commanding the apostles to baptize, the Lord said: "And teach them to observe all things I have commanded you." Therefore "the doctrine of religion," right knowledge, and life in accordance with the commandments are required of the baptized. "They added," he tells them, "to the words of the Creed the prayer which Our Lord taught in short words to His disciples, *because it contains the teaching for good works in sufficient manner.*"[38] The homily expounds the prayer line-by-line and at the end restates its importance as a guide for good life and good works, to accompany the right belief taught in the creed.

At the beginning of his next lecture, the first on baptism, Theodore defines a sacrament as "a representation of unseen and unspeakable things through signs and emblems," and therefore "words are needed to explain the power of signs and mysteries."[39]

The remainder of the lectures are almost completely devoted to a description of the rites of baptism and eucharist and a theological interpretation of these rites. The final lecture, however, concludes with a warning against unworthy communion and an exhortation to use the "medicine of repentance" administered in God's name by the priests as "physicians of sins."

Theodore's style is not congenial to us, his theology has been condemned as leading to Nestorianism, and his interpretation of the liturgy is rejected by modern commentators. He was, nevertheless, a teacher of wide influence and high repute among his contemporaries, and the formal structure of his presentations (creed, Lord's Prayer, and sacraments) still commends itself.

AMBROSE OF MILAN

The works of Ambrose of Milan provide clear Western parallels to the great Eastern catechists. Three writings of Ambrose—*Explanatio Symboli, De Sacramentis,* and *De Mysteriis*—are specifically catechetical.

Ambrose tells us that he gave daily instruction to the catechumens *de moralibus* during Lent at the time when the lives of the Patriarchs and the precepts of Proverbs were being read. References in his homilies *De Abraham* indicate that they were preached to those preparing for baptism at the time. Book I of these homilies does deal with right conduct, while Book II follows Philo in treating the mystical sense of the narrative. It certainly appears that other exegetical homilies of Ambrose on the books read during Lent were of the same character; this leads us to believe that this instruction was the occasion for many of the patristic biblical homilies. Egeria, you may remember, included biblical exegesis among the matters presented to the candidates for baptism.

Ambrose says that the enrollment of the *competentes*, or seekers of baptism, took place on Epiphany, on which day he extended an invitation to the catechumens to enroll. The creed was taught to the *competentes* (*traditio symboli*) on Palm Sunday. The *explanatio symboli* is a transcript of the ceremony as Ambrose conducted it. He speaks of this as following the scrutinies and exorcisms of the candidates. Clearly it is a high point in the preparation, which follows not only instruction and exorcism but public examination. Ambrose repeats the text three times in the homily, and tells candidates to memorize it, not to write it down. It will be easier to remember, he tells them, if they do not write it but keep it in mind for the *redditio*.

We shall probably be less willing than Ambrose to assure catechumens that the twelve apostles wrote the creed, which is therefore in twelve articles, but we can admire the simplicity and directness with which he teaches the meaning of the twelve articles of the creed.

He begins his post-baptismal lectures by saying that it would not have been right to give a reasoned account of the sacraments earlier because faith must precede reason. Baptism is the sacrament of conversion, and the purpose of catechesis before baptism is to bring the candidates to faith—thus instruction is joined to exorcism and scrutinies,

> in order that trained and instructed thereby, you might become accustomed to walk in the paths of our elders and to tread in their steps, and to obey the divine oracles; to the end that you might, after being renewed by baptism, continue to practice the life which befitted the regenerate.[40]

He mentions the *disciplina arcani* which would have prevented him from speaking of the sacraments to the uninitiated even if he had wished, but concludes:

> It were better that the light of the mysteries should reveal itself unasked and unexpected than be preceded by some discourse.[41]

All of our mystagogues, even those who describe the baptismal rites (but not the eucharist) in their final pre-baptismal lecture, speak of this discipline which conceals from catechumens the mysteries of the sacraments, but there seems here to be a conviction that it is *better* to wait until after the sacraments have been received to explain their meaning. They are first to be seen with the eyes of faith, and only then can they be examined in the light of reason. Those being taught to conform their lives to the Gospel are given moral instruction. Instruction in the sacraments is reserved for those living the sacramental life.

Ambrose's method of exposition is to describe the rites in detail, and then to explain their meaning by means of a number of Old Testament typologies. In fact, Ambrose's mystagogical work is significant for its mystical interpretation of the Song of Songs. With its exposition of the rites of baptism and eucharist in such detail, the *De Sacramentis* is a major source for our knowledge of early Latin liturgy, Ambrose expounds the Lord's Prayer and recommends the psalter to the new Christians as a source for their own prayers.

It is difficult not to compare the work of Ambrose to that of Cyril of Jerusalem. There are differences of theological emphasis between them, but the pattern of their work is so similar that it is reasonable to assume that both are following an established pattern of Christian catechesis, which the Antiochines, exemplified by Chrysostom and Theodore, had varied slightly.

Candidates for baptism are instructed in Christian living, in the Bible, and in the creed. The Lord's Prayer is expounded, either to the newly-baptized or to those about to be baptized, not only as a prayer to be memorized and recited, but as a model for their own prayer. And in the days immediately following baptism, instruction is given in the meaning of the sacraments for their new life in the risen Christ.

AUGUSTINE OF HIPPO

Although Augustine wrote several treatises on the theology of baptism and himself took part in the catechesis of candidates, he wrote neither a treatise on the rites of Christian initiation nor a complete course of catechetical instruction. F. van der Meer, in his book *Augustine the Bishop*, has collected from various primary and secondary sources most of what Augustine tells us about the preparation of candidates for baptism,[42] but it tells us little or nothing new about such preparation.

Augustine did make one unique contribution, however, his treatise *De Catechizandis Rudibus*, which might be translated *Instruction for Beginners*. It is not a course of catechetics, but an explanation of what to say to an inquirer to move him or her to enroll as a catechumen. The treatise consists of an explanation of what to do, followed by two examples, a shorter and a longer one. This is not formal liturgical catechesis, but what I would call evangelism—a first approach to the uninitiated who come asking questions.

Augustine considers whether the catechist is dealing with a single inquirer, with whom a conversation is appropriate, or with a group which must be addressed in a sort of sermon. He also considers the varied educational backgrounds from which inquirers may come. He then deals with reasons why the catechist may be unhappy about his or her task. What he actually says, although interesting, is not as important as is the clear understanding that what is taught is conditioned by the person of both teacher and pupil. The catechist needs to be in tune with the Gospel which he or she is proclaiming, if the message is to be heard.

The content of this preliminary instruction is, Augustine says, a story, a *narratio*, of the mighty acts of God from creation to the present. Theories are not to be propounded but the story, the *kerygma*, proclaimed. God acted in history; he did not expound propositions. The appeal of the story should be that God loved the world, so that the hearer is moved by the love of God. As a spur to the will, Augustine would conclude with teaching about the Last Things and the punishment of the wicked, and provide some warnings against heretics. This is not essentially different from apostolic preaching in Acts, although his model instruction is more extensive.

We must remember that this is not the catechesis itself, but only the opening instruction which will encourage inquirers to enroll and begin the course of instruction which will lead to the *traditio symboli*, the teaching of the creed, and to biblical, moral, and sacramental teaching. Its purpose is not so much to instruct as to convert, and Augustine is quite concerned that it be tailored to the individual inquirer.

The picture which emerges is of a highly specific beginning, which motivates the convert to enroll as a catechumen and begin the more formal instruction, leading to the sacramental life in Christ.

* * * * * *

The method followed in this essay has been to build up piece-by-piece from the examination of early Christian authors a picture of the process of becoming a Christian in the third, fourth, and fifth centuries.

The initial contact is made by the inquirer. Augustine addressed his treatise to the Carthaginian deacon Deogratias whose ministry this was, so we may assume that normally some minister of the church was the person who interviewed inquirers and sought to convince them to enter the catechumenate. Earlier, Hippolytus described sponsors bringing inquirers to the bishop.

After initial admission to the catechumenate they began a period of religious and cultural readjustment to a Christian lifestyle as hearers of the word. When they were ready, and when the church was prepared to accept them as seekers of baptism, they moved into an intensive period of preparation marked by daily instruction, exorcism, and other liturgical acts. It is to this period that the formal catechetical lectures on Scripture and creed belong. The creed was solemnly delivered to the candidates for baptism and formed the basis for their moral and doctrinal formation. Instruction in the Lord's Prayer, and by extension in the life of Christian prayer, was given either immediately before baptism or as part of the post-baptismal mystagogy.

Some of the classical mystagogues explained the baptismal ceremonies in the final instruction before baptism, but more often this was deferred until after baptism, when sacramental instruction was combined with moral exhortation for the living of the new life in the risen Christ.

This classical pattern apparently developed in the second

and third centuries and continued on even beyond the end of the adult catechumenate in the early Middle Ages.

Notes

1. Burton S. Easton, *The Apostolic Tradition of Hippolytus* (Cambridge: Cambridge University Press, 1934) 25.

2. English translation from Geoffrey J. Cuming, *Hippolytus: A Text for Students*, Grove Liturgical Study, vol. 8 (Bramcotte, Notts: Grove Books, 1976) 15.

3. Ibid. 17.

4. Ibid. 22.

5. English translation from C.W. Butterworth, *Clement of Alexandria*, Loeb Classical Library (Cambridge: Harvard University Press, 1960) 253.

6. English translation from J. Stevenson, *A New Eusebius*, rev. W.H.C Frend (London: SPCK, 1987) 198.

7. Ibid. 199

8. English translation from William Telfer, *Cyril of Jerusalem and Nemesis of Emesa*, Library of the Christian Classics, vol. 4 (Philadelphia: Westminster, 1955) 68.

9. Ibid. 33.

10. English translation from John Wilkinson, *Egeria's Travels* (London: SPCK, 1971) 144.

11. Ibid. 276-277.

12. Telfer, *Cyril of Jerusalem* 96.

13. Ibid. 123-124.

14. Ibid. 124-125.

15. Wilkinson, *Egeria's Travels* 145.

16. Telfer, *Cyril of Jerusalem* 193-194.

17. See Edward Yarnold, "The Authorship of the Mystagogic Catecheses Attributed to Cyril of Jerusalem," *Heythrop Journal* 19 (1978) 143-161.

18. Wilkinson, *Egeria's Travels* 145.

19. English translation from Frank F. Cross, *St. Cyril of Jerusalem's Lectures on the Christian Sacraments* (London: SPCK, 1960) 60.

20. Ibid. 66.

21. Ibid. 65.

22. Ibid. 68.

23. Ibid. 74.

24. Ibid. 65.

25. Antoine Wenger, *Jean Chrysostome: Huit catéchèses baptismales*, Sources chrétiennes, vol. 5 (Paris: Cerf, 1957).

26. A. Popadopoulos-Keremous, *Varia Graeca Sacra* (St. Petersburg, 1909).

27. See Paul W. Harkins, tr., *St. John Chrysostom: Baptismal Instructions*, Ancient Christian Writers, vol. 31 (Westminster, MD: Newman Press, 1963) 17-18.

28. English translation from Harkins, *St. John Chrysostom* 29-30.

29. Ibid. 32f.

30. Ibid. 141.

31. Ibid. 152.

32. Ibid. 195.

33. Ibid. 53.

34. Ibid. 34.

35. Ibid. 130.

36. English translation from A. Mingana, *Woodbrooke Studies*, vol. 5 (Cambridge: W. Heffer and Son, 1932) 19-20.

37. Ibid. 112.

38. English tanslation from A. Mingana, *Woodbrooke Studies*, vol. 6 (Cambridge: W. Heffer and Son, 1933) 1.

39. Ibid. 17.

40. English translation from J.H. Srawley, *St. Ambrose on the Sacraments* (London: SPCK, 1950) 122.

41. Ibid. 123.

42. See F. van der Meer, *Augustine the Bishop* (London and New York: Sheed and Ward, 1961) 353-361.

3

Four Syrian Fathers
on Baptism

THE PURPOSE OF THIS STUDY IS TO EXAMINE BRIEFLY FOUR WORKS OF
the Syrian Fathers on baptism: the Baptismal Instructions of
St. John Chrysostom; the Hymns on the Epiphany attributed
to St. Ephraem Syrus; the Mystagogical Catecheses of Theodore of Mopsuestia; and the Liturgical Homilies of Narsai. I
have chosen these works because of the preeminent positions
of their presumed authors in the development of the thought
and practice in the Syrian Church. My purpose will not be to
deal with the details of the rites themselves—both others and I
have done that elsewhere—but to see what they say about the
meaning of the rites, and particularly to examine the figures,
metaphors, and types which they use to explain the initiatory
rites to their readers.

I believe that there is in these four writers a consistent pattern of liturgy, and of theological interpretation, a pattern of
which the East Syrian tradition is the heir. We have been all
too accustomed to impose Western or Byzantine standards of
interpretation on the rites of the Syrian Church, and we need
to hear again the voices of the great Syrian doctors expounding their own liturgy of Christian initiation. I have dealt only
with the baptismal rite, and not with the baptismal eucharist
which was an integral part of that rite, since the subject of eucharistic theology is too vast for any consideration here.

JOHN CHRYSOSTOM

In 1961 the *Anglican Theological Review* published my attempted reconstruction of the baptismal liturgy known to St. John Chrysostom, on the basis of Antoine Wenger's then recently published edition of eight new baptismal catecheses.[1] Since then Thomas M. Finn has produced a much more extensive study[2] and Paul W. Harkins has translated into English not only Wenger's series of homilies but also those published by Papadopoulos Keraemeus in *Varia Graeca Sacra*.[3] My purpose here is not to go back over this ground, but to consider Chrysostom's explanations of the rite he describes, and particularly the types and figures in which he expounds it.

The first figure which Chrysostom uses of baptism is "spiritual marriage," and he addresses the newly enrolled *photizomenoi* as "a bride about to be led to the holy nuptial chamber."[4] He compares the complete change in life style which the bride underwent in her culture with the change which baptism will work in the life of the catechumen. As the bridegroom comes at night to bring the bride back to his own house, so the Lord comes at night to claim the initiate for his own.[5] Commenting on Psalm 45:10-11, Chrysostom identifies the "father's house"—which the Psalmist urges the bride to forget—with the old life of sinfulness and idolatry which the catechumen must put away.[6]

The figure looses something of its relevance to us whose customs of marriage differ so widely from those Chrysostom knew, but in a society in which the bride had never seen her intended husband until he arrived at her house on the wedding night, the "mystery" in her leaving her father and mother and cleaving only to her husband "suddenly in a single moment" is a striking analogy for the new life which the Christian begins in the font. In a passage reminiscent of Ezekiel 16, Chrysostom contrasts the love of the bridegroom with the depravity of the bride:

> He came to her who was about to become his bride and found her naked and disgracing herself. He threw around her a clean robe, whose brightness and glory no word or mind will be able to describe. How shall I say it? He has thrown himself around us as a garment: *For all you who have been baptized into Christ*

have put on Christ. Suddenly the beggar and outcast has become a queen and stands beside the King.[7]

Chrysostom then passes over into a description of the union of Christ and the church into which the neophyte is born. He refers his description of her beautiful clothing to the verse "All glorious is the princess within,"[8] to show that he is not speaking of outward things. He also speaks of the dowry gifts which Christ bestows upon his bride, citing Ephesians 5:25-27 to show that it is by the bath of baptism that he takes away the former ugliness, and cleansing the bride with his own precious blood, presents her to himself in the beauty of regeneration.[9]

Chrysostom also speaks of the enrollment for baptism as an elistment in military service,[10] and refers to the catechumens as "new soldiers of Christ."[11] He describes the armor which Christ provides for combat against the incorporial powers: the breastplate of righteousness, the shield of faith, and the sword of the Spirit.[12] He does not really develop this idea, however, and speaks more often of the Christian as an athlete arrayed for combat in the spiritual arena.

The pre-baptismal anointing and signing with the cross mark the candidate for baptism as a spiritual combatant,[13] just as a wrestler before his combat is rubbed down with oil. The catechumens, he says, are in a wrestling school, where they practice and exercise, but with baptism the contest itself begins:

> These thirty days are like the practice and bodily exercises in some wrestling school. Let us learn during these days how we may gain the advantage over that wicked demon. After baptism we are going to strip for the combat against him; he will be our opponent in the boxing bout and the fight.[14]

The roots of this idea are clearly in the Pauline epistles, and it is a theme to which Chrysostom continually returns.

Another striking figure is that of the smelting furnace in which God melts down our corrupted nature, and "lets the grace of the Spirit fall upon it instead of flames." The old nature is broken down and a new person is produced.[15] Chrysostom says clearly that the Holy Spirit is the sacramental agent of baptism, "for it is not a man who does what is done, but it is the grace of the Spirit which sanctifies the nature of the water and touches your head together with the hand of the priest."[16] His figure of the smelting furnace fed with the fire of the Spirit speaks eloquently of the personal action of God the Holy Spirit in the baptismal water.

Chrysostom follows this figure by a reference to the breaking of the potter's vessel in Psalm 2.[17] His point is that the potter's vessel is of unfired clay and can be remolded into a different shape, whereas a vessel that had been fired would be irremediably destroyed. It is, of course, the action of the Holy Spirit in baptism which fires us, but Chrysostom's point is that even then God's power is great enough to lead us back through repentence to our former state. He does not explain how God forgives post-baptismal sin, but he states clearly that God does.[18]

Perhaps the best statement of Chrysostom's view of the sacramental efficacy of baptism is this passage:

After this anointing the priest makes you go down into the sacred waters, burying the old man and at the same time raising up the new, who is created in the image of his Creator. It is at this moment that, through the words and the hand of the priest, the Holy Spirit descends upon you. Instead of the man who descended into the water, a different man comes forth, one who has put off the old garment of sin and has put on the royal robe.[19]

He goes on to explain that it is not only the priest who touches the head of the candidate, "but also the right hand of Christ."[20] In an earlier passage in the same homily he says: "It is the grace of the Spirit which touches your head together with the hand of the priest."[21] His point is that the priest is only a minister. "The one fulfilling all things is the Father and the Son and the Holy Spirit, the undivided Trinity. It is faith in this Trinity which gives the remission from sin; it is this confession which gives to us the gift of filial adoption."[22]

This is the very heart of Chrysostom's theology of baptism. It is the action of the Triune God, joining us to the likeness of the death and resurrection of Christ so that we become new people, filled with the Holy Spirit, united with Christ, children of the Father. The teaching of St. Paul in Romans 6:5-8 underlies what Chrysostom is saying, and all of his figures converge on seeing the divine gift of the heavenly washing as the passage from death to life. "We arise," he boldly proclaims, "at the moment that we are buried."[23]

Chrysostom also compares baptism to the Exodus from Egypt. This is, of course, a patristic commonplace. The figure is developed as an allegory. Egypt is the world of sin the Christian leaves behind. The demons, like the host of Pharaoh, are drowned in the water; slavery is ended; and we are led by the new Moses, not into the desert, but into heaven. Moses' face was veiled from the Israelites, but we see the glory of God in the face of Christ. Moses fed them with manna and water from the rock. Christ feeds us on the food of eternal life.[24]

Of greater interest is the passage which precedes this, in which Chrysostom comments on John 19:34. He calls the water and blood which came from the side of Christ symbols of baptism and the mysteries. Amazingly he says: "He did not say: There came out blood and water, but first water came forth and then blood, since first comes baptism and then the mysteries." The accepted reading of the gospel text is, nonetheless, *aima kai hudor*. Wenger, in his notes, comments that Chrysostom has been confused by 1 John 5:6, but goes on to note that he cites the words in this same inverted order in his major commentary on St. John's Gospel.[25]

But for Chrysostom, the symbolism of the gospel sacraments streaming forth from the side of the dying Christ suggests a still greater mystery.

> It is from both of these that the Church is sprung through the bath or regeneration and renewal by the Holy Spirit, through baptism and the mysteries. But the symbols of baptism and the mysteries come from the side of Christ. It is from his side, therefore, that Christ formed his Church. Just as he formed Eve from the side of Adam.[26]

As God created Eve from the side of the sleeping Adam, so from the side of the new Adam sleeping in death, he brings forth the church, constituted by the sacraments of baptism and the eucharist. Baptism, therefore, is for Chrysostom constitutive of the church.

We may now proceed from the consideration of Chrysostom's theology of baptism to an examination of his interpretation of the different actions of the rite.

We have already seen that he likens the enrollment of the *photizomenoi* to enlistment in Christ's army and to betrothal to the heavenly Bridegroom. The enrollment is followed by daily instruction and exorcism.[27] For the exorcism the catechumens stand naked and barefoot, with outstretched arms.[28] This is because we are the booty and spoils of war. We are the devil's captives, and are about to be freed by Christ. The King has conquered the devil in battle, and we are now led into his captivity, which is a passage from slavery to freedom. Those to be exorcized therefore appear as captives, acknowledging the sovereignty of God, into whose control they have been brought. The purpose of the exorcisms is to banish the devil who had held them captive, and to prepare the hearts of the catechumens for the royal presence.

The catechumen, according to Chrysostom, is truly defenseless. The catechumen's slavery to the devil has been ended, but he or she has not yet been brought under the Lordship of Christ. The catechumen is, in fact, "a sheep without a seal," a barren and deserted inn, which must be prepared to become a royal palace.[29] Chrysostom uses the term "seal" (*sphragis*), as Ephraem does, to designate the pre-baptismal anointing and signing with the cross, and the reference here clearly is to the seal of the King which the sheep will receive in baptism.

He speaks of the baptism as taking place at the celebration of the Pascha, so that the neophytes may be a part of the victorious King's triumphal procession, and also be partners in his crucifixion and resurrection.[30]

The first act of the actual baptism takes place on Good Friday at the ninth hour, the hour at which the good thief entered paradise, and at which the darkness covering the earth during the crucifixion was dissolved.[31] It is at this hour that the renunciation of Satan and the adherence to Christ take place. This is described as a contract, the wedding contract with the Bridegroom.[32] It marks the catechumen's actual change of sides in the cosmic warfare, and is therefore also the candidate's entry into the spiritual arena. The adherence is immediately followed by the anointing with "spiritual myron." The priest anoints the forehead, placing the seal, that is, the sign of the cross.[33] The "sheep without a seal" has now passed into the ownership of the Good Shepherd, and is sealed with the cross, the mark of the King whose service the catechumen has now entered.

There is no indication in the text that the Holy Spirit is given by the sealing with myron. It is called *pneumatikon*, spiritual, but Chrysostom always speaks of the Spirit as being given at the actual moment of baptism. The anointing is to prepare the athlete for combat, and the bride for the wedding.[34] The use of perfumed oil is thereby identified with his figures of baptism. The sign of the cross is a sure defense against the wrath of the devil, who cannot look upon it.[35] It is therefore the chief weapon of the Christian warrior/athlete.

The following events are described as taking place "in the full darkness of night."[36] Presumably there was the lapse of a day between the renunciation and the actual baptism, since we know that the baptism took place at the Pascha, but the text is somewhat less than clear on this point. The catechumens strip off their clothes, and their bodies are completely anointed.[37] The continuation of the anointing begun with the signing of the forehead links the following baptism with the preceding renunciation and adherence. Chrysostom introduces the image of Adam and Eve naked and not ashamed in Eden as a type of this removal of clothing. It is symbolic of a return to innocence and of the new creation about to be accomplished, as one stands once again naked and unashamed before one's Maker. "Do not feel shame here," he warns, "There can be no serpent here, but Christ initiating you into the regeneration that comes from the water and the Spirit."[38] The actual baptismal washing follows at once, and

> as soon as they come forth from those sacred waters, all who are present embrace them, greet them, kiss them, rejoice with them, and congratulate them, because those who were heretofore slaves and captives have suddenly become free men and sons and have been invited to the royal table.[39]

The baptismal washing completes the initiatory act, and the neophyte is welcomed into the eucharistic fellowship of the church with the kiss of peace, symbolic of the joining of souls in Christ so that the Christian community became, like its apostolic model, of one heart and one soul.[40]

Wenger, in commenting upon this rite, mentions the obvious fact that it does not contain a post-baptismal consignation. It should be clear, however, that in the context of the Syrian baptismal liturgy this is normal, rather than exceptional.[41] The *sphragis* is given before baptism. The imposition of hands occurs at the moment of baptism. The Spirit is given in baptism "through the words and hand of the priest," so that the neophytes are temples of the Holy Spirit. They are partners of the new Adam, reborn into the new humanity, as athletes and soldiers for Christ, in whose death and resurrection they now share.

EPHRAEM SYRUS:
THE HYMNS ON THE EPIPHANY

Ephraem Syrus has not left us a set of catechetical lectures like those of Chrysostom or Theodore of Mopsuestia, but he has expounded his understanding of baptism in his sermons and especially in his hymns. Edmund Beck, O.S.B., the distinguished editor of much of Ephraem's work, contributed to the first volume of *L'Orient Syrien* an article "Le Baptême chez S. Ephraem," which examined the baptismal teaching of the great Syriac doctor.[42] There would be little profit in attempting to repeat or improve upon his work, which the interested reader may consult directly. Dom Beck, however, excludes the hymns On the Epiphany from his discussion, because he is uncertain of their genuineness, and his desire is to make clear the teaching of Ephraem himself, not that of the Syrian Church.[43] We shall therefore content ourselves with looking at the explanations of baptism given in the hymns On the Epiphany[44] without entering into the question of their authenticity, since it is precisely the teaching of the Syrian Church with which we are concerned.

It is clear, not only from these hymns, but from the other works of Ephraem, that the liturgy of baptism consists principally of a pre-baptismal chrismation (*rushma*) and the baptismal washing. Hymn Three sings of the chrism and Hymn Four of the washing.

Ephraem's Seventh Hymn On Virginity also sings of the chrism, and is in many ways parallel to Epiphany Three in content, although not in structure.[45] Virg. 7:5 says: "With visible oil is painted the hidden image of the hidden king"; Epiph. 3:1: "The secret with the visible is mingled: the chrism anoints visibly—Christ seals secretly." Clearly the anointing is seen as "sacramental," that is, as an efficacious sign. "By chrism" the bodies of the baptizands "are sealed as holy and become temples for God."[46]

The structure of Hymn Three On the Epiphany appears to be simply a catalog of scriptural uses of oil applied to the anointing of those about to be baptized. It is the oil which Elijah multiplied, which Jacob poured upon the rock, with which Moses sealed and anointed Aaron and his sons, with which Saul was anointed king, with which David was anointed with the Spirit, and with which the sinful Mary anointed Jesus.

Naaman is introduced as an example of how a person may be separated from the unclean, and the Christian is described as separated from those outside by the chrism, just as the dirt Naaman took home with him separated him from the unbelievers. Later the hymn mentions the sealing with oil of lepers at their cleansing before the priest leads them to the washing.

> The type has passed and the truth has come; Lo! with chrism have ye been sealed, in baptism ye are perfected.[47]

The close relationship of the chrismation is here established, as is its link with the anointing of prophets and priests in the Old Covenant and with the messianic anointing of Jesus. Unlike the Seventh Hymn On Virginity which speaks of the oil as the friend, disciple, and minister of the Holy Spirit,[48] this hymn speaks of the oil as bringing the whole Trinity to dwell in the Christian:

> The Spirit dwelt in [David] and made song in him. Your anointing which ye have is greater, for Father, Son, and Holy Ghost, have moved to come down and dwell in you.[49]

Ephraem, if it be Ephraem, contrasts the seal of circumcision which separated the Chosen People from the Gentiles with the new seal of chrism. Circumcision sealed the goats as well as the sheep, and it is only the seal of Christ, given through the pre-baptismal chrismation, which marks the lambs of the Good Shepherd, and puts the wolf to flight; in-

deed the power of the Lamb of God changes the wolves themselves into sheep. Circumcision is a type of chrismation, but
only a type.

Hymn Four goes on to describe baptism itself, in which the
old vesture of mortality is put off and the new vesture of immortality is put on.[50] In this hymn he speaks of Christ as fulfilling the whole of the Mosaic covenant:

> Revelations beheld thee, proverbs looked for thee,—
> Mysteries expected thee, similitudes saluted thee,
> Parables showed types of thee.
> The covenant of Moses looked forward to the Gospel:—
> All things of old time flew on and alighted thereon,
>   in the new Covenant.
> Lo! the prophets have poured out on him their
>   Glorious mysteries:—
> The priests and kings have poured out upon him
>   their wonderful types:—
> They have all poured them all out of him.
> Christ overcame and surpassed by his teachings
>   the mysteries,—
> By his interpretations the parables;
> As the sea into its midst—receives all streams
> For Christ is the sea, and he can receive—
> The fountains and brooks, the rivers and streams,
> That flow from the midst of the Scriptures.[51]

Hymn Five is a second baptismal hymn, beginning like the
preceding one with "descend." The neophyte is to put on the
Holy Spirit from the waters of baptism, for "he is the fire that
secretly seals also his flock, by the Three spiritual Names,
wherein the Evil One is put to flight."[52] The baptism of Naaman by Elisha which cleansed his leprosy, and of Israel by
Moses in the sea are types of the forgiveness of sin in Christian
baptism.[53] The anointing of King David by Samuel after which
he put on the armor to slay Goliath is a type also, for Christians are anointed as heirs of the Kingdom, and the armor we
receive from baptism humbles the devil.[54]

Hymn Seven is a collection of spiritual references to water—
all seen as types of baptism: Rebecca watering her flock; Moses with the flock of Jethro, baptizing the Chosen People in the
sea, and seeking to buy water from the sons of Lot; Gideon
choosing his soldiers by how they drank the water; David at

the well of Bethlehem; God in the vision of Isaiah 63 coming as
the one who has trodden the winepress of Edom (i.e., as deliv-
erer of his people); Jeremiah burying his linen girdle in the
water; Solomon anointed as king at the river Siloam;[55] Jesus
with the Samaritan woman, and sending the blind man to
wash in Siloam; Pilate washing his hands; and Peter drawing
in the fish. It adds to these some general remarks about the desirable properties of water, and urges:

> The diver brings up—out of the sea the pearl,
> Be baptized and bring up from the water—
> Purity that therein is hidden—
> The pearl that is set as a jewel—
> In the crown of the Godhead.[56]

Almost any reference to water, no matter how remote, is
sufficient to bring the mystery of baptism into view.

A more interesting reference is found in Hymn 8:5-6 to the
three Hebrew children of Daniel 3 who were thrown into the
fiery furnace:

> That visible fire that triumphed outwardly,
> Pointed to the fire of the Holy Ghost,
> Which is mingled. Lo! and hidden in the water,
> In the flame baptism is figured,
> In that blaze of the furnace.

We might conclude our discussion of these hymns by citing
the twelfth which deals with the fall of Adam. "In baptism," it
says, "Adam found again that glory that was among the trees
of Eden." It is, in fact, an undoing of the harm that was then
done. Instead of the leaves of trees with which Adam and Eve
had to clothe themselves after the fall, God clothes them with
glory in the water. "Baptism is the well-spring of life, which
the Son of God opened by his Life; and from his side it has
brought forth streams."[57]

For the Epiphany hymns, the Holy Spirit is active both in
the chrism and in the water, and the Spirit causes the Holy
Trinity to dwell in the person who is baptized. The water and
oil act outwardly, but God acts inwardly to claim the neophyte for his own and to protect the neophyte from Satan. Incorporated into the flock of the Good Shepherd, freed from
sin, and made a temple for the divine indwelling, the new

Christian is for Ephraem the fulfillment of the Old Covenant and the fruit of the Gospel poured out upon all humankind.

We might conclude this brief study by citing two passages from other, and undisputed, works of Ephraem, which seem to sum up his teaching:

> In those who are signed in baptism, which conceives
>   them in its breast
> In place of the form of the first Adam, which has been
>   corrupted.
> In the worshipful name of the Trinity,
> Father and Son and Holy Spirit.[58]

We note the close connection of the signing with the baptism itself, and the importance of the Threefold Name which accomplishes the rebirth.

> Therefore, because the Spirit was with the Son, he came to John to receive from him baptism, that he might mingle with the visible waters the invisible Spirit; that they whose bodies should feel the moistening of the water, their souls should feel the gift of the Spirit; that even as the bodies outwardly feel the pouring of the water upon them, so the souls inwardly may feel the pouring of the Spirit upon them.[59]

What is said in Epiphany 3:1 of the chrism is here said of the water of baptism. The visible and invisible are mingled and through the external signs God acts to renew our fallen nature, as the Holy Spirit brings us into union with the Trinity.

THEODORE OF MOPSUESTIA

Theodore of Mopsuestia was a contemporary and friend of John Chrysostom, and in Theodore's mystagogical lectures we find a description of the rite of baptism parallel to that of John. The lectures were composed in Greek, but survive only in Syriac translation.[60] The only substantial difference between the rite described by Theodore and that described by Chrysostom is the inclusion by Theodore of a post-baptismal consignation. There appears to be some doubt as to the genuineness of the passage, however.[61] Theodore also describes more ceremonial elaboration in the rites themselves.

Theodore begins his explanation by stating that every sacrament consists in the representation of the unseen and un-speakable things through signs and emblems.[62] Commenting on this, Danielou has remarked:

> Rejecting typology because he refused to see a relationship be-tween historic realities, he was led to interpret sacramental symbolism in a vertical sense, as the relationship of visible things to invisible. Nevertheless, this is not the only aspect un-der which he sees them: symbols of heavenly realities, the sac-raments are for Theodore also a ritual imitation of the historic actions of Christ.[63]

We will not, then, be surprised to hear Theodore say:

> We draw nigh unto the sacrament because we perform in it the symbols of the freedom from calamities from which we were unexpectedly delivered, and of our participation in these new and great benefits which had their beginning in Christ our Lord.[64]

Theodore describes baptism first as a participation in the as-cension of Christ, in which he raises us to his heavenly king-dom. The candidate for baptism comes to enroll as a new citi-zen of the heavenly Jerusalem. In order to enter into this new citizenship, the candidate must be freed from the service of the Tyrant, and this has been accomplished by the death of Je-sus Christ, who now intercedes on the candidate's behalf against Satan.[65]

He also describes baptism as a symbolic second birth, "be-cause you will in reality receive the true second birth only af-ter you have risen from the dead."[66] In the sacrament we re-ceive the signs and symbols, and the assurance through the word of Christ that we shall indeed participate in the second birth in the future. In support of this, Theodore cites Our Lord's words to Nicodemus, commenting that he expounded to him only the symbolic birth, since the reality of the resur-rection would have been too much for Nicodemus' hearing.[67]

> He called baptism a second birth because it contains the symbol of the second birth, and because through baptism we partici-pate as in a symbol in this second birth. Indeed, we receive from baptism participation in this second birth without any question or doubt.[68]

Again Theodore reminds his hearers that it is the death of Christ which accomplishes this, and quotes Romans 6:3-4 and 1 Corinthians 15:20. Death has been abolished by Christ, "and we are baptized with such a faith because we desire to participate in his death, in the hope of participating also in the resurrection from the dead."[69]

All of this, for Theodore, is accomplished by the power of the Holy Spirit, whose grace is an earnest of the benefits which we shall receive.[70] He quotes Ephesians 1:13-14, Romans 8:23, and 2 Corinthians 1:21-22 in support of this. The last passage might be rendered this way in English: "God has *confirmed* us with you in Christ, and has *anointed* us; he has *sealed* us and given us the *first fruits of the Spirit* in our hearts." Whether or not St. Paul intended these to be technical terms, they are certainly so taken by Theodore, who sees here the basis of his baptismal theology:

> The power of the holy baptism consists in this: it implants in you the hope of future benefits, enables you to participate in the things which we expect, and by means of the symbols and signs of the future good things, it informs you with the gift of the Holy Spirit, the first fruits of whom you receive when you are baptized.[71]

Looking at Theodore's description of the actual rites, we find his figure of new citizenship carried through his explanation of the enrollment of the catechumens, and of the duties of their sponsors. The determination of the catechumen to seek baptism shows the candidate's intention of separating oneself from the servitude of the Tyrant, and the ensuing struggle is symbolized by the exorcisms. "You have," he says, "in the ceremony of exorcism, a kind of law-suit with the Demon, and by a Divine verdict you receive your freedom from his servitude."[72] He sees in the attitude of the catechumen during the exorcism, standing silent, naked and barefoot, on garments of sackcloth, a sign of one's captivity to Satan, and Theodore quotes Isaiah 30:3-4 which speaks of Isaiah going naked and barefoot as a sign of captivity.[73]

At the end of the second homily he likens the priest to a major-domo in the house of the Lord and says that we make our contracts with the master through him, since it is unbe-

coming for the master, even of a great earthly house, to con-
descend to making contracts with servants.

The abjuration of Satan is described in great detail. The one
recurring typological theme in the account is the fall of Adam,
to whom the conduct of the catechumen, through the power of
Christ, is to be a contrast. The renunciation of Satan is followed by the engagement to follow Christ:

> I abjure Satan and all his angels, and all his service, and all his
> deception, and all his worldly glamour, and I engage myself,
> and believe and am baptized in the name of the Father, and of
> the Son, and of the Holy Spirit.[74]

This is, for Theodore, a very practical thing, and he does not
hesitate to identify the "angels of Satan" with the pagan poets,
the philosophers, and the heretics, among whom he names
Mani, Marcion, Valentinus, Paul of Samosata, Arius, Eunomi-
us, and Apollinarius.[75]

The priest then draws near, and in Theodore's description
of his vestments, we see a clear example of his approach to the
explanation of the rites:

> The priest draws near to you . . . clad in a robe of clean and ra-
> diant linen, the joyful appearance of which denotes the joy of
> the world to which you will move in the future, and the shin-
> ing colour of which designates your own radiance in the life to
> come, while its cleanness indicates the ease and happiness of
> the next world.

> He depicts these things to you by means of the garments in
> which he is clad, and by the hidden symbols of the same gar-
> ments he inspires you with fear, and with fear infuses love into
> you, so that you may through the newness of his garments look
> into the power which it represents.[76]

Theodore then describes the signing of the forehead with
the chrism. It is a sign that "you have been stamped as a lamb
of God and a soldier of the heavenly King."[77] Both of these are,
of course, familiar figures, but Theodore contents himself with
the obvious explanations of the seal as a sign of ownership
and service and of citizenship in the kingdom of heaven. The
godfather then places a linen cloth over the head of the initiate
as a sign of freedom, since a slave is not allowed to do military
service.[78]

The candidate then removes his or her garments, and Theodore returns to the Adam theme to explain this. The removal of the clothing is symbolic of the putting off of mortality, since it was by the sin of Adam, resulting in the decree of death, that the necessity for wearing clothing arose. The candidate, like Adam in Eden, then comes to the font naked and unashamed.[79]

The anointing of the whole body follows at once. Theodore calls the chrism the "covering of immortality," and the total anointing symbolizes that our whole nature will put on immortality in the resurrection "according to the working of the Holy Spirit which shall then be with us."[80] Clothing is a sign of mortality and our incorporation into Adam in sin. The removal of the clothing signifies innocence and a return to Eden. The body is then covered with the chrism, the robe of immortality, which we receive symbolically in baptism, and finally at the resurrection.

Before the actual baptism, which follows at once, Theodore says the priest must invoke the Holy Spirit upon the water to "impart to it the power both of conceiving that awe-inspiring child and becoming a womb to the sacramental birth."[81] In the womb of the font, the neophyte is spiritually reborn and becomes potentially immortal and incorruptible by the power of the Holy Spirit. It is, of course, only at the resurrection that these potentialities are realized.

Theodore makes use of two figures we found also in Chrysostom. He calls the water a furnace where the neophyte is remade and refashioned, and he speaks of the potter's vessel which is remade and refashioned in water, and then hardened by the fire of the Spirit.[82]

The actual baptism is described as it was by Chrysostom. It is seen as conforming to the symbolic pattern of the Lord's own baptism:

> When therefore the priest says "in the name of the Father" remember the sentence "this is my beloved Son in whom I am well pleased," and think of the adoption of children which is conferred upon you by the Father; and when he says "and of the Son" think of the One who was near to the One who was baptized, and understand that he became to you the cause of the adoption of children; and when he says "and of the Holy

Spirit" think of the One who descended like a dove and lighted upon him, and expect from him the confirmation of the adoption of children.[83]

Baptism is, therefore, the action of the Holy Trinity. It is summed up this way by Theodore:

> You have now received baptism which is the second birth; you have fulfilled by your baptism in water the rite of burial, and you have received the sign of the resurrection by your rising out of the water; you have been born and have become a new man; you are no more part of Adam who was mutable and burdened and made wretched by sin, but of Christ who was completely freed from sin through resurrection.[84]

Following the baptism the neophyte wears a "wholly radiant" garment. When a person receives the resurrection "in reality," that person will not need any clothes, as Theodore indicated when he described the removal of the garments before baptism, but since the garments are now received "sacramentally and symbolically" they are needed, and those which the person wears symbolize the happiness which is in symbol now, but is in the future in reality.[85]

The post-baptismal signing of the forehead follows. We have seen that this is not in Chrysostom, and it may be an addition to the text of Theodore. Its meaning in the text as we have it, nonetheless, is quite clear:

> When Jesus came out of the water he received the grace of the Holy Spirit who descended like a dove and lighted on him, and this is why he is said to have been anointed. It is right therefore that you should also receive the signing on your forehead.[86]

The signing itself is a doublet of the pre-baptismal signing, but the explanation carries through the symbolic conformity of the liturgical rite to the baptism of Christ. This is the same explanation of the post-baptismal signing found in the mystagogical lectures attributed to Cyril of Jerusalem, although probably written by his successor John.[87] In any case, Theodore appears to ignore this consignation in explaining the effects and meaning of the sacrament. The neophyte proceeds to the eucharistic banquet, and Theodore to a description of the rite of the eucharist.

Although he approaches the theology of baptism differently from Chrysostom, his only real difference is in ascribing the gift of the Spirit to the post-baptismal unction, instead of to the baptism itself, but Theodore is sure that it is the power of the Spirit which makes us in baptism children of God and one Body of Christ. He does not, therefore, disconnect the Spirit from the action of baptism, but rather sees it as central to the sacrament.

NARSAI

The final author we shall consider is the Nestorian poet Narsai, who founded the school of Nisbis in the latter half of the fifth century. His poetic homilies on baptism and the eucharist follow so closely the account of Theodore of Mopsuestia that they might almost be described as poetic renditions of Theodore's text. The similarity is so great both in the structure of the rites described and in the details of their interpretation that the lack of a post-baptismal consignation in Narsai itself suggests that there was none in Theodore's original text. The late Dom R. Hugh Connolly has edited and published in English Narsai's liturgical homilies.[88]

Like Theodore, Narsai sees the meaning of baptism in our rescue by Christ from the effect of the fall of Adam:

> By Adam did the Deceiver, who sows error in the world, lead [us] astray; and a Son of Adam was jealous and avenged the wrong of all his race . . . and he consented to die that they should not be styled slaves of the evil ones. As an athlete he went down to the contest on behalf of his people; and he joined battle with Satan and vanquished and conquered him. On the summit of Golgotha he fought with the slayer of men, and he made him a laughing-stock before angels and men. Over the death of men the arrogant-minded was boasting; and by the death of one Man his boasting came to naught. His death and his life men depict in baptism, and after they have died with him they have risen and been resuscitated mystically. In the new way of the resurrection of the dead they travel with him; and they imitate upon earth the conduct of the heavingly beings . . . As athletes they have gone up from the vat of baptism; and watchers and men have received them lovingly.[89]

The identity of thought with that of his master Theodore seems clear. Narsai also stresses the relationship of the visible oil and water to the inward actions of Christ and the Spirit. "By outward things," he says, "God gives assurance of his works [done] in secret."[90] He uses the familiar figure of the furnance in which humanity is remolded.

> The furnace of the waters his purpose prepared mystically; and instead of fire he has heated it with the Spirit of the power of his will. His own handiwork has made a craftsman over his creation, that it should recast itself in the furnace of the waters and the heat of the Spirit.[91]

The priest is an important figure in Narsai's exposition, again following Theodore's lead. "Ah, priesthood," he exclaims, "how greatly is it exalted above all." To the priest God has committed the "great signet of his divinity" with which he will seal the Lord's sheep committed to his care. He has taught him the art of tracing the image of life on the tablet of the waters, of being a "painter of the Spirit."[92] The priest is a physician who mixes the divine drug given into his hands. "With the external sign (rushma, sphragis) he touches the hidden diseases that are within; and then he lays on the drug of the Spirit with the symbol of water."[93] Narsai uses an extended figure of the priest as a general in the army of the King of kings who instructs the faithful in spiritual archery. The arrows are words with which they renounce the devil and adhere to Christ, and the priest "stands at the head of their ranks and shews them the mark of truth that they may aim aright."[94]

It is unnecessary to follow in detail the many points at which Narsai simply restates what Theodore has already said. We shall therefore look briefly at Narsai's explanation of the rushma, the pre-baptismal signing, and the washing itself.

Oil and water and the word of the priest are the means by which the door of the treasure-house of life are opened. They remake the clay of human nature into pure gold.[95] The power is not in the oil, however, but in the Triune Name hidden in it, which cuts into the soul as the oil touches the body. The oil is a shield, "the image of Divinity on the head of a man," armor against evil spirits, and "the great brand of the King of kings."[96]

By the voice of [the priest's] utterances he proclaims the power that is hidden in his words, and declares whose they are, and whose name it is with which they are branded . . . The name of the Divinity he mixes in his hands with the oil; and he signs and says 'Father' and 'Son' and 'Holy Spirit'.[97]

It is not accurate to say that Narsai considers the *rushma* to be the giving of the Holy Spirit in the sense that later Romans or Byzantines would understand the phrase, but he says that the Spirit gives power to the holy oil:

The Spirit gives power to the unction of the feeble oil, and it waxes firm by the operation that is administered in it. By its firmness it makes firm the body and the faculties of the soul, and they go forth confidently to wage war against the Evil One. The sign of his name the devils see upon a man; and they recoil from him in whose name they see the Name of honour. The name of the Divinity looks out from the sign on the forehead; and the eyes of the crafty ones are ashamed to look upon it.[98]

The reference here must surely be to the *sphragis* of Revelation 7:3, and perhaps to the *tau* of Ezekiel 9:4. It is God's brand, his signature upon the forehead of the initiate which marks this person as his forever. This is completely in line with the explanations of Chrysostom and Theodore. It is not what modern writers usually mean by the seal of the Spirit, but it is certainly more than a simple exorcism. It seals the servant of the living God to the day of redemption, and is to be taken in close connection with the immediately following baptismal washing.

Narsai begins his description of baptism proper in the homily called C by Connolly, by rhapsodizing upon the power of the Spirit come into the baptismal water, and upon the ministry of the priest who, striking the water like Moses, commands it to bring forth life, by the power of the Creator. "That word which the waters heard, and brought forth creeping things: the same they hear from the mouth of the priest and bring forth men."[99]

With the name of the Divinity, the three Names, he consecrates the water, that it may suffice to accomplish the cleansing of the defiled. The defilement of men he cleanses with water: Yet not by the water, but by the power of the name of the Divinity which there lights down.[100]

The effect of the washing is, of course, the participation in the death and resurrection of Christ:

> In the grave of the water the priest buries the whole man; and he resuscitates him by the power of life that is hidden in his words. In the door of the tomb of baptism he stands equipped, and he performs there a mystery of death and of resurrection. With the voice openly he preaches the power of what he is doing . . . how it is that a man dies in the water, and turns and lives again . . .

> He verily dies by a symbol of that death which the Quickener of all died; and he surely lives with a type of the life without end. Sin and death he puts off and casts away in baptism, after the manner of those garments which our Lord departing left in the tomb. As a babe from the midst of the womb he looks forth from the water; and instead of garments the priest receives him and embraces him.[101]

We might note here the reference to the font as both a tomb and a womb, picking up the ideas of both resurrection and new birth. Narsai says that the neophyte is received from the font and adorned as a bridegroom on the day of neophyte's marriage-supper. We have already seen this image in Chrysostom, and the identification of the eucharist with the marriage-supper of the lamb is common. The image of the bride-chamber is also common among Syrian Gnostics.[102] As we have already seen, there is no post-baptismal consignation in Narsai, and the neophyte is adorned and welcomed into the eucharistic assembly for the celebration of the marriage-feast, the spiritual food for the newborn.

* * * * * *

At this point we conclude our brief examination of the rite of baptism in the Syrian Fathers. Even in this sketchy form it should be clear that there is a real Syrian theological and liturgical tradition with roots in Antioch as well as Edessa, and that John, Ephraem, Theodore, and Narsai are witnesses to the same tradition.

Notes

1. L.L. Mitchell, "The Baptismal Rite in Chrysostom," *Anglican Theological Review* 43 (1961) 397-403; A. Wenger, *Jean Chrysostome: Huit catéchèses baptismales*, Sources chrétiennes, vol. 50 (Paris: Cerf, 1957). Homilies from the Stavronikita series edited by Wenger will be cited as St.

2. T.M. Finn, *The Liturgy of Baptism in the Baptismal Instruction of John Chrysostom*, Catholic University of America Studies in Christian Antiquity, vol. 15 (Washington, D.C.: Catholic University Press, 1957.

3. P.W. Harkins, *St. John Chrysostom: Baptismal Instructions*, Ancient Christian Writers, vol. 31 (Westminster, MD: Newman, 1963); A. Papadopoulos Keraemeus, *Varia Graeca Sacra* (St. Petersburg, Russia, 1909). The homilies from this series will be cited as P.K. For the convenience of the reader, page numbers in Harkins' translation, which includes both series, will follow the citation with the symbol H.

4. St. 1:1,d (H 23).

5. P.K. 3:1 (H. 161).

6. St. 1:6-10 (H. 125f.).

7. P.K. 3:3-7 (H. 162f.).

8. Psalm 45:12.

9. St. 1:16-17 (H. 29); P.K. 3:9-10 (H. 163f.).

10. St. 1:1 (H. 23); 1:8 (H. 25); 2:1 (H. 43).

11. St. 1:18 (H. 30); 1:40 (H. 39); 4:6 (H. 68).

12. St. 3:11 (H. 59).

13. St. 2:23 (H. 51f.).

14. P.K. 1:29 (H. 140f.); see St. 3:8 (H. 58).

15. P.K. 1:22 (H. 138f.).

16. St. 2:10 (H. 47).

17. P.K. 1:23-26 (H. 139f.).

18. St. 3:23 (H. 63).

19. St. 2:25 (H. 52). We find the same idea in St. 2:11 and P.K. 1:20; 2:10.

20. St. 2:26 (H. 52).

21. St. 2:10 (H. 47; see P.K. 2:12-14).

22. St. 2:26 (H. 52f.).

23. P.K. 2:12 (H. 152).

24. St. 3:23-27 (H. 63-65).

25. Wenger, *Huit catéchèses* 160, n. 1.

26. St. 3:16-17 (H. 61f.).

27. St. 2:12 (H. 47).

28. St. 2:14 (H. 48); P.K. 2:14 (H. 153f.).

29. P.K. 3:16 (H. 155).

30. P.K. 2:7 (H. 150).

31. P.K. 3:19 (H. 166).

32. P.K. 3:26 (H. 168).

33. St. 2:23 (H. 51f.); P.K. 3:27 (H. 169). Harkins translates *sphragis* as "the sign [of the cross]" in St. 2 which obscures the reference to the seal. P.K. 3 uses the word *stauron*, and so he is correct that the outward form of the *sphragis* was the sign of the cross.

34. P.K. 3:27 (H. 169).

35. Ibid. and St. 2:23 (H. 52).

36. St. 2:24 (H. 52).

37. Ibid.

38. P.K. 3:28-29 (H. 170).

39. St. 2:27 (H. 53).

40. P.K. 3:32 (H. 171).

41. Wenger, *Huit catéchèses* 99f. This question has been much discussed, most recently in E.P. Siman, *L'Experience de l'Esprit par l'église d'après la tradition Syrienne d'Antioche*, Théologie historique, vol. 15 (Paris: Beauchesne, 1971) 88f.

42. E. Beck, "Le Baptême chez S. Ephrem," *L'Orient Syrien* 1 (1956) 111-137.

43. Ibid. 111. See also E. Beck, *Des Heiligen Ephraem des Syres Hymnen de Nativitate*, Corpus Scriptorum Christianorum Orientalium, vol. 187 (Louvain: E. Peeters, 1959) ix-xi.

44. Syriac text edited by E. Beck, Corpus Scriptorum Christianorum Orientalium, vol. 186, 144-191. German translation, Corpus Scriptorum Christianorum Orientalium, vol. 187, 131-177; English translation in Nicene and Post-Nicene Fathers (2nd series), vol. 13, 265-289.

45. Syriac text of *de Virg.* in Corpus Scriptorum Christianorum Orientalium, vol. 223, 24-28; Latin and French teanslation in Beck, *Des Heiligen* 125ff., 134f.; German translation in Corpus Christianorum Orientalium, vol. 224, 24-29.

46. Epiph. 3:9.

47. Epiph. 3:18.

48. Virg. 7:6.

49. Epiph. 3:16.

50. Epiph. 4:1-3.

51. Epiph. 4:21-25.

52. Epiph. 5:2.

53. Epiph. 5:6-7.

54. Epiph. 5:9-11.

55. 1 Kings 1:38. So the Peshitto. The Hebrew has Gihon.

56. Epiph. 7:18.

57. Epiph. 12:5.

58. *Hymnus De Virginitate* 7:5.

59. *Sermo De Domino Nostro* 53, in Post Nicene Fathers, vol. 13, 329; Syriac text in Corpus Scriptorum Christianorum Orientalium, vol. 270, 51f. (This is no. 55 in Beck's text.)

60. A. Mingana, *Woodbrooke Studies*, vol. 6 (Cambridge: W. Heffer and Sons, 1933). We shall cite his English translation. There is also a French version: R. Tonneau and R. Devreese, *Les Homilies catéchètiques de Théodore de Mopsueste*, Studi e Testi, vol. 145 (Vatican: Biblioteca Vaticana Apostolica, 1949).

61. See Siman, *L'Experience de l'Esprit* 78, 88; L.L. Mitchell, *Baptismal Anointing* (London: SPCK, 1966); 2nd edition (Notre Dame: University of Notre Dame Press, 1978) 41.

62. Mingana, *Woodbrooke Studies* 17.

63. J. Danielou, *The Bible and the Liturgy* (Notre Dame: University of Notre Dame Press, 1956) 14.

64. Mingana, *Woodbrooke Studies* 22.

65. Ibid. 24ff.

66. Ibid. 49.

67. Ibid. 50f.

68. Ibid. 51.

69. Ibid. 52.

70. Ibid. 53.

71. Ibid. 53f.

72. Ibid. 35.

73. Ibid. 32.

74. Ibid. 43.

75. Ibid. 40.

76. Ibid. 45f.

77. Ibid. 46.

78. Ibid. 49.

79. Ibid. 54.

80. Ibid.

81. Ibid. 55.

82. Ibid. 57f.

83. Ibid. 67.

84. Ibid.

85. Ibid. 68.

86. Ibid.

87. Mystagogical Catecheses 3:1-2 (ed. Cross, London: SPCK, 1960) 22f.

88. R.H. Connolly, ed., *The Liturgical Homilies of Narsai*, Texts and Studies, vol. 8.1 (Cambridge, 1909).

89. Ibid. 53f.

90. Ibid. 45.

91. Ibid. 41, see also 36, 48.

92. Ibid. 34.

93. Ibid. 43.

94. Ibid. 44.

95. Ibid. 42.

96. Ibid. 43.

97. Ibid. 44.

98. Ibid. 45.

99. Ibid. 47-50.

100. Ibid. 50.

101. 51f.

102. See C.J. de Catanzaro, "The Gospel of Philip," *Journal of Theological Studies* 13 (1962) 35-71 *et alibi*.

4

Ambrosian
Baptismal Rites

THE AMBROSIAN LITURGY OF THE CHURCH OF MILAN HAS A HISTORY as ancient and venerable as that of Rome. Some scholars have held it to be the ancient Roman rite, whereas others claim it as the source of the Gallican rites of France and Spain. Certainly we cannot neglect the testimony of this historic Western rite in our modern discussions of Christian initiation.[1]

DOCUMENTARY SOURCES

Our earliest sources for the baptismal rites of the Church of Milan are the writings of St. Ambrose himself, particularly the two treatises *De Sacramentis* and *De Mysteriis*.[2] These are mystagogical addresses to the newly baptized, and from them, and from references in Ambrose's other works, we can form at least a partial picture of the ancient rites of Christian initiation at Milan.

The next group of documents date from the ninth and following centuries. They are the Ambrosian sacramentaries,[3] the *Manuale Ambrosianum*[4] of the eleventh century, and *Beroldus*,[5] a twelfth-century description of the ceremonies of the cathedral church by its master of ceremonies for the guidance of those who performed them.

The Ambrosian rite is, of course, a living rite and is still

used in the old archiepiscopal province of Milan, and both the
Missale Ambrosianum and the *Rituale* exist in modern editions.
It is the intention of this study to compare the rites described
by Ambrose with those of the later period, with reference to
the modern books when it seems relevant.

ENROLLMENT AND PREPARATION OF CANDIDATES

St. Ambrose tells us that he invited the catechumens to enroll as *competentes*, or candidates for baptism, on Epiphany.[6]
By the eleventh century this ceremony had been moved to
the Sunday *de Samaritana* at the beginning of Lent, on which
day, after the gospel, the deacon says: "Whosoever wishes to
give in any names, let him bring them forward now."[7] However, the Ambrosian rite preserves to this day an announce-
ment of the date of Easter after the gospel on Epiphany,[8] and
it seems reasonable to conclude that this was the occasion on
which Ambrose urged the catechumens to seek baptism.[9] He
mentions the signing of the *competentes* with the cross,[10] presumably at the time of their giving their names, but he gives
no details.

Ambrose gives little information about the preparation of
the *competentes*. He does tell us that he instructed them daily
de moralibus at the time of the daily lessons from Genesis and
Proverbs,[11] and in his *De Abraham* we have a series of these
daily sermons.[12] From *Beroldus* we learn that the lessons from
Genesis and Proverbs were read daily (except Saturday and
Sunday) after terce and none.[13] After terce the two lessons
were read, separated by a *psalmellus*. The same order prevailed
after none, but they were followed by a *canticum* and the gospel. *Beroldus* expects the Mass to proceed from this point with
the *Dominus vobiscum*, *Kyrie*, and *oratio super sindonem*, but
most scholars believe that orginally the eucharist was not celebrated on the Lenten weekdays, so that Ambrose's instructions would have been given at the pro-anaphora rather than
at a full eucharist.[14] The *Manuale* gives the texts of the *psalmelli*
and *cantica* and the incipits of the lessons.

Beroldus and the *Manuale* describe scrutinies on the Lenten
Saturdays. Neither *De Sacramentis* nor *De Mysteriis* mention
these, but the *Explicatio Symboli* which precedes *De Sacramentis*

in two of the earliest manuscripts[15] begins: *Celebrata hactenus mysteria scrutaninimum*, without giving any details.[16] The ceremonies described by *Beroldus* cannot have existed in the form he knew them in Ambrose's time, but it is possible that they represent developments of earlier ceremonies.

The medieval rite took place after Mass. Ashes were blessed and placed upon a goatskin in the midst of the church in the form of a *chrismon* (that is, a *chi, rho*). The deacons and subdeacons then went to the door of the church where the *competentes* (whom *Beroldus* assumes to be children) were waiting. *Beroldus* directs the deacon to ask the questions which follow of the subdeacon, but there can be no doubt that originally the *competentes* were asked directly:

> *What do they seek? R. Faith.* He asks: *Are their parents worthy? R. They are worthy.* Again he asks: *Do they renounce the devil and his pomp? R. They renounce.* He asks: *The world and its pomp? R. They renounce.* And the deacon says: *Be mindful of your words, that they may never leave you. R. We shall be mindful.*[17]

De Sacramentis gives a different form of the renunciations and places them on Holy Saturday after the *effata*,[18] but the final sentence of this dialogue is substantially the same as *De Sacramentis* I, 2, 5, from which source it may have been introduced into the later Ambrosian rite.

The *competentes* were then brought into the church and made to stand around the *chrismon* of ashes. The clergy then breathed upon the ashes and exorcised the *competentes* using the Exorcism of St. Ambrose.[19] The presbyters signed them with the cross. They were then dismissed with a blessing.[20] *Beroldus* describes the anointing of catechumens on the breast with holy oil on the Saturday of Lazarus, with the formula "I anoint thee with the oil of salvation in Christ Jesus the Lord unto eternal life."[21] The anointing took place before the scrutinies.

THE TRADITIO SYMBOLI
AND THE CONSECRATION OF THE OILS

Ambrose makes no mention of the *traditio symboli*, the delivery of the text of the creed to the candidates, in either *De Mys-*

teriis or *De Sacramentis*, but in one of his epistles he mentions the ceremony and places it on Palm Sunday.

> On the following day, which was the Lord's Day, after the lessons and the tract, I was delivering the creed to certain candidates in the baptistry of the basilica.[22]

In the later rite the ceremony has been moved to the preceding Saturday, and is placed *post missam cantatam*.[23] However, it is clear from St. Ambrose's reference that in his day the ceremony took place between the *missa catechumenorum* and the *missa fidelium*.[24] By the time of *Beroldus* the *traditio* had become simply an ancient form, removed from its prominent place in the Sunday eucharist to the previous day after Mass. The *competentes* were admitted with the words: "Children, enter the house of the Lord. Hearken to your father, teaching you the way of knowledge."[25] The archbishop addressed them: "For those that are to be reborn: Sign yourselves and hear the Creed" and then he recited the creed three times for them, the godmothers signing the infants on the brow each time. There is no mention of an explanation of the creed in either *Beroldus* or the *Manuale*, and probably none was given as the *competentes* were expected to be infants, although such an explanation is found in both the Roman and Gallican books such as the *Gelasian Sacramentary* and the *Missale Gallicanum Vetus*. There is little doubt that originally such an explanation was given at Milan. The *Explicatio Symboli*[26] is probably a sermon preached by Ambrose at the *traditio*.

Ambrose is silent about the consecration of the chrism and the blessing of the oil of the catechumens, but the medieval rite provides for these on Maunday Thursday between the *oratio super oblatam* and the *sursum corda*. This Ambrosian material is unique, differing from the corresponding Roman forms both in text and in its position in the Mass.[27]

THE EFFETA AND FINAL RENUNCIATIONS

Ambrose describes the baptismal rites as taking place on the Sabbath and beginning with the *effeta* or *aperitio*.[28] This rite, based on our Lord's healing of the deaf mute,[29] was performed by the bishop[30] who touched the ears and nostrils of the candidate. The *effeta* has dropped out of the Ambrosian rite, although it is found in the Roman sacramentaries.[31]

The *competentes* were then brought into the baptistry where they were anointed by a presbyter and a deacon as *athletae Christi*.[32] The renunciations followed in the form:

> Dost thou renounce the devil and his works?
> I renounce.
> Dost thou renounce the world and its pleasures?
> I renounce.
> Be mindful of thy words, and never let the contents of
>   thy bond pass from thy memory.[33]

This is different both from the later Ambrosian form previously quoted and the Roman form, although, as we have seen, the final admonition has formed a permanent part of the Ambrosian scrutinies.[34] *De Sacramentis* gives the impression that these questions are asked by the deacon, but *De Mysteriis* clearly states that the questioner is the *summus sacerdos*.[35]

THE CONSECRATION OF THE FONT IN ST. AMBROSE

The consecration of the font followed. *De Sacramentis* describes it thus:

> For as soon as the priest enters, he makes an exorcism over the element of water; afterwards he offers an invocation and a prayer, that the font may be consecrated and the presence of the eternal Trinity may come down.[36]

> The priest comes; he says a prayer at the font; he invokes the Name of the Father, the presence of the Son, and of the Holy Ghost; he uses heavenly words. What heavenly words? They are those of Christ, that we should baptize in the Name of the Father and of the Son and of the Holy Ghost.[37]

De Mysteriis adds:

> But when it has been consecrated by the mystery of the saving cross, then it is fitted for the use of the spiritual laver and the cup of salvation.[38]

The picture emerges of an exorcism of the water, followed by an invocation of the Trinity with the signing of the water with the cross, repeating our Lord's words of institution. The figure is that of the baptism of Christ. The voice of the Father is heard; the Son and the Spirit descend into the water. *Beroldus* speaks of a *benedictio* and *adjuratio* of the water by the archbishop, which seems to correspond to Ambrose's description.[39] The prayers for this blessing in the *Manuale* are still found in the preconciliar *editio typica* of the *Missale Ambrosianum*.[40]

THE MEDIEVAL AMBROSIAN FORM
OF THE BENEDICTIO FONTIS

The later rite is a part of the Easter Vigil, which begins with the blessing of the new fire and paschal candle,[41] followed by the reading of six lessons, each with a chant and a collect.[42] The *benedictio fontis* begins with the collect *Omnipotens sempiterne Deus, adesto magnae pietatis tuae mysteriis* . . . found also in the Roman rite,[43] but then proceeds with different forms. First, two prayers are said, one over the water and the other for the *competentes*. Then follows the great prayer over the font, beginning *Adiuro te, creatura aquae*. The opening passage of this prayer is similar to the *exorcismus aquae fontis* in the *Missale Gallicanum Vetus*[44] and to the *consecratio fontis* in the Gelasian Sacramentary,[45] but it is longer and contains more biblical references. Beginning with the division of the earth and sea, and the flowing of the four streams from the *fons paradisi*, it continues with references to Christ's miracle at Cana, his walking on the water, and his baptism in the Jordan. It then identifies the *lignum passionis* with the wood which sweetened the waters of Marah, speaks of Christ as producing water from the stony rock, cleansing Naaman the Syrian, naming the water Siloam when he healed the blind man, and concludes with references to the water flowing from his side and to the command to baptize in the Triune Name. All is then reprised in a concluding sentence: *Efficere ergo aqua exorcizata* . . . This is followed by another prayer, *Sanctificare per Verbum Dei* . . ., which is also found in the Mozarabic *Liber Ordinum*.[46] This interesting and beautiful prayer contains a direct quotation from Ambrose's *Expositio Evangelii Secundum Lucam*,[47] but the relationship between the two may be much later than Ambrose himself.

In any event, we find in the later rite the elements described by Ambrose: the exorcism, and the prayer of blessing with the use of our Lord's own words.[48]

Beroldus and the *Manuale* direct the pouring of chrism into the font at the end of this prayer, but Ambrose says nothing of this. The medieval custom at Milan was for the archbishop to baptize three boys to be named Peter, Paul, and John.[49]

THE THREEFOLD IMMERSION

Ambrose describes the baptism proper in this manner in *De Sacramentis*:

> Thou camest to the font, thou wentest down in it; thou didst watch the high priest, thou didst see the levites and the presbyter in the font.

> Thou wast asked, "Dost thou believe in God the Father Almighty?"

> Thou saidest, "I believe," and didst dip; therefore thou wast also buried with Christ: for he who is buried with Christ, rises again with Christ. A third time thou wast asked, "Dost thou believe also in the Holy Ghost?" Thou saidest, "I believe, and didst dip a third time, that the triple confession might absolve the fall of thy former life.[50]

This triple immersion as the candidate responds to the creedal questions, as in the *Apostolic Tradition* of Hippolytus,[51] has disappeared from the medieval Milanese books. The three questions are asked, but in a Roman form, and the baptism follows the third response. *Beroldus* describes it this way:

> And they shall hold them out to the cardinals in the fonts and while they hold the boys the archbishop asks them: *What do ye seek?* They reply: *To be baptized.* Again he asks: *Do ye believe in God the Father Almighty, Maker of heaven and earth?* They reply: *We believe.* He asks: *And in Jesus Christ his only Son our Lord, who was born and suffered?* They reply: *We believe.* He asks: *Do ye believe in the Holy Ghost, the Holy Catholic Church, the communion of Saints, the remission of sins, the resurrection of the flesh, everlasting life?* They reply: *We believe.* And straightway he continues: *Baptize them in the Name of the Father and of the Son and of the Holy Ghost.* And straightway they baptize them, saying their names: *I baptize thee*, the first dip: *in the Name of the Father*, the second dip: *and of the Son*, the third dip: *and of the Holy Ghost. Amen.*[52]

This is substantially the same form as in the Gregorian and Gelasian Sacramentaries. The typically Ambrosian *et in cruce eius* has disappeared, and the declarative formula has been adopted for the actual baptism. The earlier tradition, represented by Hippolytus and Ambrose, used no declarative form, but baptized in response to the creedal questions.

THE POST-BAPTISMAL ANOINTING
WITH CHRISM

Ambrose describes the unction with chrism (*muron*) that follows the immersion. This was performed by the bishop (*sacerdos*) with the following formula: "God, who hath regenerated thee by water and the Holy Ghost, and hath forgiven thee thy sins, himself anoint thee unto eternal life."[53] *Beroldus* directs that the archbishop "anoints the aforesaid baptized children on their foreheads in the form of a cross," but Ambrose simply says *supra caput*. The prayer is similar to that found in the Gelasian Sacramentary (where, however, the anointing is performed by a presbyter) and which found its way into the First Prayer Book of Edward VI, to be used by the priest, anointing the infant upon the head immediately following the baptism.

> Almighty God, the Father of our Lord Jesus Christ, who hath regenerated thee by water and the Holy Ghost, and hath given unto thee remission of all thy sins; he vouchsafe to anoint thee with the unction of his Holy Spirit and bring thee to the inheritance of everlasting life.[54]

THE FOOT WASHING

The foot washing which followed the chrismation is mentioned in both *De Sacramentis* and *De Mysteriis*. In the former treatise, Ambrose comments upon the failure of the Church at Rome to observe this ceremony, and cites the witness of the Gospel and the testimony of St. Peter himself, *qui sacerdos fuit ecclesiae romanae*.[55] The washing was begun by the bishop and continued by the presbyters. It sounds as though the evangelical account of the foot washing were read, but there is no definite statement to this effect. Although the Roman Church does not know the foot washing, it is found in the *Missale Gothicum*, *Missale Gallicanum Vetus*, the Bobbio Missal, and the Stowe Missal. The clear unanimity of the Celtic, Gallican, and Ambrosian books in a non-Roman ceremony traceable to the works of Ambrose himself lends great weight to Mgr. Duchesne's theory of the common Milanese origin of these rites.

SEAL OF THE SPIRIT

Following the foot washing, the newly baptized were clothed in white robes (*vestimenta candida*),[56] and sealed with the *spiritale signaculum*. This "seal" is clearly not the same as the post-baptismal unction, and is separated from it by the foot washing and the clothing with white robes. The *Apostolic Tradition* also has a seal which is separated fom the anointing by the clothing. In Hippolytus the first anointing is performed by the presbyter with the formula: "I anoint thee with holy oil in the name of Jesus Christ," while after being clothed, the neophyte is brought to the bishop who lays his hand upon their head with prayer, after which he pours "the oil of thanksgiving" upon the forehead of each and says: "I anoint thee with oil in the Lord, the Father Almighty, and Jesus Christ, and the Holy Ghost." The text continues: "And signing them on the forehead he shall say: The Lord be with thee; and he who is signed shall say: And with thy spirit. And so he shall do to each one."[57]

Ambrose describes the spiritual seal in this way:

> At the invocation of the priest, the Holy Spirit is bestowed, the spirit of wisdom and understanding, the spirit of counsel and strength, the spirit of knowledge and godliness, the spirit of holy fear, as it were the seven virtues of the Spirit.[58]

> God the Father hath sealed thee, Christ the Lord hath confirmed thee, and hath given the earnest of the Spirit in thine heart, as thou hast learned from the Apostolic lesson.[59]

> Therefore God anointed thee, the Lord signed thee. How? Because thou wast signed with the image of the cross itself unto his passion, thou receivedst a seal unto his likeness . . .[60]

Form and Matter of the Seal

The first question raised by this description is whether the catalog of the sevenfold gifts of the Spirit is a liturgical formula, or simply a biblical quotation used to explain what was done. The principal argument against its being a liturgical form is that it is also quoted in *De Mysteriis* 7, 42, and *De Mysteriis* never quotes liturgical texts, presumably because the *disciplina arcani* forbade their inclusion in a work intended for the general reader. Those, like Dom Connolly and Dom Morin, who believe that it is a part of a liturgical form, feel that its similarity to the biblical passage made it possible to include it in *De Mysteriis*, where the passage is simply introduced by *accepisti signaculum spiritale*, without any reference to the invocation of the priest.

There is also a question as to what liturgical action accompanied the giving of the seal. The most reasonable assumption is, of course, that the bishop made the sign of the cross on the neophyte's forehead, and it is certain that this was done at some point in the rite, as it is mentioned in *De Sacramentis* VI, 2, 7 quoted above. However, the description of *Beroldus* directs the bishop to make the sign of the cross on the forehead at the post-baptismal unction. Clearly there is confusion between the *unctio* and the *signaculum spiritale*. The Sacramentary of Bergamo has only one anointing after baptism. It is performed by the bishop (*sacerdos*) who signs the neophytes with chrism using the Ambrosian formula for the anointing *supra caput* previously quoted. This same prayer occurs in the *Manuale* where the presbyter is directed to make the cross of chrism *in cerebro infantum*. In both these cases the final clause of the formula is augmented to read: "he himself anoints you with the chrism of salvation, in Christ Jesus our Lord unto eternal life."

Magistretti discusses this change in wording in the preface to his *Pontificale*, noting that this prayer, together with another which begins with the same words but continues by invoking the sevenfold gifts of the Spirit, occurs in the Gelasian and Gregorian Sacramentaries. His suggestion is that the fuller form came into use when the presbyters began to anoint in the absence of the bishop.

The Rites of St. Ambrose and Hippolytus

It seems that Ambrose is describing a rite similar in this respect to that described by Hippolytus. After the immersion with the threefold interrogative form, the neophytes are anointed *supra caput*, that is, by having oil poured over their head, with the formula quoted by Ambrose. Their feet are then washed, and they are clothed with their white robes and brought back to the bishop who signs them on their forehead, making the sign of the cross and using a formula containing the enumeration of the sevenfold gifts of the Spirit. The existence in the Gelasian Sacramentary of two prayers for two anointings, each having the same incipits would lead to the conjecture that Ambrose knew a form similar to that in the Gelasian book. The later Ambrosian rite, probably under Roman influence, reduced its anointings to one: the sign of the cross made on the forehead by the archbishop, or on the head by a priest who baptized in his absence. This would accord with the regulation of Innocent I that presbyters were not to anoint the brow with chrism.[61] The Ambrosian *Pontificale* contains no rite of confirmation, and Magistretti is certainly right when he identifies the *signaculum spiritale* of the *De Mysteriis* with the Roman laying on of hands, as far as it concerns its effects.[62] The Roman rite of confirmation has been introduced into Milan, and, in fact, the Ambrosian *Pontificale* is no longer in use. However, there is no evidence of the laying on of hands ever having been a part of the Ambrosian initiatory rites.

THE BAPTISMAL EUCHARIST

After the receiving of the seal, the neophytes were admitted to the eucharist. *De Sacramentis* is perhaps best known for the fragments of the eucharistic prayer, or *canon missae*, which it quotes. The Ambrosian liturgical books all provide separate *missae pro baptizatis* for the Easter octave distinct from the regular Masses. The Masses for the newly baptized are in the "winter church," and the other Masses in the "summer church." It was presumably at these Masses celebrated *pro baptizatis* that Ambrose delivered the addresses which we know as *De Sacramentis*. During these addresses Ambrose makes allusion to the lesson read in church, and J.H. Srawley, in the introduction to his edition of Ambrose's *On the Sacraments* and *On the Mysteries*, has prepared a table collating the passages mentioned by Ambrose with the lessons in the *Manuale* and Sacramentary of Bergamo.[63] This table shows that the lessons do not actually correspond in all cases with those in the liturgical books, but that in seventeen cases biblical passages quoted in *De Sacramentis* were read in church at some time during the baptismal cycle, and in only one case does the passage quoted by Ambrose as *quod audisti hodie legi* fail to appear in the lectionary. From this we may conclude that the newly initiated Christians participated in a daily eucharist throughout the Paschal octave, during which they received instructions in the meaning of the initiatory rites from the archbishop or his deputy. The pericopes which have been preserved in the liturgical books are not identical with those used in Ambrose's day, although many of these same lessons occur during the cycle, assigned to a different day.

THE RITE OF MILAN IS AMBROSIAN

This survey of the baptismal rites of Ambrose and the Church of Milan demonstrates, in this writer's opinion, that the rite of Milan can justifiably be called the Ambrosian rite, if not in the sense that Ambrose wrote it, at least in the sense that it is clearly continuous with the liturgy which he knew. It has, of course, undergone considerable modification and expansion, influenced, no doubt, by its powerful southern rival at Rome, but in the preservation of distinctive ceremonies—such as the foot washing and distinctive formulae—it has remained itself.

A comparison of this rite with, for example, that described by John Chrysostom, Cyril of Jerusalem, or Theodore of Mopsuestia, and with that of the *Apostolic Tradition* of Hippolytus,[64] will show a basically similar structure with great variety in detail. The post-baptismal anointing, whether given by the bishop or the presbyter, raise questions not easily answered as to the relation of baptism to confirmation in Christian initiation, but the clear similarity of sequence described by Ambrose and Hippolytus speaks to a Western tradition of two anointings, one of the head (which might be administered by a presbyter), and one of the forehead, the signing which was the prerogative of the bishop, and which Ambrose associated with the sevenfold gift of the Holy Ghost.

* * * * * *

In conclusion we can do little better than quote the prayer of the *Manuale Ambrosianum* which concludes the baptismal rites:

Having celebrated and perfected the sacraments of the divine baptism, let us give unwearied thanks to the Lord of heaven and earth, to God the Father Almighty, and let us humbly ask him that he grant us and all his family to be partakers of the glorious resurrection of our Lord Jesus Christ.[65]

Notes

1. Except for those passages indicated as my own translations, the translations of Latin texts are those found in E.C. Whitaker, *Documents of the Baptismal Liturgy* (London: SPCK, 1970) and in J.R. Srawley, ed. and T. Thompson, trans., *St. Ambrose on the Sacraments and On the Mysteries* (London: SPCK, 1950).

2. The vindication of the Ambrosian authorship of the *De Sacramentis* by Dom Connolly in *The De Sacramentis, A Work of St. Ambrose* (Oxford: Oxford University Press, 1942) has been generally accepted by modern scholarship.

3. The principal Ambrosian sacramentaries are the Sacramentary of Biasca (10th century) (ed., Odilo Heiming, *Das Ambrosianische Sakramentar von Biasca*, Corpus Ambrosiano Liturgicum, vol. 2 [Münster: Aschendorff, 1969]) and the Sacramentary of Bergamo (9th century) (ed. Angelo Paredi, *Sacramentarium Bergomense*, Monumenta Bergomensia, vol. 4 [Bergamo: Edizioni "Monumento Bergomensia, 1962]).

4. M. Magistretti, *Monumenta Veteris Liturgiae Ambrosianae*, vols. 2-3 (Milan, 1905); reprint (Nordeln, Lichtenstein: Kraus Reprint, 1971).

5. M. Magistretti, *Beroldus, sive Ecclesiae Ambrosianae Mediolanensis Kalendarium et Ordines* (Milan, 1894); reprint (Farnborough: Gregg International Publishers, 1968).

6. *Expositio Evangelii Lucae* IV, 76.

7. *Manuale Ambrosianum*, part II, 135.

8. *Beroldus* 80.

9. The Ambrosian Epiphany preface is baptismal and speaks of the blessing of the font "hodie."

10. *De Mysteriis* 4, 20. Also *De Sacramentis* 2, 4, 13.

11. *De Mysteriis* 1, 1.

12. In at least three places in *De Abraham* Ambrose addresses "qui ad gratiam baptismatis tenditis." Lib I, 4, 25; 7, 39; 9, 89.

13. *Beroldus* 86ff.

14. For example, A.A. King, *Liturgies of the Primatial Sees* (London: Longmans, Green and Co., 1957) 338.

15. *St. Gall 288* and *Vat. antiqua Lat. 5760.*

16. R.H. Connolly, *The Explanatio Symboli ad Initiandos* (Cambridge: Cambridge University Press, 1952) 6.

17. *Beroldus* 92.

18. This will be described below.

19. *Manuale*, Part II, 469 (*Ordo ad Catechumenum Faciendum*).

20. Ibid. 143.

21. *Beroldus* 94.

22. Epistle 20:4 (trans. LLM) (PL 16:1037)

23. *Manuale*, Part II, 169; *Beroldus* 94f.

24. See quotation above.

25. *Beroldus* 95; *Manuale*, Part II, 170.

26. In Bernard Botte's edition, *Des sacraments, des mystères, l'explication du symbole*, Sources chrétiennes, vol. 25 bis (Paris: Editions du Cerf, 1961) 46-59, or Connolly's cited at n. 16 above..

27. *Beroldus* 106. The forms are in Magistretti, *Pontificale in Usum Ecclesiae Mediolanensis* (Milan, 1897) 97ff.

28. *De Sacramentis* I, 1, 2-3; *De Mysteriis* I, 3-4.

29. Mark 8:32f.

30. "Sacerdos" is the equivalent of "episcopus" in Ambrose. He always uses "presbyter" for the second order of the ministry.

31. Wilson, *The Gregorian Sacramentary* 54; Mohlberg, *Sacramentarium Gelasianum* 68.

32. *De Sacramentis* I, 2, 4.

33. Ibid.

34. See note 17 above.

35. *De Mysteriis* 3, 8.

36. *De Sacramentis* I, 5, 18.

37. Ibid. II, 5, 14.

38. *De Mysteriis* 3, 14.

39. *Beroldus* 111.

40. *Manuale*, Part II, 205-207. In the Missal these forms are found at the end in the "Repertorium."

41. The Ambrosian "Exsultet" differs substantially from the Roman.

42. *Manuale*, Part II, 202—205.

43. Mohlberg, ed., *Sacramentarium Gelasianum* 72, n. 444.

44. Mohlberg, ed., *Missale Gallicanu Vetus* 40, no. 165.

45. *Sacramentarium Gelasianum* 73, n. 446.

46. Férotin, ed., *Liber Ordinum* (Paris, 1904) col. 29-30.

47. *Expositio Evangelii Secundum Lucam* X, 48.

48. Matthew 28:19.

49. *Beroldus* 112.

50. *De Sacramentis* II, 6, 16; II, 7, 20.

51. Easton, ed., *Apostolic Tradition* XXI.

52. *Beroldus* 112.

53. *De Sacramentis* II, 6, 24.

54. *Liturgies of Edward VI* (Parker Society ed.) 112.

55. *De Sacramentis* III, 1, 6.

56. *De Mysteriis* 7, 34.

57. Easton, *Apostolic Tradition* 47f.

58. *De Sacramentis* III, 2, 8.

59. *De Mysteriis* 7, 42.

60. Ibid.

61. *Epistula xxv ad Decentium*.

62. *Pontificale* xiif.

63. J.H. Srawley, *On the Sacraments and On the Mysteries* 35-37.

64. See my article, "The Baptismal Rite in Chrysostom," *Anglican Theological Review* (October 1961) 397-403. See also the other essays in this volume.

65. *Manuale*, Part II, 209 (translation LLM).

5

Mozarabic
Baptismal Rites

AMONG THE BAPTISMAL RITES OF THE WESTERN CHURCH, THAT OF
the Visigothic or Mozarabic liturgy occupies a unique position,
for it retains in a single baptismal service, even when the bishop is not the minister, the three liturgical actions which, with
the admission to the eucharist, constitute Christian initiation in
our oldest sources, namely, baptism in water, anointing with
oil, and the laying on of hands. Tertullian in *De Baptismo* described the anointing with chrism and the laying on of hands
as following the baptismal washing,[1] and the same sequence is
found in the *Apostolic Tradition*,[2] but in later practice the laying
on of hands and the anointing tended to become alternatives.[3]

Although the term Mozarabic may correctly be applied to
the totality of the rites and ceremonies used by the Church of
Spain from the conversion of the country until the introduction of the Roman rite in the eleventh century, we shall be concerned principally with the rite of the *Liber Ordinum*, known to
us principally through eleventh century manuscripts edited by
Dom Marius Férotin, and with the description of the rite by St.
Ildefonso of Toledo in the seventh century.

According to Ildefonso baptism may be administered only
twice in the year, at Easter and Pentecost, "at the *sedes* of legiti-
mate bishops and in their presence."[4] The proper minister of
the sacrament is the bishop, and presbyters in nearby towns

are forbidden to baptize, although those "in the churches of distant parishes" may do so. The right to administer the sacrament, Ildefonso said, is confined to the *sacerdos*, that is, the bishop and the presbyter, although in case of necessity anyone might baptize and at any time.[5] The four centuries which separate Ildefonso from the *Liber Ordinum* saw the end of these restrictions, and baptism *quolibet tempore* by the parish priest became the norm, although the Easter Vigil remained the solemn time for baptism.

THE PALM SUNDAY RITES

The ancient rites of the catechumenate had disappeared in Spain by the time of Ildefonso, and the solemn rites of baptism began with the *Dies Unctionis* or Palm Sunday, at matins, with the anointing of the *effeta*. Ildefonso tells us that the oil used for this purpose was blessed by a priest,[6] and the *Antifonario Visigotico* of the cathedral of Léon preserves the form.[7] The candidates were led across a carpet of goatskin as a token of penitence, were exorcised, signed with the cross, and finally anointed on the ears and mouth after the example of Our Lord in Mark 7:32,[8] while the priest said "Effeta, effeta, with the Holy Spirit unto an odor of sweetness, effeta," and the choir replies "He hath done all things well: he maketh the deaf to hear and the dumb to speak."[9]

The ears are anointed, says Ildefonso, "that he may receive the hearing of faith," and the *effeta* was followed by the delivery to the candidates of the Apostles' Creed, "the rule of faith."[10] The creed thus delivered to the *competentes*, or seekers after baptism, on Palm Sunday was "returned" on Maunday Thursday.[11] When the candidates were adults, this, of course, meant they they repeated the creed back to the priest on that day, as evidence that they had committed it to memory.

> For no one writes the Creed so that it can be read but it is to be thought about, lest forgetfulness obliterate things which your eyes have not read. Let your memory be your book. What ye are to hear, that ye will believe: and what ye are to believe, that ye will recite and make return of it.[12]

At the offertory of the Mass, the vessel containing the chrism was placed upon the altar,[13] and presumably consecrated, although no extant Mozarabic book actually mentions the consecration.

The Palm Sunday rites in Spain must have been among the most impressive of the year. The procession of palms, the exorcism and anointing of the *competentes*, the delivery of the creed, and the consecration of the chrism must have made it an outstanding event in the annual liturgical cycle. The significance of the day is well summed up in its gospel, from the twelfth chapter of St. John, describing both the anointing of Jesus at Bethany and the triumphal entry.[14]

THE EASTER VIGIL
AND BLESSING OF THE FONT

The baptism proper, as we have seen, took place at the Easter Vigil. The ceremony began with the blessing of the great paschal candle and the reading of twelve lessons from the Old Testament. The third lesson is from Isaiah 55: "Ho, every one that thirsteth, come ye to the waters . . ." After the lesson had begun, the bishop, with the assistant clergy, all carrying lighted candles, processed to the baptistry, which had been sealed with the bishop's ring during Lent.[15] The bishop prayed that "this font which has been sealed may be re-opened with the keys of thy mercy, and impart to those that thirst a most sweet cup of water."[16]

Ildefonso describes the blessing of the font, which followed, as being with the sign of the cross, exorcism, and the pouring in of oil.[17] The blessing provided in the *Liber Ordinum*[18] conforms to this pattern. The water was first exorcised and purged of all evil which might make it unsuitable for holy use. Then followed the principal prayer of blessing, *Sanctificare per Verbum Dei . . .*, which, with minor differences, is also found in the *Manuale Ambrosianum*.[19] Its first section is a *laus aquae*, describing both the natural and supernatural virtues of water: trodden by the feet of Christ; preserving the Hebrews and destroying the Egyptians at the Exodus; brought forth from the rock by Moses; making our crops to grow; and refreshing our bodies in the summer heat. The second section goes on to ask God to make the water of the font to be the means of washing away the bitter taste of the fruit of Eden and of breaking through the wall of fire which bars us from the garden of paradise, that we may receive again the likeness of God and know ourselves to be redeemed and reborn.

The bishop then made the sign of the cross over the font and poured in blessed oil in the Name of the Trinity. Presumably the oil was that blessed on Palm Sunday to anoint the catechumens. A final prayer of blessing followed, which asked:

> Grant that those who take from this laver a new life and set aside the record of the old and are accorded the gift of the Holy Spirit by the laying on of hands may both put away their present faults and lay hold on eternal gifts.

The structure of the blessing of the font, comprising first an exorcism and then a blessing, is common to Mozarabic, Gallican, and Ambrosian baptismal rites, and distinguishes them from the Roman. The close relationship between these non-Roman Western rites is further brought out by the common use of non-Roman prayers. We have already noted the similarity of the blessing in the *Liber Ordinum* to the Ambrosian form. The other surviving Mozarabic form, that included in the sixteenth-century *Missale Mixtum* of Cardinal Ximenes, is also found in the *Missale Gallicanum Vetus*.[20]

THE BAPTISM

The actual baptism followed the blessing of the font. The candidate first made a threefold renunciation of the devil, then replied *Credo* to the traditional three questions, affirming the candidate's belief in Father, Son, and Holy Spirit:

> N., do you believe in God the Father Almighty? R. I believe.
> And in Jesus Christ his only Son our Lord? R. I believe.
> And in the Holy Ghost? R. I believe.[21]

Finally, the candidate received a single immersion "in the name of the one Deity," while the Trinitarian baptismal formula was recited: *Et ego babtizo te in nomine Patris et Filii et Spiritus sancti, ut habeas vitam eternam.*[22] The addition of the phrase "that thou mayest have eternal life" is another point of contact with the Gallican sacramentaries.[23]

The substitution of a single immersion for the traditional threefold washing is a distinct peculiarity of the Mozarabic rite. Ildefonso, although recognizing that some orthodox Christians do practice threefold immersion, in commemoration, he says, of the three days burial of Christ:

> But because the heretics by this number of immersions are accustomed to rend the unity of the Godhead, it is by God's guidance that the Church of God observes the practice of one sprinkling only.[24]

When the neophytes emerged from the water, a hymn of joy for their liberation from sin was sung, and the priest (*sacerdos*) at once anointed them with the holy chrism, making the sign of the cross on the forehead of each, saying:

> The sign of eternal life which God the Father Almighty has given through Jesus Christ his Son to them that believe unto salvation. Amen.[25]

In the manuscripts this formula is accompanied by musical notation, and we may assume that it was solemnly sung by the bishop or by the presbyter who officiated in his stead. We may note that the Roman rite expressly forbade presbyters to sign the foreheads of the faithful with chrism, and Pope Innocent I directed presbyters, when they baptized, to sign only the top of the head. This restriction, although it is quoted by Isidore of Seville and Ildefonso, does not appear to have been observed in Spain.[26]

The anointing was followed at once by the laying on of hands, performed also by the officiating *sacerdos*. Two prayers are provided by the *Liber Ordinum* to accompany the imposition: one for use *quolibet tempore* and the other in *Vigilia Paschae*.[27] That for the vigil is longer, but the content of both prayers is the same. They ask the outpouring of the sevenfold gifts of the Holy Spirit upon those who have been washed with the water of baptism and anointed with chrism. It is not clear, particularly in the shorter prayer, however, whether it is with the laying on of hands or the anointing that the bestowal of the Spirit is associated. It speaks, for example, of God completing the grace of the sacrament by the unction with chrism which he has commanded to follow the ministration of baptism. The same prayer, after naming the seven gifts of the Spirit which it asks God to pour upon the neophytes, concludes:

And so grant that being strengthened in the Name of the Trinity, they may by this chrism be accounted worthy to become Christs, and by the power of Christ to become Christians.[28]

As we can readily see from this, the anointing and the laying on of hands were taken in the closest possible connection.

MEANING OF THE ANOINTING

Ildefonso tells us that the chrism with which we are anointed entitles us to the name of Christian, correctly deriving *Christus* and *Christianus* from *chrisma*. This identification did not, of course, originate with Ildephonsus and the Mozarabic liturgy. Tertullian, in the third century, had said:

Coming out from the washing we are thoroughly anointed with the blessed unction . . . from which you are called *Christs* from the *chrism*, that is the anointing which gave its name even to the Lord, when it became spiritual, since he was anointed with the Spirit by God the Father.[29]

This same interpretation of the anointing as the bestowal of the Christian name, found also in Augustine,[30] is the usual teaching of the Spanish Fathers and, as we have seen, is expressed in the post-baptismal prayer in the Mozarabic liturgy.

Ildefonso, like Tertullian, identifies the chrism with the unguent compounded by Moses at God's command in Exodus 30:22-25 out of liquid myrrh and spices, with which he anointed Aaron, and with which the high priest and the king were traditionally anointed. The difference, for him, is that in the New Covenant not only the pontiffs and kings, but all Christians are anointed with the holy oil, since we are the most holy members of the Eternal King and Priest.[31] We are, in the words of the First Epistle of Peter, "a chosen race, a royal priesthood." All that the anointing of the kings and priests of the Old Covenant implied is summed up and fulfilled in the Messianic anointing of Jesus, the Christ, and through the baptismal unction, Christians receive their name and are united with his royal priesthood as members of his Body.

Its Christological significance does not exhaust the meaning of the anointing with chrism for Ildefonso, however. He sees in it the fulfillment of many New Testament types. Tertullian provided the clue when he spoke of Jesus as *spiritu unctus a*

Deo patre, referring to Acts 10:38. Ildefonso can therefore go on to describe the visible anointing as the *sacramentum* of the invisible unction of the Holy Ghost.[32]

> As the outward man is anointed with the holy chrism, the inward is washed with the anointing of the Holy Ghost.[33]

This is the anointing from the Holy One of 1 John 2:20-27, the Holy Spirit abiding in us to teach the things of God and to inflame us with the fire of divine love. The sign of the cross which is traced upon the neophyte's forehead with the chrism is the sign with which we are sealed unto the day of redemption.[34] The anointing, by incorporating us into Christ, becomes the unction of the Holy Ghost with which he was himself anointed so that the Spirit of Christ dwells and reigns in us. There can be little doubt that Dom Paul de Puniet is correct when he says: "For the Spaniards, to receive the anointing with chrism is to receive the Holy Ghost."[35]

THE IMPOSITION OF HANDS

The anointing, as we have seen, was followed immediately by the laying on of the hands of the *sacerdos*. "It is therefore wholesome," says Ildefonso, "that after the example of Christ a hand in blessing is placed upon the faithful by the priest."[36] The example is that of Mark 10:13-14, so frequently used as scriptural warrant for infant baptism, but here used more accurately as warrant for laying hands upon the newly baptized *infantes*. The laying on of hands appears to be a priestly blessing with which the baptismal rite is brought to a fitting close. This is not strictly true, however, since the Spanish Church was aware of the tradition that the imposition of hands was the vehicle for the gift of the Spirit, and Ildefonso reproduces almost verbatim a section from Isidore of Seville which states plainly that after baptism the Holy Spirit is given with the imposition of hands, citing as scriptural precedent Acts 19:1-17 and Acts 8:14.[37] This tradition, nevertheless, like that of the threefold immersion, does not seem to have been generally received in Spain. Insistent as the Spanish Fathers were that the laying on of hands was an integral part of the baptismal rite, it is the anointing which is foremost in their minds.

Isidore of Seville, for example, follows his definition of a sacrament with the statement that baptism and chrism, and the body and blood of Christ are sacraments.[38] Although he speaks elsewhere at great length about the laying on of hands, it is the washing and anointing which he singles out as the "sacramental acts" of Christian initiation. To the anointing he ascribes both the *sanctificatio Spiritus* and participation in the royal priesthood of the Body of Christ.[39] Similarly, Pacien of Barcelona, the fourth-century writer who made the oft-quoted statement, "My name is Christian and my surname is Catholic," speaks of the *lavacri et chrismatis potestas* of the bishops, which he explains as the authority to baptize and to give the Holy Spirit.[40] Clearly, it is the anointing which he believes gives the Holy Spirit. In a sermon on baptism he gives his view more fully. Baptism consists of three acts: washing, anointing with chrism, imposition of hands. Through this total rite the whole person is reborn and renewed in Christ by the power of the Holy Spirit.[41]

THE PRESBYTER AS MINISTER OF BAPTISM

We have already seen that Ildephonsus considered the proper minister of baptism to be the bishop. This is also the teaching of the earlier Spanish Fathers and councils.[42] The bishop might, however, delegate this right to baptize to a presbyter. The chrism was blessed by the bishop and given by him to those presbyters whom he authorized to baptize, and the rite was then considered to be performed *quasi de manu episcopi*.[43] In this case the officiating presbyter performed the laying on of hands.

The case of baptism administered by one who was not a *sacerdos* was quite different. The right of deacons, and even the laity, to baptize in case of necessity was recognized in Spain at least as early as the pre-Nicene Council of Elvira, but they were forbidden to perform the anointing and laying on of hands. These rites, if the person thus baptized survived, were to be supplied by the bishop.[44]

We can see therefore that the Spanish Church considered the ministration of baptism, like the eucharist, to belong to the bishop. In both cases he might, and frequently did, designate presbyters to act as his deputy, but it was recognized that the presbyter was acting for the bishop, and in the case of baptism with chrism consecrated by him. The bishop might not, however, delegate his functions to one who was not a *sacerdos*, and although one baptized with water by a lay person was, if he or she died, considered *fidelis*, the anointing and imposition of hands were to be supplied by the bishop, if possible. The Spanish Church did not further restrict the imposition of hands to its bishops. The baptismal rite was retained as a unity, and the imposition of the hand of a presbyter, acting with the blessing and permission of his bishop, was considered *quasi de manu episcopi*.

FIRST COMMUNION

To return to the text of the rite itself, the *Liber Ordinum* tells us that after the imposition of hands, the heads of the candidates were veiled, and they were communicated.[45] Ildephonsus says that they were taught the Lord's Prayer before they received the eucharist.[46] It appears that the neophytes were normally communicated from the reserved sacrament, although undoubtedly they originally received the body of Christ at the Easter Mass. The *Liber Ordinum* continues its description of the Easter rites with the fourth lesson. The Mass which ends the vigil would then have been the climax of the liturgical year, celebrating not only the resurrection of Christ but also that of the neophytes born anew in him.

THREEFOLD STRUCTURE OF THE RITE

The basic structure of the Mozarabic solemn baptismal rites does not differ substantially from that of other Western liturgies. When the liturgy was performed at the solemn seasons by the bishop in his cathedral, it was much the same throughout the West, although the laying on of hands was more prominent in the Spanish rite.[47] The Spanish baptism *quolibet tempore* performed by the parish priest, on the other hand, differed markedly from the custom of other countries. In Spain the integrity of the baptismal rite was retained, and the officiating presbyter, acting in the bishop's name and with his permission, baptized, anointed (with episcopally consecrated chrism), and laid on hands. The *impositio manuum* was neither deferred until the bishop might personally "confirm" the neophytes, as in the Roman rite, nor omitted, as in the Eastern and Gallican rites. Similarly, the administration of first communion remained a part of the baptismal rite, even for children, in spite of the separation of the rite from the eucharist. Although the Spanish Church recognized that the washing with water was the essential act which would suffice *in periculo mortis*, it did not forget that baptism consisted of washing, anointing, and the laying on of hands, and that it was as a result of this complete rite that we were crucified and raised up with Christ, made members of his royal and priestly Body, the church, and received the indwelling grace of the Holy Spirit.

Notes

1. Tertullian, *De Baptismo* 7, 8. Unless otherwise identified, all translations in this chapter are from E.C. Whitaker, *Documents of the Baptismal Liturgy* (London: SPCK, 1970).

2. *Apostolic Tradition* 21, 22.

3. See Bede, *Super Acta Apostolorum Expositio* 8.

4. Ildefonso, *De Cognitione Baptismi* 108 (in PL 96).

5. Ibid. 116.

6. Ibid. 27.

7. L. Brou and J. Vives, eds., *Antifonario visigótico mozárabe de la Catedral de Léon*, Monumenta Hispaniae Sacra, Serie Liturgica, vol. 5 (Barcelona-Madrid, 1959) 243f.

8. Ildephonsus, *De Cognitione Baptismi* 21.

9. *Antifonario visigótico* 245; M. Férotin, ed., *Liber Ordinum* (Paris: 1904; reprint: Farnborough: Gregg International Publishers, 1969) col. 27.

10. *Liber Ordinum* col. 184-187.

11. Ildefonso, *De Cognitione Baptismi* 34.

12. *Liber Ordinum* col. 184-187.

13. *Antifonario Visigotico* 249.

14. F.J. Perez de Urbel and A. Gonzelez y Ruiz-Zorilla, eds., *Liber Comicus*, Monumenta Hispaniae Sacra, Serie Liturgica, vol. 2 (Madrid: 1950), vol. 1, 319.

15. *Liber Ordinum* col. 217; Ildefonso, *De Cognitione Baptismi* 107.

16. *Liber Ordinum* 218.

17. Ildefonso, *De Cognitione Baptismi* 109.

18. These are not given in the account of the Easter Vigil and must be found in the form for baptism *quolibet tempore*, col. 29-31.

19. See "Ambrosian Rites," *Studia Liturgica* 1 (1962) 247. Reprinted as Chapter 4 in this volume.

20. This beautiful blessing, expounding the Pauline theme of death in Adam and rebirth in Christ, apparently represents the use of a different local church from the *Liber Ordinum*. The *Missale Mixtum* does not include the baptismal rites but gives its blessing of the font as part of the rites of Holy Saturday. It is of particular interest to Anglicans as ten of its sixteen petitions were incorporated into the blessing of the font in the *First Prayer Book* of Edward VI.

21. *Liber Ordinum* col. 32 (trans. LLM).

22. Ibid.; Ildefonso, *De Cognitione Baptismi* 112, 117.

23. See *Missale Gothicum* 260; *Missale Gallicanum Vetus* 174; *Bobbio Missal* 248.

24. Ildefonso, *De Cognitione Baptismi* 117.

25. *Liber Ordinum* col. 33.

26. Innocent I, Epistle 35; Isidore, *De Ecclesiasticis Officiis* 27; Ildefonso, *De Cognitione Baptismi* 131.

27. *Liber Ordinum* col. 33-34, 36-37.

28. Ibid. col. 34.

29. Tertullian, *De Baptismo* 7 (trans. LLM).

30. Augustine, *Contra Littera Petiliani* II, 104; *De Civitate Dei* 17:49; *Enaratio in Psalmum* 44, 19.

31. Ildefonso, *De Cognitione Baptismi* 133.

32. Ibid. 124-125.

33. Ibid. 124 (trans. LLM).

34. Ephesians 4:30; see Ezekiel 9:4 and Revelation 7:3.

35. Paul de Puniet, "Onction et Confirmation," *Revue d'histoire ecclésiastique* 13 (1912) 459.

36. Ildefonso, *De Cognitione Baptismi* 137.

37. Ibid. 139; see Isidore, *De Ecclesiasticis Officiis* 2:27.

38. Isidore, *Etymologiarum Libri VI* 39.

39. Ibid. 50-51; *De Ecclesiasticis Officiis* 2:26; *De Fide Catholica* 2:25.

40. Pacien, Epistle I (*De Catholica Nomine*), in PL 13.

41. Pacien, *Sermo de Baptismo* 6.

42. Pacien, Epistle 1; Braulion, Epistle to Eugene of Toledo 4.

43. Council of Toledo, Canon 20; Council of Barcelona, Canon 2; Braulion, Epistle to Eugene 4.

44. Council of Elvira, Canons 38 and 77.

45. *Liber Ordinum* col. 219.

46. Ildefonso, *De Cognitione Baptismi* 132.

47. It does not appear to have survived at all in the Ambrosian

and Gallican rites and was normally reduced to an extension of the bishop's hands toward the candidates in the Roman rite. It was the signing of the forehead with the cross in chrism which was considered to be the matter of confirmation.

6

Baptismal Catechesis
in the Reformation Period

THE SIXTEENTH CENTURY IS NOT ONLY THE ERA OF THE REFORMA-
tion, it is the "Age of Discovery." While it is certainly true that
the continents Europeans "discovered" were already both
known and inhabited, it is undeniably true that interaction between Europeans and the native peoples of the Americas and
East Asia began to take place at hitherto unprecedented rates.
One might have expected that the potential conversion of vast
populations who had never heard the Christian Gospel would
have resulted in the revitalization of the classic rites of the catechumenate which had remained a dead letter in the Latin liturgical books for centuries through lack of unbaptized adults
to evangelize. One might equally have expected that the newly reformed churches, convinced as they were of the religious
and theological ignorance of the majority of Catholics, and influenced by the humanistic ideals of the Renaissance, would
have reformed and revived the process by which Christians
classically have been formed. In point of fact, neither happened. The catechumenate was simply ignored, although the
Council of Trent states:

> On adults, however, the Church has not been accustomed to
> confer the Sacrament of Baptism at once, but has ordained that
> it be deferred for a certain time.[1]

We find, for example, that in 1536 the people of the Fisher Coast in India were baptized en masse, in number about ten thousand, and then left without instruction or pastoral care, either before or after baptism, for six years.[2] It was among these people that St. Francis Xavier labored to teach the rudiments of the faith into which they had been baptized:

> On Sundays I assemble all the people, men and women, young and old, and get them to repeat the prayers in their own language . . . I give out the First Commandment which they repeat, and then we say all together, Jesus Christ, Son of God, grant us grace to love thee above all things. When we have asked for this grace, we recite the Pater Noster together, and then cry with one accord, Holy Mary, Mother of Jesus Christ, obtain for us grace from thy Son to enable us to keep the First Commandment. Next we say an Ave Maria, and proceed in the same manner through each of the remaining nine commandments. And just as we say Twelve Paters and Aves in honour of the ten Commandments, asking God to give us grace to keep them well.[3]

This is unquestionably catechetical instruction, but it is being given to those already Christian and might be termed "remedial catechesis."

The pattern was the same in South America, where Indians were baptized with only a minimal pre-baptismal instruction, and the catechism was used for the instruction of both children and adults after their baptism.[4]

In 1552 the first Council of Lima declared that Indians should be admitted only to the sacraments of baptism, matrimony, and penance until they were better instructed. Permission was given to bishops to administer confirmation to them, if they thought it desirable, and many Indians were in fact confirmed. The sainted Turibio, Archbishop of Lima and Apostle of Peru, confirmed half a millon people between 1584 and 1590.[5] The same council required the license of the bishop himself to admit Indians to the reception of the eucharist, and the custom arose of admitting the most faithful to communion annually at Easter.[6]

I cite these examples of the practice of Catholic missions to make clear exactly how dead the idea of the ancient catechumenate before baptism really was. Even in such circumstances as those in the mission fields which would lend themselves easily to the revival of the ancient discipline there was no cate-chumenate. The most rudimentary grasp of what they were doing sufficed to admit adults to holy baptism, while many never received what was considered sufficient instruction for admission to the eucharist.

If the catechumenate was indeed dead in the sixteenth cen-tury, catechesis was a primary interest of the Christian hu-manists of the Renaissance. Erasmus, in his *Paraphrase on St. Matthew's Gospel*, proposed that during Lent baptized boys be required to attend catechetical sermons which would explain to them the meaning of their baptismal profession:

> Then they would be carefully examined in private by ap-proved men whether they sufficiently retain and remember the things which the priest has taught. If they be found to retain them sufficiently, they should be asked whether they ratify what their godparents promised in their name at baptism. If they answer that they ratify them, then let that profession be renewed in a public gathering of their equals, and that with solemn ceremonies, fitting, pure, serious, and magnificent, and such things as become that profession, than which there is none more sacred . . . These things indeed will have greater au-thority if they are performed by the bishops themselves.[7]

What Erasmus proposes is a post-baptismal catechumenate. He assumes the universality of infant baptism and the impos-sibility of catechizing infants; therefore, he proposes his cate-chumenate for baptized boys "when they arrive at puberty." The "solemn ceremonies" to be "performed by the bishops themselves" were certainly understood by the Reformers to be confirmation, and we find developing in the Churches of the Reformation a pattern of infant baptism, catechesis, confirma-tion, and admission to communion.

Late medieval rituals had instructed godparents and par-ents to teach their baptized children the Lord's Prayer, Hail Mary, and Apostles' Creed as a preliminary to confirmation, which by the sixteenth century was normally not administered to children under seven.[8]

The rather quaint English of the Sarum *Manuale* of 1516 il-lustrated the tendency:

God faders and godmodyrs of thys chylde whe charge you that ye charge the foder and te moder to kepe it from fyer and water and other perels to the age of VII yere. and that ye lerne or se yt be lerned the *Pater Noster, Aue Maria*, and *Credo*. After the lawe of all holy churche and in all goodly haste to be confirmed of my lorde of the dyocise or of hys depute.[9]

We might note that the Council of Cologne in 1536 suggested for the first time that a child should not be confirmed before the age of seven, because "he will understand, not to say remember, too little or nothing of those things that are done."[10]

There is also a tradition from Wycliffe and Hus that post-baptismal instruction is concluded with a solemn profession of faith accompanied by "the apostolic rite of the laying on of hands":

Whoever being baptized has come to the true faith and purposes to portray it in action, in adversities and reproaches, to the intent that the new birth may be seen revealed in his spirit of life and thankfulness, such a one ought to be brought to the bishop, or priest, and be confirmed. And being questioned with regard to the truths of the faith and the sacred precepts, and also with regard to his good will, his firm purpose and works of truth, he shall testify and declare that he has all such things. Such a one should be confirmed in the hope of the truth he has attained, and in deed aided by the prayers of the church, so that there may come to him an increase of the gifts of the Holy Spirit for steadfastness and the welfare of the faith. Finally, by the laying on of hands to confirm the promises of God and the truth held in virtue of the name of the Father and of his Word and the kindly Spirit, let him be received into the fellowship of the church.[11]

Martin Luther

Luther's concern for catechetical instruction and religious literacy is well known, but he had few kind words for confirmation, which he called *Affenspiel* (monkey business) and *Gaukelwerk* (mumbo jumbo). In a sermon in 1522 he conceded:

I would permit confirmation as long as it is understood that God knows nothing of it, has said nothing about it, and that what the bishops claim for it is untrue.[12]

In 1533 he preached:

> Confirmation should not be observed as the bishops desire it. Nevertheless we do not find fault if every pastor examines the faith of the children to see whether it is good and sincere, lay hands on them, and confirm them.[13]

From these concerns of Luther arose what is called the "catechetical type" (*Catechismus* or *Beichtvehör*[14]) of confirmation among Lutherans. Its focus was the preparation of communicants, and during the Reformation period this catechetical confirmation did not usually involve any concluding rite. It centered in the preaching of catechetical sermons and the reading of the catechism from the pulpit, usually before the gospel. The sermons were for the entire congregation, and were given about four times a year. The sermons themselves were preached daily, or at least several times during the week. Catechetical instruction was also conducted in connection with confession and preparation for communion. "Because the average communicant was so poorly instructed, he was to become in effect a catechumen each time he went to Communion."[15] The content of the catechesis was the Ten Commandments, the Lord's Prayer, holy baptism, the Lord's Supper, and the Christian life.

Typical of the preparation for first communion in the form of several days of catechetical review (*Beichtwochen*) is this description from 1564:

> Such an examination and exercise takes place here at Onoltzbach on weekdays for the city children at twelve o'clock, for one hour each day, between Easter and Pentecost, and for the village children who belong to the parish, on Sundays and the festivals at one o'clock during the period of Reminiscere and Exaudi. In this way all may receive the Lord's Supper on Pentecost after each one has made his confession on the previous day.[16]

The confession is presumably of faith, not of sins, as described in the Pfalz-Neuburg Church Order of 1543,[17] which directs that those who wish to receive first communion should be publicly examined at vespers on the eves of the feasts of Easter, Pentecost, and Christmas, and if they are prepared they should be admitted.

In some places this catechetical instruction was concluded by a public rite along traditional lines, as in the Liegnitz Church Order of 1535:

> When the children have matured in age and grace, they shall again be presented by the parents and sponsors to the ministers in the presence of the congregation that they may make a public confession of their faith. This is to take the place of confirmation.[18]

Martin Bucer

There is also another strain in Lutheran practice which seems to relate more directly to the Wycliffe-Hus tradition, and to the concerns of Erasmus. The central figure in this line of development is Martin Bucer, who in 1534 urged the revival of confirmation in the ancient form in which "bishops laid their hands on the baptized and thereby gave them the Holy Spirit according to the example of the apostle in Samaria, Acts 8."[19]

In 1538 Bucer was called to Hesse to reform the church there, and his ideas were put into effect in the Zeigenhain Order of Church Discipline of that year.[20] It directed that the children who were prepared through catechetical instruction to receive first communion should be presented by their parents and sponsors to the pastors before the congregation. The whole collegium of ministers publicly examined the children in the chief articles of the Christian faith.

> When they had answered the questions and publicly surrendered themselves to Christ the Lord and His churches, the pastor shall admonish the congregation to ask the Lord, in behalf of the children, for perseverence and an increase of the Holy Spirit, and conclude this prayer with a collect.

> Finally the pastor shall lay his hands upon the children, thus confirming them in the name of the Lord, and establish them in Christian fellowship. He shall thereupon also admit them to the Table of the Lord.

Repp comments:

> Here Bucer was influenced also by Erasmus in establishing a confirmation rite. But he did not limit himself, as did Erasmus, to a rite in which the youths themselves made a confession of the faith which their sponsors had made for them; under Lu-

ther's influence he associated the rite also with first Communion. This is the first formal association of the rite of confirmation with the Lord's Supper.[21]

The Cassel Church Order of 1539 is based upon this, and has influenced all subsequent Lutheran practice. Consequently Bucer has been called the father of Lutheran confimation. The Cassel rite provided this formula to accompany the imposition of hands:

> Receive the Holy Spirit, protection and guard against all evil, strength and help to all goodness from the gracious hand of God the Father, Son, and Holy Spirit.[22]

Bucer is also the author of the section on the sacraments in the *Consultation* of Hermann, Archbishop of Cologne. Usually known as *Einfaltigs Bedencken*, the manuscript was composed in German in 1543 and translated into Latin in 1545 and English in 1548. A copy of the Latin version was in the library of Thomas Cranmer, Archbishop of Canterbury, and it is generally recognized as one of the sources of The Book of Common Prayer.

In *Einfaltigs Bedencken* baptism is administered to infants on Sundays and other Holy Days at the celebration of the eucharist, during which the parents and godparents are expected to receive communion. Bucer recognizes that the older tradition was for the infants themselves to receive, "but seeing this custom is worn away not without a cause," he directs the parents, godparents, and kinfolk to receive the eucharist "with singular desire of the Spirit that they may receive the Communion of Christ to themselves which they obtain in baptism for their infants."[23] Bucer uses the term "catechism" to describe an exhortation of considerable length addressed to the godparents prior to the baptism of the infants. Among the questions put to the godparents in this catechetical rite was this:

> Will ye then be godfathers to this infant, and count him for a very son of God, a brother and member of Christ, and as soon as he cometh to the use of reason, if peradventure he shall lose his parents, or if they shall be negligent in this behalf, will ye take charge of him, that he may learn the ten commandments, the articles of our faith, the Lord's prayer, the sacraments, both at home and in the congregation, that from his childhood he

may begin to understand the mystery of baptism and the benefits of Christ given to him therein, and afterwards when he is
well instructed in the religion of Christ, that he confess his faith
in the congregation with his own mouth, and through the participation of Christ that he give himself to obedience towards
God and the congregation?[24]

This is followed by an exhortation to the parents, kinfolk, and
godparents to bring the child to school when he is old enough,
"that he may be instructed more fully in the mysteries of
Christ and in other things," and generally repeats what was
previously asked. We might note too that Archbishop Hermann, for whom *Einfaltigs Bedencken* was written, was the
same archbishop who presided over the Council of Cologne in
1536—the council which had been concerned that children be
old enough when they were confirmed to understand what
was happening.

It is obvious from the catechetical rite that Bucer is concerned about the absence of the catechumenate and is making
an attempt to provide a post-baptismal catechumenate. And in
the section on confirmation Bucer reasserts his belief that the
solemn personal profession of faith before God and the congregation is of divine institution and found in both Old and
New Testaments.

At which confession of faith and profession of obedience in the
congregation they were to be solemnly confirmed of the congregation in religion through prayer and some token of God's
confirmation, which under Moses consisted in sacrifices and
oblations and, in the time of the gospel, in laying on of hands
and participation in the supper of the Lord . . . Seeing then that
this confession of faith and giving of ourselves to the obedience
of Christ and commendation of his church . . . cannot be done
in baptism, when infants be baptized it must needs to done for
them that were baptized in their infancy, when they be meetly
well instructed of religion, and when they somewhat understand those great benefits that be given in baptism.

But when they solemnly profess their faith and obedience before the congregation the very nature of faith requireth again
that the congregation pray for them solemnly and desire for
them the increase of the Holy Ghost that he will confirm and
preserve them in the faith of Christ and obedience of the con-

gregation, and that he will ever lead them into all truth. And forasmuch as such prayer . . . cannot but be effectuous, it pertaineth to the ministry of the congregation to strengthen them with the confirmation of the Holy Ghost, for whom the church hath prayer. Therefore our elders following the example of Christ and the apostles, did use the laying on of hands as a sign of this confirmation.[25]

It is this purified rite of confirmation which is to be revived in Cologne, with the imposition of hands, not anointing, as its matter. It is to be administered by appointed visitors twice yearly, since the bishops cannot visit the churches that often. The office itself consists in a rather extensive catechism of the candidates taken from the Cassel Church Order, a solemn profession of faith by the young people, and the imposition of hands with prayer for the confirmation of the Holy Spirit.

It seems clear that in the Lutheran Reformation tradition a post-baptismal catechumenate was considered essential, and in the line of tradition represented by Bucer, it was part of confirmation and admission to communion.

John Calvin

In the *Institutes of the Christian Religion* John Calvin made his contribution:

How I wish that we might have kept the custom which existed among the ancient Christians before this misborn wraith of a sacrament came to birth! Not that it would be a confirmation such as they fancy, which cannot be named without doing injustice to baptism; but a catechizing, in which children or those near adolescence would give an account of their faith before the church. But the best method of catechizing would be to have a manual drafted for this exercise, containing and summarizing in simple manner most of the articles of our religion, on which the whole believers' church ought to agree without controversy. A child of ten would present himself to the church to declare his confession of faith, would be examined in each article, and answer to each; if he were ignorant of anything or insufficiently understood it, he would be taught. Thus, while the church looks on as a witness, he would profess the one true and sincere faith, in which the believing folk with one mind worship the one God.[26]

We may note the suggestion that a set catechism was the proper method of catechesis, a suggestion apparently adopted from the Reformers by the Council of Trent, which subsequently issued its own catechism. It was Calvin's firm belief that this was the original meaning of confirmation, and in a passage added to the *Institutes* in 1543 he described his view of the primitive rite:

> In early times it was the custom for the children of Christians after they had grown up to be brought before the bishop to fulfill the duty which was required of those who as adults offered themselves for baptism. For the latter sat among the catechumens until, duly instructed in the mysteries of the faith, they were able to make confession of their faith before the bishop and the people. Therefore, those who had been baptized as infants, because they had not then made confession of faith before the church, were at the end of their childhood or at the beginning of adolescence again presented by their parents, and were examined by the bishop according to the form of the catechism, which was then in definite form and in common use. But in order that this act, which ought by itself to have been weighty and holy, might have more reverence and dignity, the ceremony of the laying on of hands was also added. Thus the youth, once his faith was approved, was dismissed with a solemn blessing.[27]

It is not necessary at this time to discuss Calvin's misreading of the practice of the primitive church. It is sufficient to see what he thought it had been, and it was this practice which came into use in the Reformed Churches. We find that Reformed practice does not differ substantially from Lutheran.

In a larger sense, the whole of life in Calvin's Geneva was a catechumenate. John Knox described it as "a school of Jesus Christ," with "edification" the purpose of Calvinist worship. Calvin was a theologian who waged a lifelong battle against what he considered theological ignorance, and so the didactic element of all worship was high. At the same time the Calvinist system at Geneva subjected the populace to a discipline so rigid and so thoroughly enforced as to make the harshest novice masters grow pale.

The Church of England

The Church of England in the sixteenth century provided

no forms at all for adult baptism. It was not until 1662 that a form for adult baptism was added to The Book of Common Prayer, an inclusion necessitated by the growth of the Anabaptists under Cromwell—with the result that the Restoration found large numbers of English adults unbaptized.

The Prayer Book of 1549 made certain changes in the pattern of Christian initiation. Since the time of Archbishop Peckham (1279-1292) confirmation had been required prior to first communion, except in extraordinary cases. This rule was retained. At the same time the confirmation of infants was abolished. Infant confirmation had been practiced as late as 1533, when the future Queen Elizabeth had been baptized and confirmed at the age of three days, and in 1536 its legitimacy had been defended by the Lower House of the Convocation of Canterbury.[28]

In 1549 a new rubric at the beginning of confirmation provides that "To the end that confirmation may be ministered to the more edifying of such as shall receive it," no one can be confirmed until the person can recite the Creed, the Lord's Prayer, and the ten commandments, "and can also answer such questions of this short catechism, as the Bishop (or such as he shall appoint) shall be his discretion appose them in."[29]

A second rubric follows Calvin and Bucer in giving as a reason for observing confimation that those baptized as infants may openly confess their faith before the church. In typical Anglican fashion, this is followed by a rubric in the medieval tradition affirming that confirmation is most appropriately administered "when children come to that age, that partly by the frailty of their own flesh, partly by the assaults of the devil, they begin to be in danger to fall into sin."

The rite itself is much more traditional than that in Bucer. It is, in fact, the *confirmatio puerorum* of the Sarum *Manuale*, with the laying on of hands substituted for the chrismation. What is of particular interest to us is that the catechism is printed between the main title and the rite, so that the catechetical instruction is seen as closely bound, not to baptism, but to confirmation.

Every parish priest is required, at least once in six weeks, to spend half an hour before evensong on some Sunday or holy day instructing and examining the children of the parish in the catechism, and to do so openly in the church. These provisions remained substantially unchanged in the 1552 Prayer Book, which removed the chrismation from baptism, and the signing of the forehead with the cross from confirmation.

The Anglican tradition of the Reformation period thus calls for the catechetical instruction of the youth of the parish on Sunday afternoons until they can say the catechism. Parents and employers are required to "cause their children, servants and prentices" to be present for these sessions. When the children can recite the catechism they are presented to the bishop for confirmation at his next visitation, and then admitted to the reception of the eucharist.

Bucer in his *Censura* of The Book of Common Prayer objected to the meagerness of its provision for catechetical instruction. He thought that learning the words of the catechism was insufficient:

> I would wish . . . that all adolescents and all young people, male and female, should attend the catechizing until they are so proficient in the doctrine of Christ that they may be excused by their pastor . . . Catechumens ought to be placed in various classes, and all the mysteries of Christ which it is necessary to believe should with such method, diligence, and power be explained and elucidated, commended and instilled into them, as will enable each to make the quicker and fuller progress and to observe whatever the Lord has commanded.[30]

The only observable effect of this aspect of Bucer's critique was the elimination of reference in the rubrics to the requirement that priests catechize the youth every six weeks, so that it spoke instead of doing it on Sundays and holy days, presumably on all of them.

The Anabaptists

There is, of course, one group springing from the Reformation which broke sharply with the medieval practice of Christian initiation. The Anabaptists abandoned infant baptism. As a rule they did not use a rite in the conventional sense, but attempted to imitate the New Testament model of Jesus' baptism in the Jordan. The baptismal theologies of the Anabaptists are a tangled skein which I shall not attempt to unravel.[31]

Although there is no such thing as a catechumenate in the

traditional sense among the Anabaptists, the Anabaptist movement itself began with "schools" for the purpose of listening to "readers" of the Bible and discussion. It was during such a "school" meeting on 21 January 1525—the day the Anabaptists were expelled from Zurich—that Geoge Blaurock, a priest, was baptized. This was the first rebaptism, and was done by a layman.[32]

Anabaptist baptism has a revivalistic character which marks the separation of the "gathered chuch" of the faithful from the "world" of Papists and Protestants. Rebaptism and the sharing of bread and wine in the Lord's Supper imitative of the New Testament accounts were their signs of fellowship. Baptism, now associated with confession of sins rather than of faith, had taken the place of penance in the lives of the converts. Thus the experience of forgiveness was followed by the ministration of baptism.

Basic to their belief was the conviction that all who had been so baptized were compelled by the great commission of Matthew 28:19-20 to proclaim true repentance and true baptism among all peoples. Of course, the Anabaptists were concerned to instruct their converts in their teachings, but do not seem to have had any organized catechumenate. For example, the spiritualist Caspar Schwenkenfeld criticized the Anabaptist Pilgram Marpeck for not insisting on an adequate catechumenate before baptism. Marpeck replied that such a period was unnecessary since repentance was brought through the Gospel as a work of God and not through any work of our own.[33] It was the Anabaptist stance that the experience of conversion and the assurance of forgiveness were the essential preparation for baptism.

Somewhat unique is the case of Balthasar Hubmaier's *Eine Form zu Taufen* as used at Nicholsberg, which contains these instructions:

> Whoever desires to receive water baptism should first present himself to his bishop so that he may be tested as to whether he is sufficiently instructed in the articles of the law, Gospel, and faith, and in the Christian life. Also he must give evidence that he can pray, and that he can intelligently explain the articles of the Christian faith. This must all be ascertained about the candidate before he can be permitted to be incorporated into the

church of Christ through external baptism unto the forgiveness of sins. If he meets these requirements the bishop then presents him to his church.[34]

Hubmaier expected that the candidates for baptism must be at least seven years of age,[35] and the rite he provides is in sharp contrast to the informal solemnity of most Anabaptist baptisms. The candidates were asked to respond "I believe" to the three paragraphs of the Apostles' Creed, to renounce the devil, to accept baptism, and to submit to the discipline of the church. The water-baptism was followed by the prayers of the church and the imposition of hands by the bishop, with the form:

> I give thee witness and authority, that thou henceforth shalt be numbered among the fellowship of Christians; that as a member of this fellowship thou shalt break bread and pray with the other Christian sisters and brethren, God be with thee and with thy spirit. Amen.[36]

Hubmaier also anticipated the dedication of children born to Anabaptist parents in a service in which the church would join the parents in praying God's blessings upon the child.[37] It seems likely that Hubmaier had in mind not so much the conversion of adults to the Anabaptist faith as the raising of children within that fellowship. This particular pattern of Christian initiation, although separated from the sacramental theology and ecclesiology which produced it, has been seen by many contemporary Christians as an appropriate one for the present age.

The presence of children for first generation Anabaptists of course produced a need and a demand for a system of catechetical instruction, but this was in fact a question of religious education rather than of a catechumenate. The Anabaptists were aware of the early catechumenate, using its existence in arguments against pedobaptists, but did not seem to have the institution themselves. They were, in fact, much more experience-oriented than either traditional Catholics or Protestants and less given to systematic expositions. George H. Williams' book *The Radical Reformation* cites examples of Anabaptist catechisms and educational systems,[38] and from these it can be seen that although they did not ritualize it, they took the catechumenal status of their children seriously.

The Anabaptist pattern of the dedication of infants with subsequent religious instruction and followed by adult baptism is today exercising a strong attraction for many whose religious heritage includes a commitment to infant baptism.[39] Certainly this practice provides a needed critique of our inherited forms. However, we must point out that in practice its "adult" character tended not to maintain itself beyond the first generation, as seen from Hubmaier's suggestion that the "believers" must be at least seven years old. Nonetheless, this pattern does place baptism, not confirmation, at the conclusion of the catechetical instruction of its "birthright members." For Anabaptists the baptismal practice was attached to a "gathered church" ecclesiology and a sacramentarian theology which denied that baptism was a means of grace. Those who advocate its readoption today must face the question of whether it can survive as an expression of a more orthodox theology of church and sacraments.

* * * * * *

In conclusion, we can observe that the Reformation period was marked by a revival of catechetical instruction associated with confirmation rather than with baptism. And with the exception of radicals looking for the spiritual experience of forgiveness and an assurance of the candidates' inability to sin, catechetical instruction was seen almost exclusively in educational terms. While many of the baptismal rites of the Reformation Churches still contain the ritual portions of the old catechumenate, exorcisms, signing, and the like, these tend to disappear in the second revision of the rite,[40] and are simple relics of past custom just as they were in the Roman ritual which made infants catechumens moments before their baptism.

Even in mission lands in the Americas or the Far East no serious attention was given to the question of adult baptism either by Catholics or Protestants outside of the Anabaptist tradition. And although the concept of the adult catechumenate was not revived for converts from paganism, the medieval practice of mass baptisms with little or no prior instruction was followed.

There was an interest in religious education, stemming from the Renaissance and from the profound conviction of many of the Reformers that their people were either theologically illiterate or grossly miseducated. And although it frequently used catechetical terms, it did not usually think of itself as a catechumenate.

The attempt to establish a preconfirmation catechumenate can best be seen as a serious attempt to adapt church institutions to the changed conditions of the modern world. And if it has largely broken down in the face of the new changes of the nineteenth and twentieth centuries, that should not blind us to the real value it had in the sixteenth. Baptism, catechesis, confirmation, first communion was the pattern which emerged from the Anglican, Lutheran, and Reformed traditions. There were substantial differences of understanding as to the nature of confirmation among and within the groups, but the pattern remained intact until this century. Pastoral concern produced this pattern, and if pastoral concern today causes us to question both the pattern and its theological basis, it can still serve as a model of the adaptability of the Christian Church to radically altered circumstances.

Notes

1. *Catechism of the Council of Trent*, trans., J.A. McHugh and C.J. Callan (New York: Wagner, 1934) 179.

2. Stephen Neill, *A History of the Christian Missions*, Pelican History of the Church, vol. 6 (Baltimore: Penquin Books, 1964) 149.

3. Ibid. 150.

4. Owen Chadwick, *The Reformation*, Pelican History of the Church, vol. 3 (Baltimore: Penquin Books, 1964) 329.

5. Ibid.

6. Neil, *History* 173.

7. Paraphrase on St. Matthew's Gospel, quoted in J.D.C. Fisher, *Christian Initiation: The Reformation Period*, Alcuin Club Collections, vol. 51 (London: SPCK, 1970) 169. See also W. Lockton, "The Age for Confirmation," *Church Quarterly Review* 100 (1925) 27-64.

8. L.L. Mitchell, "What Is Confirmation?" *Anglican Theologican Review* 55 (1973) 202ff.

9. *Manuale ad Usum Percelebris Ecclesie Sarisburiensis*, ed., A.J. Collins, Henry Bradshaw Society, vol. 91 (Chichester: Henry Bradshaw Society, 1960) 32.

10. Mansi, *Conciliorum Omnium Amplissima Collectio*, vol. 32, col. 1258 (Florence: 1798). For English see Fisher, *Christian Initiation* 185.

11. *Confessio Fidei Fratrum Waldensium.* English translation quoted in Fisher, *Christian Initiation* 168.

12. *Uom Eelichen Leben* ("The Sermon on Married Life") quoted in Arthur C. Repp, *Confirmation in the Lutheran Church* (St. Louis: Concordia Press, 1964) 17.

13. *Predigt am Sontag Latare Nachmittags,* quoted in Repp, *Confirmation* 17.

14. In this entire section I am following Arthur Repp's excellent discussion in chapter one of his *Confirmation in the Lutheran Church.*

15. Ibid. 22.

16. George Karg, quoted in Repp, *Confirmation* 25.

17. Aemilius Ludwig Richter, ed., *Die evangelischen Kirchenordungen des sechzehnten Jahrhunderts* (Nieuwkoop: B. de Graaf, 1967) 27.

18. Repp, *Confirmation* 45.

19. E.A. Achelis, *Lehrbuch der Praktischen Theologie,* vol. 2 (Leipzig: J.C. Hinrichs, 1911) 315.

20. E. Schling, ed., *Die Evangelischen Kirchordnung des XVI Jahrhunderts* 8 (Tübingen: J.B. Mohr, 1957) 104. English translation is in Repp, *Confirmation* 45.

21. Repp, *Confirmation* 32.

22. E. Sehling, ed., *Evangelischen Kirchenordnung,* vol. 8, 124. English translation in Fisher, *Christian Initiation* 180.

23. Quoted in Fisher, *Christian Initiation* 57.

24. Ibid. 64.

25. Ibid. 195.

26. Jean Calvin, *Institutes of the Christian Religion,* ed., J.T. McNeill, trans., F.L. Battles, Library of Christian Classics, vol. 21 (Philadelphia: Westminster Press, 1960) 1460.

27. Ibid. 1451.

28. S.L. Ollard, "Confirmation in the Anglican Communion," in *Confirmation or the Laying on of Hands,* vol. 1 (New York: Macmillan, 1926) 62f.

29. F.E. Brightman, *The English Rite,* vol. 2 (London: Rivingtons, 1915) 776 (spelling modernized).

30. Fisher, *Christian Initiation* 249. See also E.C. Whitaker, *Martin Bucer and the Book of Common Prayer,* Alcuin Club Collections, vol. 55 (Great Wakering: Mayhew-McCrimmon, 1974) 113.

31. George H. Willians, ed., *The Radical Reformation* (Philadelphia: Westminster Press, 1962) 300-319. See also Rollin S. Armour, *Anabaptist Baptism,* Studies in Anabaptist and Mennonite History, vol. 11 (Scottdale, PA: Herald Press, 1966).

32. Williams, *Radical Reformation* 120-123.

33. Armour, *Anabaptist Baptism* 123.

34. Ibid. 143.

35. Ibid. 55.

36. Ibid. 144.

37. Ibid. 132.

38. Williams, *Radical Reformation*.

39. David G. Perrey, *Baptism at 21* (New York: Vantage Press, 1973). Aidan Kavanagh, "The Norm of Baptism: The New Rite of Christian Initiation of Adults," *Worship* 48 (1974) 143-152.

40. Luther's First and Second *Taufbuchlein*, Zwingli's two orders of baptism, The 1st and 2nd Prayer Books of Edward VI. All are in Fisher, *Christian Initiation*.

REVISING THE RITES

7

The Roman Catholic Church

THE REVISION OF THE RITES OF CHRISTIAN INITIATION IN THE ROMAN Catholic Church has been part of the general revision of all rites, as mandated by the Second Vatican Council. The Constitution on the Sacred Liturgy specifically directed the restoration of the catechumenate for adults, the revision of the rites for the baptism of adults and of infants, the drawing up of a new rite of the admission to communion of converts who have already been baptized, and the revision of the rite of confirmation "so that the intimate connection of this sacrament with the whole of Christian initiation may more clearly appear."[1] All this was mandated in the light of the council's theological assertions:

> [Christ] willed that the work of salvation which they [i.e., the apostles] preached should be set in train through the sacrifice and sacraments, around which the entire liturgical life revolves. Thus by Baptism men are grafted into the paschal mystery of Christ; they die with him, are buried with him, and rise with him. They receive the spirit of adoption as sons "in which we cry, Abba, Father" (Romans 8:15) and thus become true adorers such as the Father seeks. In like manner so often as they eat the Supper of the Lord they proclaim the death of the Lord until he comes.[2]

The constitution continues by explaining that this is the reason why those who responded to Peter's sermon were baptized and "continued steadfastly in the teaching of the apostles and in the communion of the breaking of bread and in prayers (Acts 2:41)." Baptism, eucharist, and the paschal mystery are set out boldly as the very foundation of the church as the Body of Christ. In light of this solid theological beginning and our retrospective knowledge of the revolution in baptismal theology and practice of which this was the opening manifesto, it seems surprising that both baptism and eucharist were not then taken up in this context, but the constitution moved in the traditional categories of the time and discussed first the general principles of liturgical reform and renewal, then their application to the eucharist, and only then, under the title "The Other Sacraments and the Sacramentals," did it discuss the reform of Christian initiation, a term which the constitution does not use.

THE UNREFORMED RITES IN ENGLISH

Following the mandate of the constitution, the American bishops authorized on 2 April 1964 an English translation of the existing rites from the *Collectio Rituum* of 1961. Although the initiation rites of the *1964 English Ritual*[3] are in many ways a colossal anachronism, they provide an excellent starting place and benchmark against which to measure the reformed, renewed, and revised rites.

The order in which the rites appeared in the *1964 English Ritual* gives an indication of their priority. First is "The Rite for the Baptism of a Child"; then "The Rite for the Baptism of More Than One Child"; "The Rite for Supplying the Ceremonies Omitted in a Private Baptism"; "Private Baptism"; and only then "The Rite for the Baptism of Adults"; and finally "The Rite for the Baptism of Adults Arranged according to the Stages of the Catechumenate." Clearly, the customary rite is that for the baptism of a single child. The possible variations follow. A most interesting opening rubric reads:

> The more solemn form of baptism is that which is celebrated with the faithful gathered together . . . The more solemn form should not be used too frequently. Nevertheless, it should be

celebrated at least once a year, especially at the time of Easter or Epiphany, in order to renew in the faithful the fervor of their baptism.[4]

In the case of adult baptism, the rite printed first is intended to be administered all at once, including two sets of renunciations, two signings with the oil of catechumens, tasting of salt, three exorcisms, the *redditio* of the creed and the Lord's Prayer, the *ephphetha*, baptism, post-baptismal chrismation, confirmation "if a bishop is present," Mass and the reception of the eucharist "if the hour is suitable."

The second alternative, not only more traditional but a preview of things to come, divides this into seven stages to be "celebrated with the greatest possible solemnity, with the Christian people assisting."[5] Although the opening rubric directs that all local ordinaries may "concede or prescribe" this form of the rite,[6] it is clearly presented as something exceptional.

THE REFORMED RITES

The reform and renewal which followed is one of the major reworkings of Christian initiation in the latter half of the twentieth century. It would be hard to underestimate its importance, not only for Roman Catholics but for other Western Christians. Certainly Aidan Kavanagh is correct that the reforms of these rites are not ceremonial in nature but "a practical vision of what the church can become through that continuing renewal process known as Christian initiation."[7]

The first of the new rites to appear was the Rite of Baptism for Children in 1969, followed by the Rite of Confirmation in 1971, and the Rite of Christian Initiation of Adults (RCIA) in 1972, with ICEL's interim English translation in 1974.[8] The "vernacular typical edition" for the United States did not appear until 1988.[9] It is nevertheless clear that it is the RCIA which is normative, and the other rites are to be interpreted in its light.

This is signaled in the first two paragraphs of the General Introduction, which first appeared with the rite for children in 1969:

Through the sacraments of Christian initiation we are freed from the power of darkness and joined to Christ's death, burial, and resurrection. We receive the Spirit of filial adoption and are part of the entire people of God, in the celebration of the memorial of the Lord's death and resurrection.

The "sacraments of Christian initiation" are then described as baptism, confirmation, and eucharist, concluding:

> Thus the three sacraments of Christian initiation closely combine to bring us, the faithful of Christ to his full stature and to enable us to carry out the mission of the entire people of God in the world.[10]

The "rite" itself consists of three steps separating four periods or stages. It is not primarily a set of texts for the conduct of religious services, but a framework for a process of conversion. In the opening Period of Evangelization and Precatechumenate there are no liturgical rites, yet this period marks the turning of the "convert" toward Christ:

> From evangelization, completed with the help of God, come the faith and initial conversion that cause a person to feel called away from sin and drawn into the mystery of God's love.[11]

This period closes with a public liturgical rite, the first step, namely, Acceptance into the Order of Catechumens. In the words of *Lumen Gentium*:

> Catechumens who, moved by the Holy Spirit, desire with an explicit intention to be incorporated into the Church, are by that very intention joined to her. With love and solicitude mother Church embraces them as her own.[12]

The catechumenate itself may last several years, but in point of fact, in the United States it normally lasts only until the beginning of Lent. During the Period of the Catechumenate, celebrations of the word are held for the catechumens, and minor exorcisms take place. The end of the catechumenate is marked by the second step: Election or Enrollment of Names. The rite normally takes place after the homily on the First Sunday of Lent. The godparents testify before the community as to the readiness of the catechumens to be enrolled for Easter baptism, and these candidates are publicly accepted (i.e., elected) and enrolled.

During the Lenten Period of Purification and Enlightenment

the scrutinies and the presentations of the creed (*traditio symboli*) and the Lord's Prayer (*traditio orationis dominicae*) take place. The scrutinies take place at Mass on the Third, Fourth, and Fifth Sundays of Lent. The readings are those of Year A. The scrutinies include prayer for the elect and exorcisms. Ideally, the presentation of the creed takes place during the week following the first scrutiny and that of the Lord's Prayer in the week following the third scrutiny.

It is during Lent that the celebration of the RCIA will have the most profound effect upon the community as the rites take place at the parish Mass on successive Sundays:

> In the liturgy and liturgical catechesis of Lent the reminder of baptism already received or the preparation for its reception, as well as the theme of repentance, renew the entire community along with those being prepared to celebrate the paschal mystery, in which each of the elect will share through the sacraments of initiation. For both the elect and the local community, therefore, the Lenten season is a time for spiritual recollection in preparation for the celebration of the paschal mystery.[13]

The Lenten preparation of the *competentes* is completed on Holy Saturday with the recitation (*redditio*) of the creed and the Lord's Prayer and the *ephphetha*, the traditional rites of preparation going back to the *Apostolic Tradition* of Hippolytus.

The third and final step, Celebration of the Sacraments of Initiation, takes place during the Easter Vigil. The candidates are presented, the water blessed, sin and the devil renounced, the interrogative creed assented to with the traditional three *credos*, rendered rather weakly as "I do," and the water baptism takes place. The baptism may be by immersion or affusion, "whichever will serve in individual cases and in the various traditions and circumstances to ensure the clear understanding that this washing is not a mere purification rite but the sacrament of being joined to Christ."[14] The "explanatory rites" of anointing, clothing with a baptismal garment, and presentation with a lighted candle follow, except that the anointing will almost invariably be omitted, since confirmation follows with its own anointing.[15] The rite concludes with the celebration of the eucharist at which the neophytes and all those involved in the baptism receive communion under both kinds.[16]

The final period is Postbaptismal Catechesis or Mystagogy. This takes place primarily at the Sunday eucharists of the Easter season, and normally extends till Pentecost Sunday. It is an occasion both for the integration of the neophytes into the community of the faithful and for all to grow together in the sacramental life of the paschal mystery.

For me to give a detailed, historically based commentary on this substantial corpus of material in the amount of space allocated to this essay would be both impossible and undesirable. The sheer bulk of literature on the subject is already large, much of it written by those with extensive personal experience of its use,[17] and their commentary and critique are readily available. I shall therefore make some general comments more appropriate to a member of another ecclesial communion whose acquaintance with the material is largely academic.[18]

A Revolution with Precedent

Ralph Keifer has described these rites as "a revolution quite without precedent,"[19] and he was certainly right. They have restored the baptismal focus of a major portion of the liturgical year, from Ash Wednesday through Pentecost. They have made it clear that the formation of Christians is the work and apostolic mission of the whole church, not simply of the clergy and a few para-professional catechists. They have reaffirmed the paschal character of initiation, celebrating it solemnly at the heart of the restored Easter Vigil, and renewing the close relationship of baptism and eucharist as the sacraments of our participation in the paschal mystery. Baptism can be seen again as the sacrament of conversion, rather than simply a means of removing the stain of original sin from infants, and the sacramental vocation of the baptized Christian has gained new recognition.

This has not happened without problems or costs. As has been widely pointed out, many congregations are not the kind of communities of faith which the formation of catechumens requires. There has been radical change and spiritual growth in a great many places. This has resulted not only in the loss and disillusionment, on the one hand, of those unready or unwilling to change, but also in the often unwelcome challenging of the established order, on the other, by lay women and men made aware of the full meaning of their baptismal priesthood through participation in the rites. New questions about the relationship of priest and lay baptized believer, of men and women, and of Catholics and other baptized Christians are raised not by the failure of the RCIA, but by its success. The reassertion of the primacy of baptism not simply by theological decree, but by allowing the baptized to experience the rites in their full power is bound to have substantial fallout. We are after all, as Kavanagh described it, "at the storm center of the universe."[20]

The revival of the catechumenate not only in the Roman Catholic Church, but in the Anglican and Lutheran Churches, is wholly the work of the RCIA. The catechumenal rites of the American Episcopal Church are copied from the RCIA, and the document itself is widely used and adapted by all those of whatever church interested in baptismal renewal. We are all in the debt of Balthasar Fischer and the committee which so boldly produced the *Ordo Initiationis Christianae Adultorum*.

The Catechumenate and Reception into Communion

The use of the catechumenal rites of the RCIA has nonetheless created one ecumenical problem. Often the distinction between catechumens and baptized Christians being received into the Roman Catholic Church from other churches is blurred. All are sometimes treated as if they were unbaptized. Two provisions of the Reception of Baptized Christians into Full Communion of the Catholic Church[21] are of great ecumenical importance:

> The sacrament of baptism cannot be repeated and therefore it is not permitted to confer it again conditionally, unless there is a reasonable doubt about the fact or the validity of the baptism already conferred.[22]

> Any appearance of triumphalism should be carefully avoided . . . Both the ecumenical implications and the bond between the candidate and the parish community should be considered.[23]

Nothing is more offensive to Christians of other communions than the once common practice of rebaptizing those who have already been baptized with water in the Name of the Trinity. Clearly the new edition of the RCIA, by rescuing this rite and these directives from the obscurity of the appendix in which they originally appeared, is attempting to mend ecumenical fences.

More is involved than good ecumenical relations, however. The principle of one baptism is at stake, and although the document is clear that baptized but uncatechized adults have a different status from catechumens, in practice their common participation in the catechumenal process obscures this. Sometimes they have even participated in the rites of the catechumenate. There are abundant practical reasons for combining the preparation of small groups of baptized but uncatechized adults with even smaller groups of catechumens, but more emphasis needs to be placed on the optional rites for the former group.[24] The theological point is well made in the document:

> Even though uncatechized adults have not yet heard the message of the mystery of Christ, their status differs from that of catechumens, since by baptism they have already become members of the Church and children of God. Hence their conversion is based on the baptism they have already received, the effects of which they must develop.[25]

The Problem of Confirmation

The place of confirmation in the mix remains a problem. In order to "reintegrate" baptism and confirmation, the RCIA directs the omission of the post-baptismal chrismation.[26] Although the other classic rites, for example, Byzantine, Ambrosian, Gallican, and Mozarabic, have a single post-baptismal anointing, the Roman rite from the time of the *Apostolic Tradition* of Hippolytus has had two.[27] The meaning of the first, an anointing by the presbyter on the crown of the head, is well expressed in the formula given in the RCIA:

> The God of power and Father of our Lord Jesus Christ has freed you from sin and brought you to new life through water and the Holy Spirit. He now anoints you with the chrism of salvation, so that, united with his people, you may remain for ever a member of Christ who is Priest, Prophet, and King.[28]

The second anointing is the *consignatio frontis*, the signing of the forehead by the bishop following the prayer for the seven-fold gift of the Spirit, which became separated from the rest of the rite when the bishop did not preside, and came to be called confirmation.

In its theologically appropriate desire to unite baptism and eucharist at the baptism of adults, the RCIA has abandoned the Roman rite's traditional restriction of confirmation to the bishop.[29] It has simultaneously, in the interest of ritual coherence, eliminated the Christological post-baptismal consignation, the other distinctively Roman feature of the baptismal liturgy. Perhaps this is of concern only to historical liturgiologists like myself, but the theological content of the first anointing is too significant to lose.

A second group of problems is raised by the theological justification given in the RCIA for the inclusion of confirmation:

> In accord with the ancient practice followed in the Roman liturgy, adults are not to be baptized without receiving confirmation immediately afterward, unless some serious reason stands in the way. The conjunction of the two celebrations signifies the unity of the paschal mystery, the close union between the mission of the Son and the outpouring of the Holy Spirit, and the connection between the two sacraments through which the Son and the Holy Spirit come with the Father to those who are baptized.[30]

Aidan Kavanagh is not alone in wondering why it is not equally appropriate to confirm children.[31] Historically, it was the insistence by the Roman Church on the sole right of the bishop to confer the *consignatio frontis* which created confirmation as a rite separate from baptism. Since that episcopal prerogative is abandoned, or at least substantially diluted in the RCIA, it is reasonable to suggest that the rite to which it gave birth should be reunited with baptism. Attempts to formulate a theology of confimation as a separate rite have not been notably successful. Gerard Austin comments:

> No other sacrament has had such a checkered history and . . . no other sacrament has been so subject to a search for meaning. If one seeks a single word to describe the history of confirmation perhaps the most precise would be "disintegration"; disintegration of the unity of the rite itself and of the significance of that rite.[32]

James Dunning writes: "It should be clear by now that to tie Confirmation as a separate "maturity rite" to any time in early or late adolescence is pastoral nonsense." What he believes does make pastoral sense is "to celebrate full initiation for children rather early (presuming a community of faith in family around them) and then 'confirm' that initiation through celebrations at important passage points in their journey."[33] This, as he observes, is the pattern of the Episcopal, Lutheran, and Methodist rites. He cites a distinction made by Daniel Stevick, a member of the Episcopal Church's Drafting Committee on Christian Initiation, between what he called "Confirmation A"—the sacramental gift of the Holy Spirit in Christian initiation, and "Confirmation B"—a catechetical rite involving the renewal of baptismal promises, with its roots in the late Middle Ages.[34] Dunning concludes:

> The Roman Catholic confirmation rite has tried to save something of both meanings. These other churches in Confirmation A celebrate an integral initiation restoring the unity of water, oil, and bread/wine. Confirmation B is celebrated at important moments, possibly including the acceptance of adult responsibilites in the church and puberty; but the times are left to the creativity of the local church and the grace of God.

One Baptism

Dunning's pastoral concerns raise naturally a deeper theological issue. The emphasis now being placed on the RCIA raises serious questions about the baptism of children as well as the confirmation of adolescents. There is only one baptism, but there is a real danger of pastors and catechists drifting into a *de facto* situation where the theology of the RCIA and that of infant baptism are really seen as different. We cannot use one set of theological categories to explain the unified initiation rite of adults and another to explain the baptism of infants and their later confirmation. Do the Rite of Baptism of Children and the Rite of Confirmation *really* proclaim the same theology as the RCIA, and do the faithful and their pastors perceive them as doing so? If the answer is not an unequivocal yes, then the rites and their celebration need to be more carefully examined.

* * * * * *

Keifer pointed out to us in 1975 that the revised rites "are in many ways out of step with the presuppositions of those who must use them . . . provide a possible critique of church life as it is presently lived . . . are not apt to be received with open arms and . . . will not be easily understood."[35] He was right. The fact that they have not been able to deliver everything which a full and perfect implementation would cause the true believers to hope for, is not reason to condemn them. Mary Collins has aptly reminded us: "After two thousand years of Sunday assemblies we continue to struggle to 'get it right'."[36] We have not been working on the revised rites of Christian initiation nearly so long.

Notes

1. Constitution on the Sacred Liturgy n. 64-71, in Austin Flannery, ed., *Documents of Vatican II* (Grand Rapids: Eerdmans, 1975).
2. Ibid. n. 6.
3. *Collectio Rituum: The 1964 English Ritual,* containing the text for the administration of sacraments and blessings approved by the National Conference of Bishops of the United States of America, April 2, 1964, and confirmed by the Holy See, May 1, 1964 (Collegeville: The Liturgical Press, 1964).
4. Ibid. p. 3.
5. Ibid. n. 4, p. 109.
6. Ibid. n. 1, p. 107.
7. *Made, Not Born* (Notre Dame: University of Notre Dame Press, 1976) 119.
8. *The Rites of the Catholic Church as Revised by Decree of the Second Vatican Council and Published by Authority of Pope Paul VI* (New York: Pueblo Publishing Co., 1976) 1-334.
9. *Rite of Christian Initiation of Adults Approved for Use in the Dioceses of the United States of America by the National Conference of Catholic Bishop and Confirmed by the Apostolic See* (Washington, D.C.: United States Catholic Conference, 1988).
10. RCIA xiv.
11. RCIA n. 37. In the Latin text and in the original ICEL translation this was n. 10. Where it is appropriate these numbers will follow the paragraph numbers of the official U.S. text in square brackets.

12. Dogmatic Constitution on the Church n. 14, in Flannery, *Documents* 366.

13. RCIA n. 138.

14. RCIA n. 213 [n. 32].

15. RCIA nn. 215, 228 [nn. 34, 224]. See the discussion below.

16. RCIA n. 243 [n. 234].

17. A short list of the works I have found most helpful includes the following: Gerard Austin, *Anointing with the Spirit* (New York: Pueblo Publishing Co., 1985); Michael Dujarier, *The Rites of Christian Initiation* (New York: Sadlier, 1979); James Dunning, *New Wine: New Wineskins* (New York: Sadlier, 1981); Aidan Kavanagh, *The Shape of Baptism* (New York: Pueblo Publishing Co., 1978); *Made: Not Born* (Notre Dame: University of Notre Dame Press, 1978)—especially the articles by Robert Hovda, Ralph Keifer, and Aidan Kavanagh.

18. During the period in which this material was appearing I was a member of the committee revising the rites of Christian initiation in the Episcopal Church and teaching initiation in the graduate liturgy program at Notre Dame.

19. *Made, Not Born* 149.

20. "For when we talk about confirmation our conversation is really about baptism; when we are dealing with baptism we are discoursing about Christian initiation; when we are into Christian initiation we are face to face with conversion in Jesus Christ dead and rising; and when we are into conversion in Jesus Christ dead and rising we are at the storm center of the universe." In *Made, Not Born* 2.

21. An appendix to the Latin text but nn. 473-501 of the English *editio typica*.

22. RCIA n. 480 [originally n. 7 in the appendix].

23. RCIA n. 475 [originally n. 3 in the appendix].

24. Rite of Welcoming the Candidates; Rite of Sending the Candidates for Recognition by the Bishop and for the Call to Continuing Conversion; Rite of Calling the Candidates to Continuing Conversion.

25. RCIA n. 400.

26. RCIA nn. 215, 216 [nn. 34, 35].

27. See L.L. Mitchell, *Baptismal Anointing* (London: SPCK, 1966); 2nd edition (Notre Dame: University of Notre Dame Press, 1978) 173 *et passim*.

28. RCIA n. 228.

29. "If the bishop has conferred baptism, he should now also confer confirmation. It the bishop is not present, the priest who conferred baptism is authorized to confirm." RCIA n. 232 [n. 228].

30. RCIA n. 215 [n. 34].

31. Kavanagh, *The Shape of Baptism* 138.

32. Austin, *Anointing with the Spirit* 30.

33. Dunning, *New Wine: New Wineskins* 104f.

34. See the following chapter.

35. *Made, Not Born* 151.

36. Mary Collins, *Contemplative Participation* (Collegeville: The Liturgical Press, 1990) 42.

8

The American
Episcopal Church

IN THE PERIOD SINCE 1964 THE EPISCOPAL CHURCH IN THE UNITED
States, like many other churches, has been embroiled in liturgical reform and renewal. Specifically, in 1964 it began a revision of The Book of Common Prayer, a labor which it brought
to term in 1979 with the adoption of the new book. In 1964 the
triennial General Convention requested the Standing Liturgical Commission to prepare a plan for the revision of the
Prayer Book. This plan was accepted by the Convention of
1967 and put into operation. It called for the creation of a number of "drafting" committees to prepare revised drafts of various portions of the Prayer Book, with members of the Standing Liturgical Commission serving as chairs of the various
committees and the Commission itself constituting a general
revision committee. The present author served from its beginning on the "Drafting Committee on Christian Initiation."

Although the details of our revision may be both local and
denominational, their development raises serious theological,
liturgical, and pastoral problems which all contemporary
Christians must face. "The situation in which we are living
seems to be calling familiar rites and meanings into question.
Customs, teaching, and ritual, which once commended themselves as self-validating, functional, and life-supporting, no
longer seem fully appropriate."[1]

The Meaning of Baptism

When the committee first met in May of 1968, it was immediately obvious that we could not simply follow in the footsteps of those who had prepared *Prayer Book Studies 1*[2] on baptism and confirmation in 1950 and "tinker" with the texts of these rites in the 1928 Book of Common Prayer. We felt compelled instead to raise the basic question of the meaning of baptism and its place in the economy of salvation. Our working answer became the opening paagraph of the introduction to *Prayer Book Studies 18*[3], the draft rite submitted to the General Convention of 1970.

> Baptism is the sacrament in which we accept salvation from sin and reconciliation with God by participation in the death and resurrection of Jesus Christ. By the Holy Spirit a person is born anew into the fellowship which, because it is responsive in faith, is used by Christ as his Body through which he continues to work and serve in the world. In Baptism, as in all the sacraments, the principal action is God's. He accepts the candidate as his own child by incorporating him into his Son, and raises him to newness of life. He gives him the power of the Holy Spirit to fulfill his vocation in this world and to reign with Christ in his eternal kingdom.[4]

Our next task, and one to which we returned again and again, was to reconsider the practice of infant baptism, particularly in the context of the American religious scene, in which all churches are voluntary associations, and in which many, both adults and young people, question the right of anyone to make binding religious promises in the name of another. Yet, to abandon infant baptism and adopt "believer's baptism" would, in one sense, simply exchange one set of problems for another, and there is certainly no real expectation among Anglicans that the church should do this. We must, nonetheless, be aware that more and more parents will refrain, for a variety of reasons, from presenting their children for baptism, and it would be unwise to develop rites that presuppose the baptism of infants. But this is precisely the assusmption upon which the two-stage initiatory rite of the modern Western Church has been built. Infants receive baptism shortly after birth, are instructed in the Christian faith during childhood, and at the age of twelve or thirteen are confirmed and admitted to holy communion.

There seems to be a real consensus among liturgical scholars that adult baptism should be a complete act of Christian initiation, as it was in the ancient church, culminating in admission to eucharistic fellowship. On the other hand, there is no consensus in the case of the baptism of children. I believe that the focus of this disagreement lies in the different understandings of Episcopalians concerning the nature of confirmation.

The Episcopal Church by no means stands alone in its confusion. Even if it were possible (and I am by no means convinced that it is) to find a clear "Anglican" teaching in the Prayer Books of 1549 and 1552, both the teaching and the practice of the Episcopal Church have been influenced by our Roman Catholic, Lutheran, and Calvinist neighbors. "Confirmation" is an American puberty rite, whether for the Episcopalian, the Lutheran, or the Reformed Jew. It is also a "sacrament," even if it is referred to as an "apostolic rite," or by some other periphrasis. It is seen by some to be an essential part of the process of Christian initiation, without which baptism itself is but a half-sacrament.[5] By others it is considered a service of renewal and ratification of baptismal vows by those who were baptized in infancy.[6] Again, some would say with J.D.C. Fisher, "the essence of Confirmation is the imparting of the Holy Spirit,"[7] while others would affirm with G.W.H. Lampe, "there should be no thought of the gift or seal of the Spirit as a grace of Confirmation."[8]

The 1968 Lambeth Conference suggested two possible lines of experimental change in the traditional Anglican pattern of initiation:

> (A) Admission to Holy Communion and confirmation would be separated. When a baptized child is of appropriate age, he or she would be admitted to Holy Communion after an adequate course of instruction. Confirmation would be deferred to an age when a young man or woman shows adult responsibility and wishes to be commissioned and confirmed for his or her task of being a Christian in society.

> (B) Infant baptism and confirmation would be administered together, followed by admission to Holy Communion at an early age after appropriate instruction. In due course, the bishop

would commission the person for service when he or she is capable of making a responsible commitment.[9]

One way to interpret the actions of the Standing Liturgical Commission would be that they proposed alternative B to the Episcopal Church in 1970, and finding that it was unacceptable, they proposed alternative A in 1973. I do not believe that this would represent the true situation.

In my opinion, suggestions A and B are not alternative practices, but alternative means of describing the same course of action. An integral rite of Christian initiation is to be administered to children, after which they are to be admitted to holy communion. Upon arrival at maturity they are to be commissioned by the bishop "for the task of being a Christian in society." The difference lies entirely in whether this "commissioning" is to be called confirmation.

G.W.H. Lampe describes confirmation as "the blessing of the bishop to a new member of his flock, and a commission to take his place as an active partner in the Church's apostolic task."[10] On the other hand, Lampe states that the "seal of the Spirit," which the papal constitution *Divinae Consortium Naturae* declares to be the form of the sacrament of confirmation, is part of baptism in Anglican practice.[11] If we accept the definitions of Lampe, we shall identify the bishop's commissioning of adult Christians for service with confirmation. If, instead, we accept the definitions of Paul VI, of Gregory Dix, and of J.D.C. Fisher, then we shall identify confirmation with "the seal of the Holy Spirit," of which the external rite is normally considered to be the signing of the forehead with a cross, or consignation, a ceremony which Lampe quite accurately points out has immediately followed water baptism in Anglican usage since 1552.

The Proposed Rites

The practical point of this discussion is that the Drafting Committee on Christian Initiation was concerned that the "seal of the Spirit" be obviously a part of the baptismal liturgy, and to this end proposed, in both *Prayer Book Studies 18* and *26*, that the cross might be made with chrism, as in the early church, the Eastern Church, the medieval Western

Church, and the 1549 Prayer Book. Whether this "signing and sealing" is confirmation, or simply a declarative act symbolizing one of the inward effects of holy baptism is a disputed matter, and the Drafting Committee did not wish to attempt to decide it. It is my personal belief that the Anglican Communion has survived through its common use of a liturgy, while allowing the greatest freedom of theological interpretation to those who used the forms of the church. I had hoped that the flexibility of the proposed forms would enable this theological discussion to continue, without disruptive effects on pastoral practice. In my view the changes made by the House of Bishops in the proposed baptismal rite of *PBS 26* at the General Convention of 1973 severely restricted that flexibility of interpretation. Fortunately, much of the flexibility was restored in 1976.

The attempt of the Drafting Committee in both *PBS 18* and *26* was to produce a rite which would be recognized by all as the complete sacrament of Christian initiation. This concern is expressed in the first rubric on page 22 of *PBS 26*, which has become the opening rubric of the baptismal rite as adopted in the 1979 Prayer Book:

> Holy Baptism is full initiation by water and the Holy Spirit into Christ's Body the Church. The bond which God establishes in Baptism is indissoluble.[12]

At the joint meeting of the Theological and Prayer Book Committees of the House of Bishops with the Standing Liturgical Commission, attended also by representatives of the General Synod Committee on Doctrine and Worship of the Anglican Church of Canada in 1972, the following statements (among others) were agreed upon:

> There is one, and only one, unrepeatable act of Christian initiation, which makes a person a member of the Body of Christ.

> The essential element of Christian initiation is baptism by water and the Spirit, in the Name of the Holy Trinity, in response to repentance and faith.

> Christian initiation is normatively administered in a liturgical rite that also includes the laying-on of hands, consignation (with or without Chrism), prayer for the gift of the Holy Spirit, reception by the Christian community, joining the eucharistic

fellowship, and commissioning for Christian mission. When the Bishop is present, it is expected that he will preside at the rite.

An act and occasion for (more or less) mature personal acceptance of promises and affirmations made in one's behalf in infancy is pastorally and spiritually desirable.[13]

These principles are, in fact, those which underlie both the rites of *PBS 18* and *26* and that actually adopted. The presidency of the bishop over the whole process of initiation was affirmed strongly by the drafting committee, and the rites consider him the normative minister of Holy Baptism, although recognizing that the parish priest presides upon most occasions, and this was written into the rubrics as finally approved.

The Sacrament of Holy Baptism

The celebration of baptism is set in the context of the eucharist as the chief service of a Sunday or other feast, both to ensure the participation of the congregation in what is essentially a communal act, and to emphasize relationship of the two sacraments of the Gospel. *PBS 26* recommended a further restriction of its ministration to those occasions in the Christian Year with which it is theologically related: Easter Vigil, Pentecost, Epiphany, All Saints, and the bishop's visitation, and this recommendation became a part of the rite in The Book of Common Prayer.[14]

The candidates for baptism are presented following the scripture readings and sermon. Essential to the rationale of both proposals is the renewal of the baptismal vows by the entire congregation in company with those making them for the first time. In this way the celebration of baptism becomes the occasion for the renewal of the baptismal convenant for all present. The one substantial difference in approach to this renewal of vows between the two proposals was the assumption of *PBS 18* that this regular on-going renewal of vows might be more pastorally and spiritually beneficial than the picking out of specific occasions for the solemn affirmation of baptismal vows. This idea did not gain acceptance with the bishops, and so *PBS 26* provided "A Form for the Affirmation of Baptismal Vows, with the Laying-on of Hands by the Bishop." *PBS 18* did not reject this idea, but it certainly did not emphasize it. *PBS 24*, Pastoral Offices, had contained an extremely flexible "Form for Commitment to Christian Service"[15] to meet this need, but it was not connected with the episcopal imposition of hands.

The baptismal vows themselves are in the traditional form, with the people responding to three questions by reciting the three paragraphs of the Apostles' Creed, the ancient baptismal creed of the Western Church.

The vows are followed by the blessing of the water, and, if it is to be used, the blessing of the chrism. The hope of the committee was that bishops would consecrate chrism upon their visitation to the parishes of their dioceses when they themselves presided at the baptismal liturgy, and then deliver the remaining oil to the pastor to use upon other baptismal occasions.

In both *PBS 18* and *26* the water baptism is followed by a prayer for the gift of the Holy Spirit. That in *PBS 18* used the phrase "Strengthen and confirm them, O Lord," whereas that in *PBS 26* says "Sustain them," in keeping with the desire of the bishops to retain the word "confirmation" for the bishop's act of commissioning. The bishop, or the priest if the bishop is not present, then signs each candidate with the cross (using chrism if desired). *PBS 18* accompanied this act straightforwardly with the formula "*Name*, you are sealed by the Holy Spirit," intending to adopt suggestion B of the Lambeth Conference and consider this consignation to be confirmation. The House of Bishops at the General Convention of 1970, however, refused to sanction even the trial use of this rite by those who were not bishops, or its use with "children under the present age normal for confirmation."[16] The rite therefore had little use in the form in which it was proposed by the Standing Liturgical Commission. The Convention did permit priests to use the "baptismal portion" of the rite, however, and in practice this meant that an alternative prayer and consignation formula for use by priests were issued. In this form it was widely tried, with generally positive results.

As a result of the limited approval given the rite, and of the consultations between the members of the Drafting Committee and the Standing Liturgical Commission and the bishops, the results of which are quoted above, a new approach was taken in *PBS 26*, and the following formula was provided for use by the celebrating priest or bishop:

> "*Name*, child of God, inheritor of the Kingdom of heaven, you have been sealed by the Holy Spirit and marked as Christ's own forever."[17]

Even this did not seem to satisfy the bishops, who amended it at the General Convention of 1973 by adding the words "by the water of baptism" after the phrase "sealed by the Holy Spirit." My objection to this change is that it accepts G.W.H. Lampe's view that the actual "sealing" is done in the baptismal water, that the "seal of the Spirit" is, in fact, the inward part of the sacrament of baptism. This is certainly a theologically tenable position, but there are many Episcopalians who would hold that the "seal" should be identified with the outward rite of the signing, closely identified with, but not identical to, the water baptism. In the form proposed, the formula was capable of either interpretation.

A compromise on this formula was agreed to and authorized for trial use during 1975. This version was presented to the General Convention of 1976 and subsequently adopted:

> N., you are sealed by the Holy Spirit in Baptism and marked as Christ's own for ever.[18]

This restores much of the ambiguity. In my opinion it leans toward identifying the *seal* with the consignation then being performed, but clearly asserts its baptismal character.

The consignation is followed by the greeting of the newly baptized by the minister and congregation, and by the holy eucharist, beginning at the prayers of the faithful, as in Justin Martyr's second-century description of the baptismal eucharist.

A rubric both in *PBS 26* and in the 1975 proposal stated that the newly baptized might receive communion, but it was deleted from the text actually presented in 1976 in *The Draft Proposed Book of Common Prayer*.[19] The reasons for the removal of the proposed rubric are not clear. There was some concern that the rubric was an attempt to authorize the reception of communion by baptized members of other churches, and some genuine opposition to the communicating of infants. Any lingering confusion about the intention of the Episcopal

Church was removed by the 1988 General Convention, which included in *The Book of Occasional Services* a rubric permitting the communion of a newly baptized infant "in the form of a few drops of wine, if the child is not weaned,"[20] and a resolution stating:

> That those baptized in infancy, may, as full members of The Body of Christ, begin receiving communion at any time they desire and their parents permit.[21]

Confirmation or Affirmation of Vows

As has already been indicated, *PBS 26* also contained a form for "Affirmation of Baptismal Vows, also called Confirmation." The bishops in 1973 amended the title to give more prominence to the name confirmation, and in The Book of Common Prayer the service is now called "Confirmation, with Forms for Reception and for the Reaffirmation of Baptismal Vows."[22] In 1973 the rubrics were amended to make it clear that the rite was expected to be a part of Christian nurture.[23] In 1976 the General Convention added a second rubric extending that expectation to those baptized as adults "unless baptized with the laying on of hands by a bishop," clearly intending to continue the Anglican custom whereby all adult members of the church have been confirmed by a bishop.[24]

According to *PBS 26* the rite is intended for those who are prepared to make a public affirmation of their baptismal faith, who return to the Christian life after having neglected or abandoned it, and those who come into the bishop's jurisdiction from another church. Beginning with the 1975 proposals these three classes of recipients were distinguished in the rite itself by the provision of different formulas for confirmation, reception, and reaffirmation, thus avoiding the suggestion that confirmation was repeatable.[25]

It is the hope of the compilers that the confirmation rite will be used in connection with the baptismal liturgy, so that the bishops on their visitation will preside at the baptismal liturgy, and then, after signing the newly baptized, lay hands on the candidates for confirmation, reception, and reaffirmation. In this case the candidates renew their baptismal vows along with those taking them for the first time. The final version of the rite includes these forms within the rite of baptism to encourage this. For occasions when the rite is conducted apart from baptism, it is also printed separately with a renewal of vows after the sermon of the eucharist.

The actual rite is quite simple. The bishop asks the candidates: "Do you reaffirm your renunciation of evil?" and "Do you renew your commitment to Jesus Christ?" They then renew their baptismal convenant. After the signing and sealing of the newly baptized, the bishop commends "these persons who have renewed their commitment to Christ" to the prayers of the congregation and prays over them for the renewal of the convenant and that God will send them in the power of the Spirit to perform the tasks he has set for them. The bishop lays hands on each candidate for confirmation and repeats either the traditional Anglican "Defend, O Lord . . ." or a slightly revised version of the form written for *PBS 26*:

> Strengthen, O Lord, your servant *N.* with your Holy Spirit, empower *him* for your service; and sustain *him* all the days of *his* life.[26]

Alternative forms are given for reception and reaffirmation. The form for reception makes it clear that the person is already a member of the one holy catholic and apostolic church and is being received into "this Communion." The form for reaffirmation asks the Holy Spirit, "who has begun a good work in you, [to] direct and uphold you in the service of Christ and his kingdom."

A single prayer that God's "fatherly hand ever be over" them and the "Holy Spirit ever be with them" concludes the rite. The peace is exchanged and the eucharist continues with the common prayers of the faithful.

What is this rite which is here called confirmation? It depends on what you believe confirmation to be. Certainly this is exactly what G.W.H. Lampe, and for that matter Luther and Calvin, considered confirmation to be. It is the kind of confirmation described in Lambeth option A. It is certainly not what J.D.C. Fisher or Paul VI mean by confirmation. Some have even suggested that the Episcopal Church has succeeded in abolishing confirmation in this new rite. I do not believe this is true, and experience with the rite since its adoption in 1976 has strengthened this belief.

Unfortunately the word "confirmation" carries so many overtones that it is almost impossible to use it in a univocal sense. I wish it were possible to retire it from use for a period of years to allow the air to clear. The intent of the revised rites is clearly that baptism be the complete rite of initiation, containing all traditional elements, including the prayer for the Holy Spirit, consignation, and admission to the eucharistic fellowship. Confirmation is a "rite of intensification," a solemn public affirmation of baptismal vows in the presence of the bishop, who imposes hands, praying that they "may continue [God's] forever and daily increase in [God's] Holy Spirit more and more,"[27] a phrase found in all Anglican confirmation rites since 1552.

My personal preference would be for the restoration of the simple formula for the baptismal consignation found in *PBS 18*. Thus, the baptismal rite would more unambiguously correspond to the classical rites of the Christian Church, such as that of the *Apostolic Tradition* of Hippolytus. On the other hand, the rite adopted clearly can be viewed in that way, and is viewed in that way by an increasing majority of those using it. There remain some, however, who see the changes made in the baptismal rite as mere ceremonial embellishments, and a few who see confirmation as a puberty rite.

The Catechumenal Process

The most obvious defect of the baptismal rite as it appears in The Book of Common Prayer is the absence of a formal catechumenal structure to bring adult candidates to the baptismal confession of faith. In 1976, following the adoption of the texts which became The Book of Common Prayer of 1979, the Standing Liturgical Commission began work on *The Book of Occasional Services*. A subcommittee, of which the present writer served as chair, prepared a section for that book entitled "Preparation of Adults for Holy Baptism," which provides a framework for a traditional catechumenate. The work is basically an adaptation of material found in the Roman Catholic Rite of Christian Initiation of Adults. These texts appeared and were authorized in 1979.[28]

Very few Episcopal parishes had had any experience with

the catechumenate in 1979, but its inclusion in *The Book of Occasional Services* not only made the resource available for those parishes preparing catechumens, but gave valuable suggestions to others as to how adult candidates for baptism could be prepared.

A second edition of *The Book of Occasional Services*[29] was approved in 1988. During the interim there had been considerable growth in the number of parishes preparing catechumens and the material was revised, with the participation of those who had been actively engaged in that work. The ongoing problem, particularly where the total numbers of candidates involved was small, was the confusing of catechumens with baptized persons wishing to reaffirm their baptismal vows and either enter or return to the communicant life of the church. Therefore, a new block of material entitled "Preparation of Baptized Persons for Reaffirmation of the Baptismal Convenant" was prepared and adopted.[30] This material, although based both on the RCIA and medieval material for the order of penitents, is much more original.

It makes clear that the rites of the catechumenate are not suitable for those already baptized, although the formational processes of catechesis is, and it includes new rites for the baptized inquirers. "The Welcoming of Baptized Christians into a Community" includes the writing of their names in the church register. It marks the transition from simple inquirer to one undergoing "a disciplined exploration of the implications of Christian living."[31] It may also be used for people transferring from another congregation.

"The Calling of the Baptized to Continuing Conversion" is a rite for Ash Wednesday, including the imposition of ashes. It is intended for those who will reaffirm their baptismal convenant at the Easter Vigil. There is a third rite, associated with the foot washing on Maundy Thursday, as a final preparation for reaffirmation.

The third new block of material is "The Preparation of Parents and Godparents for the Baptism of Infants and Young Children."[32] It uses material which already existed: "The Blessing of Parents at the Beginning of the Pregnancy" from the *Book of Occasional Services*, "Thanksgiving for the Birth or Adoption of a Child" from the Prayer Book, and the baptismal rite. It is designed to give content to the rubric in The Book of Common Prayer[33] requiring the preparation of parents and godparents.

* * * * * *

The revised rites have already (1991) had a profound effect on the liturgical lives of parishes. Baptisms are being regularly celebrated at the principal eucharist on Sundays and especially on the great baptismal feasts. More and more bishops are seeing their role to be the presidency of the entire initiation process and not simply to confirm. The adult catechumenate has gained a foothold, and the national church is sponsoring training programs for catechists.

Most significantly, I believe, the essential link between baptism and the eucharist has been restored, and baptism is seen as leading to membership in the eucharistic community of the church. Some confusion about confirmation remains. It is clear that the Episcopal Church wishes to have a rite with this name, but there is still disagreement about what it means. In any case, to paraphrase Eugene Fairweather, the gap between baptism and eucharist is closed and the scandal of a class of apparently half-initiated Christians abolished.[34] I agree with Professor Fairweather that it would be most logical to call the consignation administered with baptism "confirmation," and use some other term for the bishop's later adult commissioning, but that does not appear to be an acceptable course to the American bishops. One thing which the history of the initiatory rites makes abundantly clear is that they have been successfully adapted and reinterpreted many times in Christian history, and this work is being carried on again to meet the new conditions of the present.

Notes

1. D.B. Stevick, *Supplement to Prayer Book Studies 26* (New York: Church Hymnal Corporation, 1973) 36.
2. *Prayer Book Studies 1* (New York: Church Pension Fund, 1950).
3. *Prayer Book Studies 18* (New York: Church Pension Fund, 1970).
4. Ibid. 13.
5. Gregory Dix, *The Theology of Confirmation in Relation to Baptism* (Westminster: Dacre, 1946).

6. For example, R.C. Miller, "Confirmation and the Ministry of the Laity," *Anglican Theological Review* 54 (1972) 359.

7. In *Crisis for Confirmation*, ed., M. Perry (London: SCM, 1967) 90.

8. G.W.H. Lampe, *The Seal of the Spirit* (London: Longmans, 1951) 317.

9. *The Lambeth Conference 1968. Resolutions and Reports* (London and New York: SPCK and Seabury, 1968) 99.

10. Lampe, *Seal of the Spirit* 316.

11. Ibid. 314, 315.

12. *The Book of Common Prayer* (New York: Church Hymnal Corporation, 1979) 298.

13. *Prayer Book Studies 26* (New York: Church Hymnal Corporation, 1973) 3-4.

14. *The Book of Common Prayer* 312.

15. *Prayer Book Studies 24* (New York: Church Hymnal Corporation, 1970) 40-41; see *The Book of Common Prayer* 428f.

16. *Services for Trial Use* (New York: Church Hymnal Corporation, 1971) 21.

17. *Prayer Book Studies 26* 17.

18. *Holy Baptism Authorized for Trial Use during 1975-1976* (New York: Church Hymnal Corporation, 1975); *The Book of Common Prayer* 308.

19. *Prayer Book Studies 36* 18; *Holy Baptism 1975-1976* 18; *The Draft Proposed Book of Common Prayer* (New York: Church Hymnal Corporation, 1976) 315 and passim.

20. *Book of Occasional Services*, 2d ed. (New York: Church Hymnal Corporation, 1988) 157.

21. The Episcopal Church, *Journal of the General Convention 1988* 158.

22. *The Book of Common Prayer* 413.

23. *Prayer Book Studies 26* 22. The word "encouraged" was changed to "expected" in the second rubric. See also *The Book of Common Prayer* 412.

24. For a critical discussion of this, see L.L. Mitchell, "The Theology of Christian Initiation and *The Proposed Book of Common Prayer*," *Anglican Theological Review* 60 (1978) 414f.

25. *A Form for Confimation, for Reception and for the Reaffirmation of Baptismal Vows Authorized for Trial Use during 1975-1976* (New York: Church Hymnal Corporation, 1975) 8; *The Book of Common Prayer* 309f, 418f. Urban T. Holmes, *Confirmation: The Celebration of Maturity in Christ* (New York: Seabury, 1975) 25, 48, 57ff, 65ff, 73 *et alibi* strongly defended the idea of the repeatability of the rite, pointing out, quite correctly, that baptismal vows can obviously be affirmed

many times, and that there is nothing different about the first time except that it is first. It is, of course, the sacramental entry into the baptismal covenant, of which the baptismal signing and sealing is an integral part, which is once and for all and can never be repeated. See also L.L. Mitchell, "The Theology of Christian Initiation," *Anglican Theological Review* (1978) 417f.

26. *The Book of Common Prayer* 309, 418; see *PBS 26*, 26.

27. *The Book of Common Prayer* 309, 418.

28. *The Book of Occasional Services* (New York: Church Hymnal Corporation, 1979) 112-125.

29. *The Book of Occasional Services, Second Edition* (New York: Church Hymnal Corpoation, 1988). The catechumenal rites are on pages 112-126.

30. *BOS* 132-141.

31. Ibid. 135.

32. Ibid. 155-158.

33. *The Book of Common Prayer* 298.

34. In *Partners in Mission: Anglican Consultative Assembly-Dublin* (New York: Seabury, 1973) 44-45.

9

Other Churches

ECUMENICALLY, THE MOST IMPORTANT DOCUMENT OF THE LAST half century on Christian initiation is not a liturgy but a theological statement, the baptismal portion of *Baptism, Eucharist and Ministry*, the Lima Document, issued by the Faith and Order Commission of the World Council of Churches in 1982 after a process of fifty years.[1] Although there is no common baptismal liturgy included, the theological agreement on the meaning of baptism and the constitutive elements of a "comprehensive order of baptism" is both the fruit of and a major contributor toward ecumenical convergence in the celebration of Christian initiation. The area of theological agreement is large and the spectrum of participating traditions broad.[2] These would seem to be the most important common statements about the meaning of baptism:

> Baptism is the sign of new life through Jesus Christ. It unites the one baptized with Christ and with his people.[3]

> By baptism Chistians are immersed in the liberating death of Christ where their sins are buried, where the "old Adam" is crucified with Christ, and where the power of sin is broken . . . Fully identified with the death of Christ, they are buried with him and raised here and now to a new life in the power of the resurrection of Jesus Christ, confident that they will also ultimately be one with him in a resurrection like his.[4]

> The baptism which makes Christians partakers of the mystery of Christ's death and resurrection implies confession of sin and

conversion of heart . . . Thus those baptized are pardoned, cleansed and sanctified by Christ, and are given as part of their baptismal experience a new ethical orientation under the guidance of the Holy Spirit.[5]

God bestows upon all baptized persons the anointing and the promise of the Holy Spirit, marks them with a seal and implants in their hearts the first installment of their inheritance as sons and daughters of God.[6]

Through baptism Christians are brought into union with Christ, with each other and with the Church of every time and place. Our common baptism, which unites us to Christ in faith, is thus a basic bond of unity.[7]

Our common baptism is therefore a call to Christian unity as well as an eschatological sign of the Kingdom. With these theological and ecumenical foundations laid, the document turns to baptismal practice. The first major ecumenical question it faces is the baptism of believers and infants. "All churches," it reminds us, "baptize believers coming from other religions or from unbelief."[8] The question, then, has to do with the baptism of infants. Lima attempts to find common ground for its discussion, beginning by stating that all baptisms take place in the church, which is the community of faith:

All baptism is rooted in and declares Christ's faithfulness unto death. It has its setting within the life and faith of the Church and, through the witness of the whole Church, it points to the faithfulness of God, and the ground of all life in faith.[9]

LITURGICAL IMPLICATIONS OF LIMA

In terms of the actual liturgy this means that a personal confession of faith is an integral part of the baptismal rite for those old enough to make such a profession. For infants, the personal response comes later in their life, "and Christian nurture is directed to the eliciting of this confession." This connection is important for those churches which practice infant baptism lest they drift into two theologies of baptism, one for adults and another for infants.

Liturgically this is expressed in the celebration and development of baptism in the setting of the Christian community. Reaffirmation of faith by the whole congregation and their pledging themselves to provide the environment of witness and service necessary for the nurture of baptized children, the formation of catechumens and their incorporation into the church is intrinsic to the celebration.

The document then addresses the relationship of baptism, chrismation, and confimation:

> In God's work of salvation, the paschal mystery of Christ's death and resurrection is inseparably linked with the pentecostal gift of the Holy Spirit. Similarly, participation in Christ's death and resurrection is inseparably linked with the receiving of the Spirit. Baptism in its full meaning signifies and effects both.[10]

There is, of course, no ecumenical consensus as to whether the Spirit is given in the water rite, the anointing with chrism, the imposition of hands, or all three. The document, nevertheless, mentions laying on of hands, anointing, and signing with the cross as additional ways which signify the gift of the Spirit and comments: "the recovery of such vivid signs may be expected to enrich the liturgy."[11] It also recognizes that some churches do not consider Christian initiation complete without "the sealing of the baptized with the gift of the Spirit" and participation in the eucharist. The commentary contains a further warning to those churches "which baptize children but refuse them a share in the eucharist . . . to ponder whether they have fully appreciated and accepted the consequences of baptism."[12]

THE LIMA BAPTISMAL LITURGY

Obviously there is more theological meat in the Lima Document that we can chew at this time, but we need to note, before moving on, its criteria for the actual celebration. In the first place, baptism is with water in the name of the Father, the Son, and the Holy Spirit.[13] Immersion is clearly preferred, as vividly expressing "the reality that in baptism the Christian participates in the death, burial and resurrection of Christ."[14]

Other elements in a complete rite include the proclamation of the Scriptures referring to baptism, the invocation of the Holy Spirit, renunication of evil, profession of Christological and Trinitarian faith, "a declaration that the persons baptized have acquired a new identity as sons and daughters of God, and as members of the Church, called to be witnesses of the Gospel." Sealing with the Spirit and participation in the eucharist complete the order, recognizing that not all churches consider them necessary.[15] Baptism is normally administered during public worship, especially at Easter, Pentecost, and Epiphany.[16]

It is not difficult to see the common practice of many churches in this statement, both those which had already reformed, restored, and renewed their initiatory rites and those, like the Orthodox, which continue to use patristic rites. We can also see the concerns of serious theologians for anomalies in present practice, and it is a worthwhile endeavor for liturgists and pastors to examine afresh their own rites in the light of this ecumenical consensus.

CONSULTATION ON CHURCH UNION

In 1973 the Consultation on Church Union (COCU), an ecumenical group representing several American denominations,[17] issued *An Order for the Celebration of Holy Baptism.*[18] It was issued "for the use, study, and critical response of all who are interested." It has been widely studied and criticized, and it has received some use, although it has not been widely used in those churches having their own liturgical books. My only personal knowledge of its use is among Disciples. Its importance far exceeds its actual use. Among the distinguished liturgists whose names are listed as members of the Commission on Worship which produced the liturgy are Horace Allen, Hoyt Hickman, Boone Porter, Charles Smith, Keith Watkins, and James White.

The service is intended to be celebrated as part of the regular Sunday liturgy of the congregation, including the reading and preaching of the word of God. After the sermon the candidates are presented and asked if they desire to "be baptized into death with Christ who breaks the power of sin," to be raised to new life in Christ, "sharing in his work of reconciling love," and to be "joined to the people of God and its ministries of service in the name of Chist." If the promises are made by sponsors in the name of a child, they (and the congregation) are asked to continue the care and Christian formation of the candidates.[19] The prayer over the water is then offered. It is described in the commentary as "the principal act of prayer in this rite of baptism."

> It should be offered with great reverence, and it is appropriate for the congregation to stand. Ancient Christian custom would have this prayer recited by the senior or principal clergyman, such as a bishop if he is present. Other participating ministers stand nearby.[20]

The influence of classical Christian baptismal liturgy and theology is obvious, not only in this description, but in the entire commentary and in the rite itself. The theological description which follows is worth quoting in full, both for its own sake and as representative of the theological level of the work:

> Traditional Christian prayers over the baptismal font resemble the prayers said over the bread and wine in the eucharist. Like the latter, they reflect the Hebrew tradition of blessing objects and giving them spiritual significance by giving thanks to God for them and blessing him for his act of creation and redemption. The prayer over the water, traditionally known as the benediction of the font, relates the water to great acts in the history of salvation. Baptism may be performed at a beach on the oceanside, or from a cup of water at the bedside of a dying man. In either case, this particular water is invested with a spiritual significance extending into broad biblical horizons. The power of God embodied in the primal ocean of creation, in the parting waves of the Red Sea, in the healing waters of Jordan, in the tomb of Jerusalem, and in the Spirit-motivated life of the Christian community—this is the power to be brought to bear here and now when this water is administered in God's name.[21]

Before the actual baptism the candidates affirm their Christian faith, using either the Apostles' Creed or three creedal questions to which they reply: "I believe." Baptism is with the traditional Western formula, by immersion or affusion, preferably with large amounts of water as in the early church.[22]

After baptism the minister *may* lay a hand upon each neophyte, marking the cross upon the forehead, using oil prepared for the purpose if it is desired. The accompanying form is:

> You are sealed by the Holy Spirit and marked with the sign of Christ's cross, that you may know him and the power of his resurrection, and the fellowship of his suffering.[23]

The use of these post-baptismal ceremonies, including the chrismation, is strongly defended in the commentary.[24] Recognizing the different disciplines of different churches, it affirms:

> The rite here given is composed as a complete rite, containing baptism in water, the invocation of the Holy Spirit with laying on of hands, and Holy Communion. When administered under properly authorized circumstances, it is assumed that the laying on of hands (and/or anointing) will constitute confirmation.[25]

The influence in the first Episcopal proposal, *Prayer Book Studies 18*, the only contemporary rite to appear in the booklet's bibliography, is clear. The commentary goes on to discuss other possibilities, such as the omission of confirmation and communion in the case of infants in churches which will not confirm and communicate them, and the possibility of using the entire rite for infants and another rite at a late date for confirmation.[26] Even with all these qualifications, the COCU order did bring the concept of a unified initiation rite to the attention of many who would never have considered adopting it from The Book of Common Prayer or the Rite of Christian Initiation of Adults.

The baptismal rite concludes with the welcoming of the newly baptized, the exchange of peace, and their participation in the eucharist.[27] The commentary concludes with a spirited defense of the inclusion of the eucharist in the baptismal rite:

> The meaning of baptism and the receiving of the eucharist are closely related. To be baptized without the intention of becoming a communicant would be a strange anomaly. It is as members of the royal and priestly people that the newly baptized, and/or their parents and sponsors, intercede in prayer, offer solemn praise and thanksgiving, and receive the sacrament of the Lord's flesh and blood . . . The reasons for administering Holy Communion to a small child are no lesser and no greater than the reasons for administering baptism to the same child. Both practices look to Our Lord's insistence that little children be permitted to come to him.[28]

Appearing as early as it did, in 1973, this liturgy had significant influence, if not on the people, at least on the liturgy com-
missions of those churches which came later to the work of reform and renewal.

LUTHERAN BOOK OF WORSHIP

The services of "Holy Baptism" and "Affirmation of Baptism" in the 1978 Lutheran Book of Worship[29] (LBW) are revisions of the forms in *Contemporary Worship 7: Holy Baptism*[30]
(CW 7) and *Contemporary Worship 8: Affirmation of the Baptismal
Covenant*[31] (CW 8) prepared by the Inter-Lutheran Commission on Worship in 1974 and 1975 for provisional use. The
chair of the drafting committee was Hans C. Boehringer, then
professor at Valparaiso University. The introduction mentions
"considerable study" of the practices of Episcopalians, Roman
Catholics, and various other churches, as well as Lutheran traditions.[32] The COCU baptismal rite, *Prayer Book Studies 26* (the
second Episcopal proposal), and the Roman Catholic Rite of
Baptism for Children, but not the Rite for the Christian Initiation of Adults, appear in the bibliography.

There are many differences of text and presentation between the two versions of the baptismal rite, but they are not
substantively different. CW 7, for example, sets its baptismal
rite within the eucharistic liturgy, for which a complete text is
given. LBW simply indicates by rubric that it follows the sermon and Hymn of the Day.[33] LBW is clearly a revision of the
provisional text, and we shall therefore follow its text.

The rite begins with the presentation of the candidates, and
prayer for them during the prayers of the people. The thanksgiving over the water stands in the tradition of Luther's Flood
Prayer (*Sintflutgebet*), being drawn from the same traditional
materials which Luther used.[34] The LBW *Manual on the Liturgy*
quotes Luther's *Small Catechism* to explain the purpose of the
thanksgiving:

> It is not the water that produces these effects, but the Word of
> God connected with the water, and our faith which relies on
> the Word of God connected with the water. For without the
> Word of God the water is merely water and no Baptism. But
> when connected with the Word of God it is a Baptism, that is, a

gracious water of life and a washing of regeneration in the Holy Spirit.[35]

The candidates then renounce "all the forces of evil, the devil, and all his empty promises," and profess their faith by reciting the Apostles' Creed in response to three questions, as in the Episcopal rite.[36]

For the baptism itself a choice is given between the traditional Western "I baptize" form and the Eastern "N. is baptized" form.[37] This choice was already in CW 7. The text prescribes the mode as a threefold affusion, but a rubric in the introduction permits baptism by immersion.[38] CW 7 contained an extensive explanation of different modes of immersion, grounding it in the early church, rather than modern Baptist practice.[39]

Immediately following the water baptism, the newly baptized kneel, and "the minister lays both hands on the head of each of the baptized and prays for the Holy Spirit." The *Manual* cites Acts 8:14-18 and 9:17 as biblical precedents for requiring the use of *both* hands.[40] A form of the traditional Gelasian prayer for the sevenfold gift of the Spirit into which the name of the individual is inserted accompanies the action. This "signals a return to the liturgical fullness of the ancient church which was lost when confirmation became a separate rite."[41] Each is then signed on the forehead with the formula:

> [Name], child of God, you have been sealed by the Holy Spirit in baptism and marked with the cross of Christ for ever.[42]

The signing of each candidate with the cross is described as "a principal part of the rite, traceable to the beginnings in the ancient church."[43] The use of "oil prepared for the purpose" for the signing is specifically authorized, and the *Manual*, following CW 7, explains the meaning of anointing and describes the preparation of the oil by adding balsam or other fragrant oil to olive oil.[44] There is no mention of the consecration or blessing of the oil, nor is the word *chrism* used.

The expressed intention to return to the "liturgical fullness" lost when confirmation became a separate rite, makes it clear that the Lutheran rite is intended to be integral, based on ancient Christian models and what was then the proposed rite of the Episcopal Church. The laying on of hands is primarily identified with "confirmation" and the gift of the Spirit, and the signing with the cross with "the indelible seal of the new Lord," but both actions are integral.

> Each one is made a child of God by the washing in the baptismal water, sealed by the Spirit with the laying on of hands, and marked now with the cross of Christ. Yet these are not three separate actions exactly nor one action with embellishments. It is one rich action of initiation.[45]

The liturgy continues with the giving of a lighted candle and the welcoming of the newly baptized verbally and with the exchange of peace.[46] It is presumed that adults and older children who are baptized will commune for the first time during the baptismal eucharist which is the completion of initiation into the Christian community.[47] "The gift of Communion is the birthright of the baptized." Although the LBW does not expect infants to receive first communion at their baptism, it does suggest that they simply come to the altar with their families "at the appropriate time," which is "as soon as children begin to participate in the congregation's life."[48]

The service of Affirmation of Baptism began in CW 8, where it followed the pattern of the Episcopal *Prayer Book Studies 26*. Like their Episcopalian colleagues, the Lutheran revisers found that their church intended to take adolescent confirmation much more seriously than the revisers had thought. Like the Episcopal rite authorized in 1975[49] and now in The Book of Common Prayer, the rite in LBW provides for three parallel occasions: confirmation, reception into membership, and restoration to membership. The imposition of hands is reserved for confirmation only.[50]

Confirmation is defined by Lutherans as "a pastoral and educational ministry of the church which helps the baptized child through Word and Sacrament to identify more deeply with the Christian community and to participate more fully in its mission."[51] It is therefore a catechetical program of which the rite marks the completion.

> Those who have completed this program were made members of the Church in Baptism. Confirmation includes a public profession of faith into which the candidates were baptized, thus underscoring God's action in their Baptism.[52]

The rite takes place following the sermon and the Hymn of the Day at the eucharist. The various groups of candidates are presented, and all reaffirm ther baptismal covenant as in the baptismal liturgy. The congregation prays for them, and they are asked if they intend to continue in the covenant:

> to live among God's faithful people, to hear his Word and share in his supper, to proclaim the good news of God in Christ through word and deed, to serve all people, following the example of our Lord Jesus, and to strive for justice and peace in all the earth?[53]

All kneel and the presiding minister offers a prayer "based on the confirmation prayer in the baptismal liturgy" praying for "a strengthening of the spiritual gifts bestowed in Baptism." The pastor then lays both hands on the heads of those being confirmed, praying:

> Father in heaven, for Jesus' sake, stir up in [Name] the gift of the Holy Spirit, confirm *his/her* faith, guide *his/her* life, empower *him/her* in *his/her* serving, give *him/her* patience in suffering, and bring *him/her* to everlasting life.[54]

The rite concludes with the exchange of the peace, and the eucharistic liturgy continues.

The pattern displayed in the rites of the Lutheran Book of Worship is parallel to that of the Episcopal Book of Common Prayer. The BCP was published as a proposed book in 1976, and the LBW appeared in 1978. The two books have many points of contact. As we shall see, this new initiatory pattern, including an integral baptismal liturgy for both infants and adults with a catechetical non-initiatory confirmation rite for adolescents is becoming common, with variations, and replacing the older infant baptism, adolescent confirmation, and first communion models.

UNITED METHODIST CHURCH

The United Methodist Church entered into the process of baptismal reform and renewal in 1976 by publishing *A Service of Baptism, Confirmation, and Renewal*,[55] an alternate text, with introduction, commentary, and instructions. A slight revision of the text appeared in We Gather Together.[56] A further revision was contained in The Book of Services[57] approved by the 1984 General Conference. Finally, as of the present writing, this material has been incorporated, with some revision, into The United Methodist Hymnal[58] of 1989. The actual status of these rites is somewhat different from that of Roman Catholic, Lutheran, or Episcopal rites. Clergy and congregations are not obligated to use them, but since they appear in the Hymnal and are authorized, they are widely used, although not necessarily without substantial local adaptation. Those accustomed to the more liturgical traditions sometimes erroneously assume that because something is in the service book of a more liturgically flexible church it will be universally used, more or less as printed. This is not always the case.

As the material is presented in the Hymnal, Baptismal Covenant I is the material we are considering; Baptismal Covenant II reprints those parts needed for the baptism of children only; Baptismal Covenant III is the traditional text of the old Methodist and Evangelical United Brethren Ritual; and Baptismal Covenant IV is a service for the renewal of baptismal vows. We will look only at I and IV.

The services are conducted during public worship of the congregation where the person's membership is to be held, preferably following the readings and sermon. An introduction explains the purpose of the rites:

> Through the Sacrament of Baptism we are initiated into Christ's holy church. We are incorporated into God's mighty acts of salvation and given new birth through water and the Spirit.

> Through confirmation and through the reaffirmation of our faith, we renew the covenant declared at our baptism, acknowledge what God is doing for us, and affirm our commitment to Christ's holy Church.[59]

A representative of the congregation presents the candidates to the pastor. They renounce sin and evil and accept Christ. Parents or sponsors respond on behalf of those too young to do so themselves, and the congregation promises:

> With God's help we will proclaim the good news and live according to the example of Christ. We will surround these *persons* with a comunity of love and forgiveness, that *they* may

grow in *their* trust of God and be found faithful in *their* service to others. We will pray for *them*, that *they* may be true disciples who walk in the way that leads to life.[60]

It is because the congregation has a vital role here described in the formation of new Christians that baptism is held as a part of public worship. The role of the congregation, not simply liturgically, but as the community of faith and the local manifestation of the universal Church into which we are baptized is one of the elements stressed both here and, as we have seen, in other contemporary baptismal rites.[61]

The congregation joins the candidates in affirming their faith in response to three creedal questions. They may recite the Apostles' Creed as in the Lutheran and Episcopal rites, or respond more simply, omitting all but the first line of the second and third paragraphs of the creed. The reason for the alternative, according to the "official" commentary,[62] is that Methodist discipline does not require individual members to affirm the Apostles' Creed, but only Trinitarian faith. It strongly recommends the use of the creed, however, unless candidates specifically object.

The Thanksgiving over the Water, similar in content to that in LBW and BCP but different in wording, is accurately described as "ancient and ecumenical" and "the central expression in words of what baptism means."[63] The title of the act which follows is "Baptism with Laying on of Hands." The water baptism with the traditional formula is followed by the pastor and others laying hands on the head of each with the words:

> The Holy Spirit work within you, that being born through water and the Spirit, you may be a faithful disciple of Jesus Christ.[64]

This restoration of the laying on of hands to baptism is a distinctive part of the new pattern based on the models of the early church and found in the Episcopal, Lutheran, and COCU liturgies. It is parallel to the inclusion of confirmation in the RCIA by Roman Catholics and represents a reintegration of the baptismal liturgy to its original fullness.

The service continues with the welcoming of the newly baptized, which may be followed by confirmation, reaffirmation of faith, or reception into the United Methodist Church or the local congregation. In the first two cases the pastor says "Remember your baptism and be thankful," and the rubrics state that "water may be used symbolically." Clearly, the purpose is to integrate the renewal experience with baptism itself.[65] The formula used during the confirmation laying on of hands is identical with that used at baptism, except that "being born" is changed to the perfect participle, "having been born."

The concluding rubric says:

> It is most fitting that the service continue with the Holy Communion, in which the union of the new members with the Body of Christ is most fully expressed. The new members may receive first.[66]

Baptismal Covenant IV is a service for the congregational reaffirmation of the baptismal covenant. While this has Methodist roots in John Wesley's Covenant Service, this service is intended for use during the Great Fifty Days, the Baptism of the Lord, and All Saints, the baptismal feasts, as well as at the New Year, as Wesley's service was. It is a renewal of baptismal vows, accompanied by the thanksgiving over the water and the symbolic use of water with the congregation. Like baptism itself, it is recommended that this be a part of the celebration of Holy Communion.[67]

The inclusion of the eucharist within the baptismal context completes the restoration of the ancient "shape." The Methodists did not recommend the restoration of chrismation, as COCU, the Lutherans, and Episcopalians did, but the clear intention is to restore the ancient rite of initiation to use in the church today.

THE PRESBYTERIAN CHURCH

In 1985 the Presbyterian Chuch (U.S.A.), as part of a comprehensive project begun in 1980 to develop a new sevice book, issued *Holy Baptism and Services for the Renewal of Baptism*.[68] The baptismal service, like the others we have examined, is intended to be part of the Sunday liturgy. This has always been a part of the Reformed tradition.[69] It also considers it especially appropriate at the Easter Vigil, the Baptism of the

Lord, the Sundays of Easter, Pentecost Sunday, and All Saints. This idea of baptismal feasts is ancient, although this particular list is appaently based on that of The Book of Common Prayer.[70] The rite is also intended to be part of the eucharist, not simply of a word liturgy.

> It is highly appropriate to follow baptism with a celebration of the Lord's Supper . . . When the two sacraments are celebrated in the same service, their intimate relationship is emphasized, for through baptism the church is created and in the Supper the church is sustained. From ancient times, Christian initiation culminated with the new Christian joining the congregation at the holy Table. Thus Christian initiation has traditionally included three actions: washing with water, anointing with oil, and celebration of the eucharist.[71]

This seems a clear intention of restoring the classic "shape" of baptism, and this is borne out in the service itself. The candidates are presented, they renounce sin and profess faith in Jesus Christ, and join the congregation in reciting the Apostles' Creed, in response to the traditional three questions.[72]

The Thanksgiving over the Water is thoroughly traditional. It is closer to the LBW version than to The Book of Common Prayer or the Methodist Hymnal, but it is not simply copied. It contains an explicit invocation of the Holy Spirit to "bless this water."

> This prayer is parallel to the great prayer of thanksgiving of the Lord's Supper. It is just as essential to baptism as its counterpart is to the Eucharist.[73]

Baptism is by pouring, sprinkling, or immersion, and its use of water is to be visible and generous. "While the quantity of water applied," the commentary tells us, "does not affect the validity of the sacrament, it does enhance the ability of the sacrament to express that of which it is a sign."[74] Alternative formulas for the act of baptizing add the words "child of the covenant" after the candidate's name, or follow the Eastern passive construction.[75]

The Blessing (and Anointing) immediately follow the water baptism. The minister lays hands on the newly baptized, calling each by name and using a prayer invoking the sevenfold Spirit.[76] This is followed by the sealing.

N., child of the covenant, you have been sealed by the Holy Spirit in baptism, and marked as Christ's own forever.[77]

This formula, based on that in The Book of Common Prayer, may be accompanied by the signing of the forehead with the cross, using oil. The commentary describes the anointing as a "literalizing of the New Testament imagery" and points out the Christological connection with the Anointed One as well as the common derivation of *Christian* and *chrism* from the Greek *Christos*.[78]

The service continues with the welcoming of the newly baptized, and ideally with their participation in the eucharist.[79]

The Services for the Renewal of Baptism include a wide variety of occasions for renewal: Public Profession of Faith, traditionally called "confirmation" in the Reformed tradition; Renewal of Baptism for Those Who Have Been Estranged from the Church; Renewal of Baptism for a Congregation; Renewal of Baptism Marking Occasions of Growth in Faith; Renewal of Baptism for the Sick and Dying; and Renewal of Baptism in Pastoral Counseling.[80] These are pastoral occasions on which either the public or private renewal of commitment to one's baptism is often appropriate.

The Public Profession of Faith is a ceremony "for those who have been baptized in infancy and nurtured within the church." It is described as "a claiming of the promises and responsibilities that baptism entails." It includes a renunciation of evil and an affirmation of faith in Christ, including the recitation of the Apostles' Creed. A prayer giving thanks for what God has done for them in baptism leads to the laying on of hands. The minister lays *both* hands upon the head of each candidate, and may mark the sign of the cross with oil on the forehead, as in the baptismal rite. There is no separate formula for the signing, however. If it is done, it is done during the form accompanying the hand laying, which—instead of asking God to "give" the sevenfold Spirit—asks "Daily increase in (*him, her*) your gifts of grace," and then names the seven gifts.[81]

The rite appears to do what it claims to do, to permit those baptized in infancy to claim the promises and responsibilities of their baptism. In this it follows the lead of the Episcopal

Prayer Book Studies 26, reflected in both The Book of Common Prayer and the LBW.

The service for those renewing their baptism after having been estranged from the church is parallel, with appropriate changes, to the presentation and the prayer before the laying on of hands.[82] The Renewal of Baptism for a Congregation is intended for the Easter Vigil or Easter. It uses traditional renunciations and affirmations, including the Apostles' Creed. The minister raises water from the font in his or her hand and lets it fall back into the font, then signs the cross over the congregation saying: "Remember your baptism and be thankful. In the name of the Father and of the Son and of the Holy Spirit." The minister may also invite "those who wish to receive the laying on of hands" to come and kneel at the font. The blessing and, optionally, anointing are performed as in the previous rites. The peace and the celebration of the Lord's Supper follow.[83] The other services are variations of this form.

These rites are at present supplementary. Their proposal is clear evidence of the movement of baptismal renewal within the Presbyterian Church and of its participation in what is becoming a more or less general agreement among many North American churches of the proper "shape" of baptism and its relationship to confirmation and other rites of reaffirmation.

UNITED CHURCH OF CHRIST

The Book of Worship of the United Church of Christ[84] was asked for by its 1977 General Synod and published by its Office of Church Life and Membership in 1986 as a "resource for the public worship of God."[85] Its introduction makes specific reference to *Baptism, Eucharist and Ministry,* and it is compiled in light of that document. It invites congregations to the imaginative use of the book in the hard work of *leitourgia,* which is "the vocation of every Christian and every local church."[86]

Its Order for Baptism has been described as "moving baptism from the periphery to the center of the church's life."[87] Its previous baptismal rite[88] had relied heavily on Jesus' welcome of little children[89] for its exposition of baptism. The new rite concludes an exposition on the meaning of baptism with this response:

This is the water of baptism. Out of this water we rise with new life, forgiven of sin, and one in Christ, members of Christ's body.[90]

Baptism takes place in the context of a service of word and sacrament or a word service. There is, as with the other rites we have examined, a single rite for both infants and adults, with a number of alternatives to meet the needs of both groups. The parents of young children, for example, are asked if they will encourage them to renounce evil and teach them so that they may be led to profess faith in Christ, whereas adults are asked the questions directly.[91]

The congregation joins the candidates in affirming faith in the Triune God. As in the Methodist rite, simple statements of belief in God, Jesus Christ, and the Holy Spirit are sufficient, although "an ancient baptismal creed" may be used. A traditional "prayer of baptism" giving thanks for water in creation, the flood, the Red Sea, the baptism of Jesus, and the well of Samaria (an interesting addition), and a petition to bless the water are included, or the pastor may pray in his or her own words.

At the baptism of infants, the child is formally named immediately before the water baptism. The traditional Trinitarian formula in either its Eastern or Western form is used for the baptism itself. The pastor may then lay hands on the head of the baptized, saying:

The Holy Spirit be upon you, [Name], child of God, disciple of Christ, member of the Church.[92]

A prayer for the newly baptized and their welcome into the congregation, which may include the giving of the lighted candle, and the leading of the newly-baptized through the congregation as a sign of entry, conclude the baptism, and the service continues.

In this liturgy baptism is clearly a part of corporate worship. The possibility of it being a part of the eucharist is raised, but no particular rationale for doing so is given. A full biblical theology of baptism is expressed, and the laying on of hands, although not chrismation, is restored to the rite.[93]

Both confirmation and reception of members are subtitled Affirmation of Baptism, and the rites provided[94] are renewals of the baptismal covenant. The rites are parallel in structure, but the laying on of hands is a part of confirmation, while members are received by extending "the hand of Christian love," which was formerly known as extending the right hand of fellowship.

In addition to these rites, there is provision in the Easter Vigil for the congregational renewal of their baptismal promises, followed by the blessing of the people with baptismal water.[95]

Although the rites of the United Church of Christ are not as comprehensive as those of some other churches, they are designed in the light of the Lima Document, and they follow the tradition of the rites of other American churches.

* * * * * *

The remarkable thing about the variety of rites examined here is the degree of congruence and convergence which has developed ecumenically in North America since 1965. There would have been much less continuity in agreement with ancient models then. The influence of the new direction taken by The Book of Common Prayer is evident, but it has by no means been slavishly copied. The Prayer Book includes the giving of a lighted candle only in an additional directive, and never mentions the possibility of sprinkling the congregation with baptismal water. Both of these are found in most of the rites of this group. Episcopalians thought the use of baptismal water to bless the congregation too "high church" to include. Others saw it differently, perhaps indicating a new thinking about "holy water" in the churches of the Reformation.

The influence of the RCIA is also evident, but more indirectly. There is no mention of the catechumenate in these rites beyond general statements that adult candidates need to be instructed, but the RCIA has often been used as a resource for such instruction.

A concern for the unity of the sacramental rite is everywhere evident. There is still confusion about confirmation, but a pattern appears to be emerging. It is renewal of baptism and an occasion for affirmation of the baptismal covenant.

Notes

1. *Baptism, Eucharist and Ministry*, Faith and Order Paper 111 (Geneva: World Council of Churches, 1982). (Hereafter BEM.)

2. The cover of the booklet mentions Eastern Orthodox, Oriental Orthodox, Roman Catholic, Old Catholic, Lutheran, Anglican, Reformed, Methodist, United, Disciples, Baptist, Adventist, and Pentecostal.

3. BEM 2 [The numbers are paragraphs in the baptism section.]

4. Ibid. 3.

5. Ibid. 4.

6. Ibid. 5.

7. Ibid. 6.

8. Ibid. 11.

9. Ibid. 12.

10. Ibid. 14.

11. Ibid. 19.

12. BEM, Commentary (14).

13. BEM 17.

14. Ibid. 18.

15. Ibid. 20.

16. Ibid. 23.

17. At that time: African Methodist Episcopal Church, African Methodist Episcopal Zion Church, Christian Church (Disciples of Christ), Christian Methodist Episcopal Church, Episcopal Church, Presbyterian Church in the U.S., United Church of Christ, United Methodist Church, United Presbyterian Church in the U.S.A.

18. Consultation on Church Union, *An Order for the Celebration of Holy Baptism with Commentary* (Cincinnati: Forward Movement, 1973). [Hereafter COCU.]

19. COCU 30f.

20. Ibid. 15.

21. Ibid. 15f.

22. Ibid. 32f, 18ff.

23. Ibid. 33f.

24. Ibid., 20-22.

25. Ibid. 23.

26. COCU did, in fact, issue such a rite, *An Order for an Affirmation of the Baptismal Covenant*, in 1980. This form is derivative of the one presently being considered and the comparable forms by then in use, particuarly Lutheran, United Methodist, Presbyterian, Episcopal, and Roman Catholic forms. I served as one of its drafters but have no knowledge that it has ever been used anywhere. It has certainly not been widely used nor has it had much influence.

27. COCU 34.

28. Ibid. 24f.

29. *Lutheran Book of Worship,* Ministers Desk Edition (Minneapolis: Augsburg, 1978). [Hereafter LBW.]

30. *Contemporary Worship 7: Holy Baptism* (Minneapolis: Augsburg, 1974). [Hereafter CW 7.)

31. *Contemporary Worship 8: Affirmation of the Baptismal Covenant* (Minneapolis: Augsburg, 1975). [Hereafter CW 8.]

32. CW 7, 9.

33. LBW 30.

34. The English text of the Flood Prayer, accompanied by a magnificent wood cut showing Luther celebrating a baptism is printed in CW 7, 3.

35. Philip H. Pfatteicher and Carolis R. Messerli, *Manual of the Liturgy: Lutheran Book of Worship* (Minneapolis: Augsburg, 1979) 177.

36. LBW 310; see *The Book of Common Prayer* 304.

37. LBW 311.

38. Ibid. 31.

39. CW 7, 14.

40. *Manual* 185 and note 19, 371.

41. LBW 31.

42. Ibid. 311.

43. Ibid. 31.

44. *Manual* 186; see CW 7, 20.

45. *Manual* 185.

46. LBW 312.

47. Ibid. 30; *Manual* 187.

48. LBW 31f.

49. *A Form for Confirmation, for Reception, and for the Reaffirmation of Baptismal Vows,* Authorized for Trial Use during 1975-1976 (New York: Church Hymnal Corporation, 1975).

50. LBW 324-327.

51. *Manual* 340.

52. LBW 324.

53. Ibid. 326.

54. Ibid. 327.

55. *A Service of Baptism, Confirmation, and Renewal: Introduction, Text, Commentary, and Instructions, An Alternate Text 1976* (Nashville: United Methodist Publishing House, 1976).

56. *We Gather Together: Services for Public Worship,* Supplemental Worship Resources 10 (Nashville: United Methodist Publishing House, 1980).

57. *The Book of Services,* Containing the General Services of the

Church Adopted by the 1984 General Conference (Nashville: United Methodist Publishing House, 1985).

58. *The United Methodist Hymnal.* (Nashville: United Methodist Publishing House, 1989) 32-54.

59. Ibid. 33.

60. Ibid. 35.

61. See BEM 12.

62. Hoyt L. Hickman, ed., *Worship Resources of the United Methodist Hymnal* (Nashville: Abingdon, 1989) 99f.

63. Hickman, *Resources* 101.

64. *Hymnal* 36.

65. Ibid. 37.

66. *Resources* glosses "Remember your baptism . . ." to "remember that you have been baptized," and ways in which the water might be used, including sprinkling the people with an evergreen branch (106f).

67. *Hymnal* 50-53; *Resources* 92f.

68. *Holy Baptism and Services for Renewal of Baptism,* Supplemental Liturgical Resource, vol. 2 (Philadelphia: Westminster, 1985). [Hereafter SLR 2.]

69. SRL 2, 48; see J.D.C. Fisher, *Christian Initiation: The Reformation Period,* Alcuin Club Collections, vol. 51 (London: SPCK, 1970) 113 (Calvin) and 119 (Knox).

70. SRL 2, 49; see BCP 312 and LBW 30.

71. SRL 2, 58.

72. Ibid. 26ff.

73. Ibid. 54.

74. Ibid. 31, 55.

75. Ibid. 38.

76. Ibid. 31.

77. Ibid. 31; see BCP 308.

78. SLR 2, 56ff.

79. Ibid. 32.

80. Ibid. 69-72.

81. Ibid. 76f.

82. Ibid. 78-81.

83. Ibid. 82-85.

84. The United Church of Christ was formed in 1957 by the merger of the Congregational Christian Church and the Evangelical and Reformed Church. It therefore includes a wide liturgical spectrum and is heir both to New England Puritans and the Mercersburg theologians of the German Reformed Church.

85. United Church of Christ, *Book of Worship* (New York: United

Church of Christ Office for Church Life and Leadership, 1986). [Hereafter BW.]

86. BW 13 and the entire introduction, 1-27.

87. Ruth Duck, "Baptism in the Church's Life: From Periphery to Center," *Prism* 3:2 (Fall 1988) 12-22. I am indebted to Professor Duck, who teaches worship at Garrett-Evangelical Theological Seminary, directly across the street from Seabury-Western, for pointing out not only her commentary but this UCC material of which I had been unaware.

88. *Services of the Church 3* (Philadelphia: United Church Press, 1969).

89. Mark 10:13-16.

90. BW 136.

91. Ibid. 142.

92. Ibid. 238-242.

93. See Duck, "Baptism" 16.

94. BW 145-165. See also Duck, "Baptism" 16-21.

95. BW 238-242.

PARTICULAR QUESTIONS

10

The Thanksgiving over the Water in the Baptismal Rites of the West

IN THE BOOK OF COMMON PRAYER OF THE EPISCOPAL CHURCH (AMERican 1979) the baptismal immersion is preceded by a prayer entitled "Thanksgiving over the Water"[1] and introduced by the invitation, "Let us give thanks to the Lord our God." The prayer is parallel in structure to a eucharistic prayer beginning with thanksgiving for creation and redemption, including the "institution narrative," and continuing with specific reference to our present action, invocation of the Holy Spirit, and concluding with doxology. Following the direction of the *Apostolic Tradition* that "Lift up your hearts" be reserved for the eucharistic offering,[2] that invitation is omitted from the opening dialogue.

The prayer begins with thanksgiving for water and its place in the economy of salvation.

> We thank you, Almightly God, for the gift of water. Over it the Holy Spirit moved in the beginning of creation. Through it you led the children of Israel out of their bondage in Egypt into the land of promise. In it your Son Jesus received the baptism of John and was anointed by the Holy Spirit as the Messiah, the Christ, to lead us, through his death and resurrection from the bondage of sin into everlasting life.

Of the many Old Testament "types" available, two are used: the activity of the Spirit over the waters of chaos in Genesis 1:2, and the crossing of the Red Sea. The most common other type, which does not find a place in this prayer, is the Flood. It was apparently felt that the water in the Flood story, in spite of its use as a type of baptism from the patristic period through Luther, did not fulfill the same function as the water in Christian baptism and would be inappropriately cited here. The baptism of Jesus is the scriptural model for rites of Christian baptism and has often been considered the dominical institution of the sacrament. It is described as the occasion of Our Lord's messianic anointing by the Holy Spirit, and is brought into relation with Jesus' own death and resurrection which will bring about ours.

The reference to the baptism of Christ provides a transition to thanksgiving for the water of baptism which follows. The sacrament is described in Pauline terms as dying and rising with Christ, and in Johannine terms as rebirth in the Spirit. The missionary command of Matthew 28:19 brings the second paragraph to a climax.

> We thank you, Father, for the water of Baptism. In it we are buried with Christ in his death. By it we share in his resurrection. Through it we are reborn by the Holy Spirit. Therefore in joyful obedience to your Son, we bring into his fellowship those who come to him in faith, baptizing them in the Name of the Father, and of the Son, and of the Holy Spirit.

The words of the missionary command lead into a specific application to the water actually in the font, upon which the celebrant invokes the Holy Spirit that it may be the means of baptismal regeneration.

> Now sanctify this water, we pray you, by the power of your Holy Spirit, that those who here are cleansed from sin and born again may continue for ever in the risen life of Jesus Christ our Savior.

The thanksgiving concludes with a Trinitarian doxology.

> To him, to you, and to the Holy Spirit, be all honor and glory, now and for ever. *Amen.*

The parallel to the eucharistic thanksgiving is not artificial, but witnesses to the church's use of the *eucharistia* form for its most important prayers of blessing. The blessing of the water in the new Roman Catholic rite, although not introduced by "Let us give thanks," has the same structure, and is similar in content.[3]

The blessing of baptismal water is one of the most ancient traditions of the Christian Church. It is attested by the *Apostolic Tradition* of Hippolytus,[4] and by St. Basil the Great, who gives it as an example of an apostolic tradition which is not mentioned in Scripture.[5] Our concern in this essay is with the forms for this blessing used in the Western Church as they witness to the development of the doctrine of salvation. We have begun with the thanksgiving in the new American Prayer Book as illustrating that doctrine and being the most recent addition to the body of Western prayers of thanksgiving over the water, with which it has much in common.

THE CLASSIC ROMAN TEXTS

Our earliest texts of the Roman baptismal rite, those found in the *Gelasianum*[6] and the *Hadrianum*,[7] are from the seventh century and contain the central prayers of the *benedictio fontis* in substantially the same form in which they appeared in the *Missale Romanum* of Pius V. The *Gelasianum* provides a short prayer, *Omnipotens sempiterne deus, adeste . . .*, which it titles *benedictio fontis*,[8] followed by a much longer prayer, or collection of prayers, *Deus, qui inuisibili potentia tua . . .*, headed item *consecratio fontis*.[9] The *Hadrianum* places all under the single heading *benedictio fontis*.[10] Later manuscripts of the *Gregorianum* insert the dialogue *sursum corda* between the two prayers, turning the second into a sort of preface and emphasizing its similarity to a eucharistic prayer.

Numerous studies have shown that even in this earliest form which we possess, the blessing is not a unity, but is composed of at least two strata, and that within each there is both a negative part, or exorcism, and a positive part, or benediction.[11] There is some disagreement concerning the precise divisions of the strata.

The short opening prayer is Gallican.[12] It is found in all Roman and Ambrosian sources, in the *Missale Gallicanum Vetus*, the Bobbio Missal, and the Stowe Missal.[13]

Almighty, everlasting God, be present at the mysteries of your great goodness, be present at the sacraments; and send forth the Spirit of adoption to create the new people whom the font of baptism brings you forth, and may what is done by the ministry of our lowliness be fulfilled by the working of your power.[14]

It is clearly an introductory prayer, asking the divine assistance for the action of the minister in celebrating the sacraments, and we need not consider it further.

The opening section of the longer prayer is undoubtedly Roman. The first sentence is parallel to the short prayer, asking the aid of God in the mysteries which we are unworthy to perform. The second sentence invokes God whose Spirit was borne upon the waters *inter ipsa mundi primordia*, a reference to Genesis 1:2, and who cleansed the world from sin through the waters of the Flood.

God, who by your invisible power wonderfully accomplish the working of your sacraments, and although we are not worthy to perform so great mysteries, do not desert the gifts of your grace, but incline the ears of your goodness to our prayers.

God, whose Spirit was borne upon the waters at the very beginning of the world, that even then the nature of waters might conceive the power of sanctification; God, who washing away the sins of a wicked world symbolized in the waters of the flood themselves the type of regeneration, that in the mystery of one and the same element might be the end of vice and the beginning of virtue.[15]

The historian of religion Mircea Eliade, writing about the religious significance of aquatic symbolism tells us:

The waters symbolize the universal sum of virtualities; they are *fons et origo*, "spring and origin," the reservoir of all the possibilites of existence; they precede every form and support every creation . . . On the other hand, immersion in water signifies regression to the preformal, reincorporation into the undifferentiated mode of preexistence . . . In whatever religious complex we find them, the waters invariably retain their function; they disintegrate, abolish forms, "wash away sins"; they are at once purifying and regenerating.[16]

It is these two aspects of the symbolism of water that are

here proclaimed: the creative and destructive, in this opening passage of the Roman *consecratio fontis*. There is less agreement that the next section of the prayer is Roman,[17] but what we have already examined is merely introductory and must be connected with some petition. Whatever its original source, the following petition for the blessing of the font and those to be baptized therein is used by the earliest surviving form to complete the thought of the opening invocations.

> Look, Lord, on the face of your Church and multiply your generations in her, you who make glad your city by the outpouring of the force of your grace, and who open the font of baptism for the renewing of the nations of the whole world, that by the command of your majesty it may receive the grace of your Only-begotten from the Holy Spirit. May he by the secret mixture of his light make fruitful this water prepared for the regeneration of men, that conceived in sanctification a heavenly offspring reborn in new creation may come forth from the immaculate womb of the divine font. May grace bear them all as a mother in a common infancy distinguished neither in body by sex nor in time by age.[18]

The principal figure here is, of course, that of the font as a womb by which Christians are brought to new birth. Today, we are more apt to emphasize the idea of death and resurrection following the teaching of St. Paul in Romans 6, but the font as a womb is a patristic commonplace.

The following section is a sort of indirect exorcism, asking God that the evil one be kept from the consecrated water.

> Therefore let every unclean spirit keep far from it at your command, Lord, let all wickedness of devilish deception stand far away, let nothing in this place be mixed with his opposing power, let him not fly about to lay his snares, let him not creep in secretly, let him not corrupt with his poisoning. May this holy and innocent creature be free from every incursion of the enemy and purified by the removal of all wickedness. Let it be a living font, regenerating water, a purifying wave, that all who shall be washed in this saving bath may by the working of the Holy Spirit in them be brought to the mercy of a perfect cleansing.[19]

This exorcism, as the text appears in the manuscripts, leads directly into a blessing of the font in the name of God and his

Christ. The two following sections, however, are generally considered to be a Gallican exorcism and blessing which have been incorporated into the Roman prayer.[20]

> Wherefore I bless you, creature of water, through the living God, through the holy God, through God who in the beginning by his word separated you from dry land and commanded you in four rivers to water the whole earth, who in the desert made your bitterness to become drinkable sweetness and brought you forth from a rock for a thirsty people. I bless you through Jesus Christ his only Son our Lord, who in Cana of Gallilee changed you into wine as a wondrous sign by his power, who walked upon you with his feet, and was baptized in you by John in Jordan, who brought you forth from his side together with blood and commanded his disciples that they should baptize in you all who believe, saying: Go, teach all nations, baptizing them in the name of the Father and of the Son and of the Holy Spirit.

And,

> Almighty, merciful God, be with us as we follow your commands, graciously breathe upon us, bless these simple waters with your mouth, that they may surpass their natural purity by which they are able to wash our bodies and be made effectual also to cleanse our minds.

This same form is found in the Stowe Missal with *exorcizo* instead of *benedico* as the verb[21] and a parallel form with *adiuro* is found in the Ambrosian rite.[22] As it occurs here, it is a rehearsal of the *Heilsgeschichte* as it involves water, concluding with the Dominical warrant for baptizing. This then leads directly into the following paragraph which asks for the blessing of the water. It is a sort of indirect epiklesis, asking God to bless the water with the breath of his mouth. As it is used in the text, it leads directly into the explicit epiklesis of the next paragraph:

> May the power of the Holy Spirit descend into the fulness of this font and the whole substance of this water be made fruitful for the working of regeneration. Here may the nature established according to your image be restored to the honor of its beginning and cleansed from all the filthiness of its old age, that every person coming to this sacrament of regeneration may be reborn in true innocence to a new infancy.

This *discendat* epiklesis is preceded in later manuscripts by two rubrics, although there are none accompanying it in *Gelasianum*.[23] The earlier directs that the priest blow three times into the water. The obvious reference is to John 20:22, where the Spirit is given by Jesus breathing on the apostles. The more immediate reference is the mention of God breathing upon the water to bless it in the previous paragraph. The latter rubric, which precedes the earlier in the texts which have both is *Hic deponatur cereus benedictus in fontem.* The lowering of the paschal candle into the font accompanies the proclamation *excelsa voce: Discendat in hanc plenitudinem fontis uirtus spiritus sancti.* This is to be followed by the breathing, in the form of the Greek letter *psi.* The lowering of the candle is the most dramatic ceremonial act connected with the blessing. In it the figure of the font as the womb from which the newborn Christian emerges into new life in the risen Christ and the force of the phrase, *Totam huius aquae substantiam regenerandis fecundet effectu,* are given ritual expression.

The text calls upon the Holy Spirit to bless the water for the restoration of humankind to its original state in the *imago Dei,* a washing away of sin, and rebirth to a *noua infantia.* It contains ideas parallel to the third paragraph, *respice, domine . . .,* and forms a unit with it. The entire prayer concludes with a doxology:

> Through our Lord Jesus Christ your Son, who will come to judge the living and the dead and the age by fire.

Although our earliest manuscripts present this as a single prayer, roughly parallel to the eucharistic prayer, it is a conflation of at the least a Roman and a Gallican form of blessing, and in itself is a difficult model to follow. A significant alternative in the medieval period is the prayer *Sanctificare per Verbum Dei,* which is found both in the Ambrosian rite and in the Visiogothic *Liber Ordinum.*[24]

NON-ROMAN ALTERNATIVES

In the *Liber Ordinum,* described by its editor Dom Marius Férotin as in use in the Mozarabic or Visigothic Church of Spain from the fifth to the eleventh centuries,[25] *Sanctificare per Verbum*

Dei follows an exorcism and is described as *benedictio fontis*. A rubric directs that it be said *sicut in missa solent dicere*. There are minor differences in text between the Mozarabic and Ambrosian versions. What follows is the text of the *Liber Ordinum*:

> Be sanctified through the Word of God, heavenly stream; be sanctified, water trodden by the feet of Christ, though pressed upon by the mountains, you are not confined, though dashed against the rocks you are not broken, though poured out over the earth you do not fail. You support the dry land, bear the weight of the mountains and are not swallowed up. You are held up by the height of heaven; poured out over everything, you wash all, yet are not washed. You were held back, hardened into ice, when the people of the Hebrews were fleeing. You again, melting on the high peaks, destroy the neighbors of the Nile and pursue with fierce raging the world like an enemy. One and the same, you are the salvation of the faithful and the punishment of the wicked. The rock struck by Moses spewed you forth: nor could you lie in the rocks when ordered by the command of Majesty to come forth. Borne by the clouds, you make fertile the field with pleasant rain. Through you a draught beneficial to grace and life is poured out upon bodies dry with the summer heat. Welling up in hidden channels or confined in the breeze, you give the lifegiving and fruitful sap, lest a dry and lifeless earth deny our bodies its accustomed produce. Through you the beginning and through you the end rejoice, or rather it is your gift from God that we know no end.

> And you, Lord, almighty God, of whose power we are not unaware, while we mention the merits of the waters, and proclaim the signs of their work, receive mercifully the sinful, and with your accustomed goodness release the captives. Restore that which Adam lost in paradise, which his wife let go, which an excess of grasping gluttony devoured. Give a saving draught to those who are badly sated with the bitterness of the apples, that you may wash away the distress of mortals and the age-old ruin be disolved by the divine antidote. Wash away the gluttony of the untilled earth; shatter the sword of flame turning every way to bar the road to paradise. Let an entrance bedecked with flowers be opened to those who are returning. May they receive the image of Godhead which they once lost through the malice of the serpent, that they may wash away in the purity of this flood whatever guilt has been contracted through their transgression. May they rise up to rest, be

brought forth to pardon, that renewed by the mystic waters they may know themselves to be redeemed and reborn. *Amen.*

The prayer divides neatly into two paragraphs, the first addressed directly to the water and the second to God, asking him to use the water to accomplish his divine purpose in the restoration of all people to their primitive innocence. The first paragraph is a veritable *laus aquae* apostrophizing the water, not only for its place in the history of salvation, but for its natural saving effects. Three biblical references are used: Christ walking on the waters, Moses bringing water from the rock, and the Hebrews crossing the Red Sea. The idea that this was accomplished by the freezing of the water presents an interesting picture. The entire prayer, in fact, is an eloquent rhetorical passage, contrasting sharply with the spare Latinity of the Roman collects. The images are vivid and the contrasts sharp. Its closing sentence seems to sum up both its content and its form: *Per te initium, per te finis exultat, uel potius ex Deo tuum est ut terminum nesciamus.*

The *nesciamus* is picked up again in the opening clause of the second paragraph: *At tu, Domine, omnipotens Deus, cuius uirtutem non nescii . . .* It makes the transition to the direct address of God. Here the theme of the return to paradise is consistently maintained, and the effects of baptism are described in terms of the restoration of our lost innocence and the lost *imago deitatis.* The newly baptized are to be Adam and Eve before the fall, the effects of which are to be washed away. The bitterness of the apple produces in human kind *indigesta* which the baptismal waters wash away. Regeneration in the sense of the removal of original sin so that the baptized may start afresh with a *tabula rasa* is the only effect of baptism to which this prayer, like the Roman blessing, refers. The Roman blessing, in fact, leans more heavily upon the idea of rebirth into a new innocence, whereas this places its emphasis on the innocence to which we are restored. The idea of the font as the place of resurrection, and baptism as a dying and rising again finds expression in the *contestatio fontis* from *Missale Gallicanum Vetus.*[26]

This remarkable prayer, a form of which appears also in the Mozarabic *Missale Mixtum* of Cardinal Ximenes[27] where it is interspersed with responsive *Amens,* was apparently a source for the blessing in the *First Prayer Book* of Edward VI.[28] The *Missale Gallicanum Vetus* is the name given to an incomplete Gallican sacramentary of the first half of the eighth century. The *contestatio* (which is the regular Gallican term for a eucharistic preface) begins: *Dignum et iustum est.* Undoubtedly the *sursum corda* separated the *contestatio* from the prayer which precedes it in the manuscript:

> It is fitting and right. It is truly fitting and right for us to give you thanks, Lord God eternal, who alone have immortality, and lest you alone should possess it, have shared it with us for the renewal of our life. You have willed to reform for the better by the working of baptism, as precious as it is blessed, that dignity of its first origin which was lost to the human race through transgression.

> Be present, we pray, at the invocation of your name. Sanctify this font, Sanctifier of the human race. Let this place be made worthy that the Holy Spirit may flow into it. Let that old Adam be buried here and the new arise. Let all that is flesh die. Let all that is spirit arise. Let the garments befouled by vices and former crimes be taken off, that the clothing of splendor and immortality may be put on, and whoever is baptized in Christ may put on Christ. Whoever shall have renounced the devil in this place, grant them to triumph over the world. Whoever shall have called upon you in this place, know them in your kingdom. May crimes be so obliterated in this font that they do not rise again. May the working of this water be made so powerful that it extinguishes the burning of the eternal fire.

> May the fonts admit to your altars those whom the altars admit to your kingdom. May every fear of death be buried here. May whoever shall here have begun to be yours not cease to be yours. May the people consecrated to you through our ministry and your mystery, be consecrated to your for eternal rewards. Through our Lord Jesus Christ.

Here we find a different set of images and other aspects of the doctrine of salvation set forth than in the blessings we have previously examined. The familiar idea of our restoration to lost innocence occurs in the opening lines. Then we find the Pauline idea of dying and rising with Christ from Romans 6 and 1 Corinthians 15. The waters are presented not simply as washing away sin, but as being both the *tomb* of the old and the *womb* of the new Adam. The old Adam, sin, "flesh" go down. The new Adam who is Christ, immortality, "spirit" arise. The waters are seen here as exercising their dual function of destroying and making alive[29]

Exuantur sordentes uiciis et discessis criminibus amictus ut splendoris et immortalis summantur has its origin in the quotation from Galatians 3:27 which follows in the text, but there is an extensive liturgical tradition for its use. St. Ambrose says:

> After this you received the white robe, as a sign that you have taken off the covering of sins [and] put on the chaste garments of innocence.[30]

Ambrose is, of course, referring to the rite of stripping before baptism and clothing in white afterward, but this rite is in turn a symbol of baptism itself as the stripping off of the old and the putting on of the new. Theodore of Mopsuestia calls the chrism with which the baptizand is anointed the "covering of immortality,"[31] and a similar phrase, "incorruptible robe," occurs in the blessing of *myron* in the Coptic and Byzantine rites.[32] The preface of the Maundy Thursday *missa chrismalis* of *Gelasianum* speaks of the chrism as a *uestimentum incorrupti muneris* which is put on.[33] This preface is undoubtedly a Gallican element. Similarly, the form for the post-baptismal anointing in *Missale Gothicum*, another major Gallican sacramentary, begins:

> I anoint thee with the chrism of holiness, the garment of immortality, which our Lord Jesus Christ first received from the Father . . .[34]

I believe that the reference is probably to the chrism in our *contestatio fontis* also. It is apparently a common Gallican idea originally stemming from the East. The clothing of the old life is removed. One stands naked as Adam did in Eden, and is *perunguitur*, anointed all over, with the chrism, as a covering of immortality, a symbol of the glory with which the Christian will be covered at the Resurrection. This is, of course, also the symbolism of the white robes in which the newly baptized are clothed.

There is no recounting of the wonders of God performed through water in this form, an omission which the *Missale*

Mixtum supplied by peceding it with an exorcism which recounts Christ's walking on the water and baptism in it.[35] There is also no recitation of the great commission to baptize, and a minimal invocation of the Holy Spirit. In fact, in spite of its *Vere dignum* beginning, this *contestatio* is less like a eucharistic prayer than the Roman form.

Theologically, the prayer begins with the assertion that God shared his unique immortality with us, an idea found in the Bible in Wisdom 2:23. It does not deal with the fall, but focuses on the restoration of the dignity of our first origin through baptism. Its insistent theme is the death of the old and the birth of the new through the baptismal water. Finally, it declares baptism as the means of union with God. Font admits to altar and altar admits to kingdom, and affirms baptism as a death to self and a resurrection to eternal union with God. It does not say, as Roman 6 does, that this is because we die and rise again with Christ in the water, but that is the doctrine of salvation through the sacraments which it expresses.

THE FIRST PRAYER BOOK OF EDWARD VI

In the 1549 Book of Common Prayer, the Blessing of the Font was not a part of the baptismal rite, but was placed after it. A rubric directed the water to be changed monthly and the blessing to be said at that time.[36]

Its opening paragraph reprises ideas from the medieval forms, but is not closely copied from any of them:

> O most merciful God, our savior Jesus Christ, who hast ordained the element of water for the regeneration of thy faithful people, upon whom being baptized in the river of Jordan, the Holy Ghost came down in the likeness of a dove: Send down, we beseech thee, the same thy Holy Spirit to assist us, and to be present at this invocation of thy holy name.

The final phrase directly translates *Adsiste quesumus, ad inuocationem nominis tui* from the Gallican-Mozarabic form above and begins a series of quotations and paraphrases of that prayer.

> Sanctify this fountain of baptism, thou that art the sanctifier of all things, that by the power of thy word, all those that shall be

baptized therein, may be spiritually regenerated and made the children of everlasting adoption, *Amen*.

O merciful God, grant that the old Adam, in them that shall be baptized in this fountain, may so be buried, that the new man be raised up again. *Amen*.

Grant that all carnal affection may die in them: and that all things belonging to the spirit, may live and grow in them. *Amen*.

Grant to all them which at this fountain forsake the devil and all his works: that they may have power and strength to have victory and to triumph against him, the world, and the flesh. *Amen*.

Whosoever shall confess thee, O Lord: recognize him also in thy kingdom. *Amen*.

Grant that all sin and vice here may be so extinct: that they never have power to reign in thy servants. *Amen*.

Grant that whosoever here shall begin to be of thy flock: may evermore continue in the same. *Amen*.

Grant that all they which for thy sake in this life do deny and forsake themselves: may win and purchase thee (O Lord) which art everlasting treasure. *Amen*.

Grant that whosoever is here dedicated to thee by our office and ministry: may also be endowed with heavenly virtues, and everlastingly rewarded through thy mercy, O Blessed Lord God, who dost live and govern all things world without end. *Amen*.

The *Amen* refrain and the final doxology are from the version of the blessing in *Missale Mixtum*. A comparison of this text with that from *Missale Gallicanum Vetus* will show both the close dependence of the blessing upon the Gallican *contestatio fontis* and also the workmanship of Cranmer, by which he expanded the clauses and inserted ideas often implicit in the Latin explicitly into the English.

The blessing in 1549 continues with the salutation and a final prayer, taken from the Sarum baptismal rite, that is a late version of the classical Roman prayer from *Gelasianum* and *Gregorianum* which we examined above. It omits the references to the changing of water into wine, the walking on the water, and Christ's baptism, and moves directly to the reference to the water flowing from the side of Christ:

> Almighty everliving God, whose most dearly beloved Son Jesus Christ, for the forgiveness of our sins did shed out of his most precious side both water and blood, and gave commandment to his disciples that they should go teach all nations, and baptize them in the name of the Father, the Son, and the Holy Ghost: Regard, we beseech thee, the supplication of this congregation, and grant that all thy servants which shall be baptized in this water, prepared for the ministration of thy holy sacrament, receive the fulness of thy grace, and ever remain in the number of thy faithful and elect children, through Jesus Christ our Lord.

The second part of this prayer deserts the Sarum-Roman model and is based the closing lines of the Mozarabic exorcism which precedes the blessing in *Missale Mixtum*.[37]

As usual, Cranmer has made free use of his sources, but his blessing is based closely on the Gallican-Mozarabic source. What he has added to it are significant scriptural references missing from that form: the baptism of Christ, the pouring of water and blood from his side, and the great commission— which contains what we might call the "words of institution" for baptism. He does not use any of the Old Testament types, although the flood is mentioned prominently in another prayer of the baptismal rite, and he omits from the prayer he copied from Sarum its references to the miracle at Cana and Christ's walking on the water, thereby making the water and blood flowing from the side of Christ, seen by both Augustine and Chrysostom as symbolic of baptism and eucharist, the only scriptural reference not used in its literal sense. The death-rebirth contrast, taken from his medieval source, becomes the dominant theological theme of the blessing, but it is focused not so much on our union with Christ as on individual salvation through death to sin.

This blessing was highly abridged in 1552, retaining only four of the Gallican-Mozarabic petitions and the final collect. Since the petition to sanctify the water was omitted, it had ceased to be a blessing of the font and become a prayer for those to be baptized, as suggested by Bucer in his *Censura*.[38] In

1662 a phrase was added to the final collect under Laudian influence, "Sanctify this water to the mystical washing away of sin,"[39] thereby restoring the blessing.

* * * * * *

The Thanksgiving over the water of The Book of Common Prayer (American 1979) with which we began our discussion is based upon all of the blessings we have considered. They were the chief models before the committee which drafted the new prayer. It is not directly copied from any of them, but it seeks to proclaim the traditional themes in a balanced way. The almost exclusive emphasis on the removal of original sin and the restoration of lost innocence in the older rites is toned down, and the idea of participation in the death and resurrection of Christ brought forward. Thanks is given for creation and redemption, through the exodus and the resurrection, and all are tied to the element of water as in the medieval prayers. More of salvation history is thus included than in the earlier Prayer Books.

An attempt has been made to avoid the excessive length, disjointed structure and duplications of the classical rites. In the process some beautiful passages have been lost and some marvelous images passed over. Certainly, as the rites have evolved in the West, the blessing of the font is one of the chief *loci* for serious theological proclamation of the meaning of baptism. We have seen this in the classical medieval forms, in the 1549 Prayer Book, and in the new American Prayer Book. Baptism is proclaimed as the sacrament of rebirth, forgiveness of sin, death and resurrection, anointing with the Spirit, and union with Christ in God.

Notes

1. *The Book of Common Prayer and Administration of the Sacraments and Other Rites and Ceremonies of the Church Together with the Psalter or Psalms of David according to the Use of the Episcopal Church* (New York: Church Hymnal Corporation, 1979) 206-207.

2. Bernard Botte, *La Tradition apostolique de saint Hippolyte*, Liturgiewissenschaftliche Quellen und Forschungen, vol. 59 (Münster: Aschendorff, 1963) 25, p. 64.

3. *Rite of Christian Initiation of Adults* (Washington, D.C.: United States Catholic Conference, 1974) 215, p. 63 (222A in the 1989 edition).

4. Botte, *Tradition apostolique* 21, p. 44.

5. *De Spiritu Sancto* 27:66 (PG 32:187).

6. *Vat. Reg. 316.*

7. *Cambrai 164.*

8. *Liber Sacramentorum Romanae Aeclesiae Ordinis Anni Circuli*, ed., L.C. Mohlberg, Rerum Ecclesiasticarum Documenta, Series Maior, Fontes, vol. 4 (Rome: Herder, 1960) 444.

9. Ibid. 445-448.

10. *Le Sacramentaire grégorienne*, ed., Jean Deshusses, Specilegium Friburgense, vol. 16 (Fribourg: Editions Universitaires, 1971) 373-374.

11. Hubert Scheidt, *Die Taufwasserweihgebete*, Liturgieschichtliche Quellen und Forschungen, vol. 29 (Münster: Aschendorff, 1936). Eduard Stommel, *Studien zur Epiklese der romanischen Taufwasserweihe*, Theophaneia, vol. 5 (Bonn: Peter Hanstein, 1950). Suitbert Benz, "Zur Vorgeschichte des Textes der romanischen Taufwasserwiehe," *Revue Bénédictine* 66 (1956) 218-255. Alexander Olivar, "San Pedro Crisologo Autor del Texto de la Fuentes Bautismales?" *Ephemerides Liturgicae* 71 (1957) 280-290.

12. Benz, "Zur Vorgeschicht" 221-222; Olivar, "San Pedro Crisologo" 281.

13. Gel. 444; Greg. 373: *Das Sacramentarium Triplex*, ed., Odilo Heiming, Corpus Ambrosiano-Liturgicum, vol. 1, Liturgiewissenschaftliche Quellen und Forschungen, vol. 49 (Münster: Aschendorff, 1968) 1287, 1303); *Das Ambrosianische Sakramentar von Biasca*, ed., Odilo Heiming, Corpus Ambrosiano-Liturgicum, vol. 2, Liturgiewissenschaftliche Quellen und Forschungen, vol. 51 (Münster: Aschendorff, 1969) 494; *Sacramentarium Bergomense*, ed., Angelo Paredi, Monumenta Bergomensia, vol. 6 (Bergamo: Edizioni "Monumenta Bergomensia," 1962) 531; *Manuale Ambrosianum*, vol. 2, ed., Marco Magistretti, Monumenta Veteris Liturgiae Ambrosianae, vol. 3 (Milan: Ulricii Hoepeli, 1905); reprint (Nendeln, Lichtenstein: Kraus Reprints, 1971) 205; *Missale Gallicanum Vetus*, ed., L.C. Mohlberg, Rerum Ecclesiasticarum Documenta, Series Maior, Fontes, vol. 3 (Rome: Herder, 1958) 164; *The Bobbio Missal*, ed., E.A. Lowe, Henry Bradshaw Society, vol. 58 (London: Harrison and Sons, 1920) 235; *The Stowe Missal*, ed., George F. Warner, Henry Bradshaw Society, vol. 32 (London: Harrison and Sons, 1915) 29.

14. Text, Gel. 444; Greg. 373 (trans. LLM).

15. Text, Gel. 445; Greg. 374 (trans. LLM).

16. Mircea Eliade, *The Sacred and the Profane* (New York: Harcourt, Brace & World, 1959) 130-131.

17. Suitbert Benz (227-230 and passim) believes it is Ravennan. Hubert Scheidt (64-65), Eduard Stommel (22), and Alexander Olivar (281) believe it is Roman.

18. Gel. 445; Greg. 374a-374b (trans. LLM).

19. Ibid.

20. Benz (232-240); Olivar (281). Gel 446; Greg. 374c-374d (trans. LLM).

21. *Stowe* 28.

22. *Triplex* 1306; *Biasca* 498; *Bergamo* has a lacuna; *Manuale Ambrosianum*, vol. 2, 205-206.

23. Greg 374, notes; Michel Andrieu, *Ordines Romani*, vol. 5, Specilegium Sacrum Lovaniense, vol. 29 (Louvain: Specilegium Sacrum Lovaniense, 1961), *Ordo L* 29:50, p. 280.

24. Ambrosian sources: *Sacramentarium Bergomense*, no. 535, pp. 165-166 (the opening of the prayer is missing from the manuscript and is supplied by the editor from ms. ambrosiano Trotti 251); *Das Ambrosianische Sakramentar von Biasca* no. 499, p. 72; *Manuale Ambrosianum*, vol. 2, p. 206. Mozarabic-Visigothic source: *Le Liber Ordinum*, ed., Marius Férotin, Monumenta Ecclesiae Liturgica, vol. 5 (Paris, 1904); reprint (Farnborough: Gregg International Publishers, 1969) col. 29-30.

25. *Le Liber Ordinum* pp. I, IX.

26. *Missale Gallicanum Vetus* 168 (trans. LLM).

27. *Missale Mixtum*, ed., Francisco Ximenes (PL 85:464-465).

28. F.E. Brightman, *The English Rite*, vol. 2 (London: Rivingtons, 1921); reprint (Farnborough: Gregg International Publishers, 1970) 738-740.

29. See note 16 above; also Mircea Eliade, *Images and Symbols* (New York: Sheed and Ward, 1969) 151-160.

30. *De Mysteriis* 34, ed., Bernard Botte, *Des Sacramentis, des mystères, explication du symbole*, Sources chrétiennes, vol. 25 bis (Paris: Cerf, 1961) 174 (trans. LLM).

31. A. Mingana, *Woodbrooke Studies*, vol. 6 (Cambridge: W. Heffer and Sons, 1933) 54.

32. J. Denzinger, *Ritus Orientalium*, vol. 1 (Würtzburg, 1863) 265. J. Goar, *Euchologium sive Rituale Graecorum* (Venice, 1730) 702. See also Leonel L. Mitchell, *Baptismal Anointing* (London: SPCK, 1966);, 2nd ed. (Notre Dame: University of Notre Dame Press, 1978) 75, 64.

33. *Sacramentarium Gelasianum* 378.

34. *Missale Gothicum*, ed., L.C. Mohlberg, Rerum Ecclesiasticarum Documenta, Series Maior, Fontes, vol. 5 (Rome: Herder, 1965) 261. Translation from E.C. Whitaker, *Documents of the Baptismal Liturgy* (London: SPCK, 1960) 152.

35. PL 85:464.

36. Brightmann, *The English Rite*, vol. 2, 738 (spelling modernized).

37. PL 85:464.

38. Whitaker, *Martin Bucer and the Book of Common Prayer* (Great Wakering: Mahew-McCrimmon, 1974) 88-91.

39. Brightmann, *The English Rite*, vol. 2, 741.

11

Confirmation in the Western Church

THE FIRST LATIN THEOLOGICAL WRITER, TERTULLIAN OF CARTHAGE, wrote in his *De Resurrectione Carnis*:

> Flesh is washed, that the soul may be cleansed; flesh is anointed, that the soul may be consecrated; flesh is signed, that the soul may be fortified; flesh is shadowed by the imposition of the hand, that the soul may be enlightened by the Spirit; flesh feeds on the Body and Blood of Christ, that the soul also may fatten upon God.[1]

This passage was cited by Pope Paul VI in 1971 in his apostolic constitution on the sacrament of confirmation.[2] To the extent, then, that there is a consistent tradition of Christian initiation in the Latin Church, we may assume that it is represented by this quotation.

EARLY TRADITION

The rite which underlies Tertullian's commentary is clearly similar to that set forth in greater detail in the *Apostolic Tradition* of Hippolytus.[3] The candidates are washed in water confessing the Name of the Father, Son, and Holy Spirit. They are anointed with chrism, as Christ was anointed with the Holy Spirit at his baptism. They are signed, presumably upon the forehead, with the sign of the cross. They receive the laying on of hands *advocans et invitans Spiritum sanctum*.[4] They receive holy communion. Further, this rite, as both Tertullian and Hippolytus describe it, formed the conclusion of a lengthy process which separated the catechumen from pagan culture and introduced him or her into the new life in Christ. Hippolytus mentions a period of at least three years of catechesis and exorcism culminating in the final renunciation of "the devil, and his pomp, and his angels."[5]

As the rite is described in the *Apostolic Tradition*, it is a single complex sacramental action which climaxes the initiation process and makes the catechumen a neophyte. This complex consists of water baptism, anointing with chrism, imposition of hand by the bishop with prayer and pouring of chrism, signing with the cross, and reception of the body and blood of Christ.[6] In spite of the headings introduced into his English edition by Gregory Dix,[7] there is no suggestion in the text of the *Apostolic Tradition* that these are three rites of baptism, confirmation, and first communion celebrated consecutively, much like morning prayer, litany, and ante-communion in eighteenth- and nineteenth-century Anglicanism.

Tertullian, on the other hand, seems to make a distinction between two stages of the rite. He says in *De Baptismo*:

> Not that the Holy Spirit is given to us in the water, but that in the water we are made clean by the action of the angel, and ready for the Holy Spirit . . .

> Next follows the imposition of the hand in benediction, inviting and welcoming the Holy Spirit . . . At this point the most Holy Spirit willingly comes down from the Father upon bodies cleansed and blessed, and comes to rest upon the waters of baptism as though revisiting his primal dwelling place . . .[8]

I believe it is essential to realize that Tertullian, like Hippolytus, is describing a single rite. He uses the analogy of the hydraulic organ to explain how God uses the hand of the priest and the baptismal water acting together to play a spiritual melody.[9] The "angel" to which Tertullian refers is the angel of John 5:4 who stirs up the pool of Bethesda to produce a healing miracle, but the primary picture which Tertullian has in mind is the baptism of Christ, in which the Holy Spirit descends on Jesus when he comes up out of the water. He, in fact, identifies the post-baptismal chrismation with the baptismal anointing of Jesus with the Spirit.[10]

Tertullian, as I have said, was describing a single rite and saw the washing, the anointing, and the laying on of hands as interrelated. He, nevertheless, planted the seed of the idea that it was the second part of the baptismal rite, the imposition of the bishop's hand, which was the outward sign of the descent of the Spirit upon the neophyte. When baptism and confirmation in later days came to be considered separate sacraments, this interpretation would be picked up to cause theological havoc. In the present century the names of Dom Gregory Dix and Fr. Lionel Thornton are identified with the view that confirmation is the "baptism of the Spirit" which is necessary to Christians, and water baptism is simply the necessary precondition for that sacrament.[11]

Our experience in the Episcopal Church in attempting to revise our rites of initiation between 1967 and 1979 leads me to conjecture that there are few full-fledged Dixians around today, but many semi-Dixians who feel that confirmation is necessary to the completeness of Christian initiation, and the full gift of the Spirit.

Both Hippolytus and Tertullian clearly knew the baptism of infants. Tertullian, as a matter of fact, was against it.[12] It is nevertheless true that the rites were directed primarily at adults. This is true also of the very similar rites described by Ambrose and Cyril of Jerusalem in the fourth century.[13] When we look at the rites of the classic Roman sacramentaries, the Gregorian and the Gelasian, on the other hand, we are dealing primarily with the baptism of children.[14] The classic pattern of the earlier rites is preserved, especially in the Gelasian Sacramentary, and it is possible to reconstruct the earlier shape of the rites as they were celebrated for adults, but in the form in which they actually appear in our surviving texts, the rites are performed over infants. This is obviously a major change, but it is scarcely reflected in the rites themselves. Adults answer in the name of the children who are "carried through" the traditional ceremonies of catechumenate, baptism, chrismation, laying on of hands, and first communion.

TWO CHANGES IN PRACTICE

It is at this point in our sources that we can observe two important changes in practice. The first is peculiar to the Roman rite, that is, the liturgy of the city of Rome and its surrounding dioceses. It is the separation of the final act of the initiation liturgy, the episcopal laying on of hands, which in Rome from the time of Hippolytus had been accompanied by a *consignatio*, a signing of the forehead of the neophyte with a cross in chrism. This *consignatio* and *impositio manus* acquire a separate identity as a sacrament of confirmation.

The Easter Vigil rite of the Gelasian Sacramentary (Vat. Reg. 316) has the ceremonies in their traditional order in a single rite. Baptism is administered as the candidates make their threefold confession of faith and are anointed with chrism by a presbyter. "Then the sevenfold Spirit is given to them by the bishop."[15] He recites a prayer for the seven gifts, imposes a hand, and signs them on the forehead with chrism. This is immediately followed by the Easter Mass with the communion of the neophytes.

When the Gelasian describes the baptism of the sick, however, the *consignatio* follows the administration of communion, and was presumably administered by the bishop upon a later occasion.[16] We know from a passage in the Sixth Book of Eusebius that it was Roman practice in the time of Pope Cornelius in the third century for the bishop to "seal" those who had been baptized by others *in extremis*.[17]

The Supplement to the Gregorian Sacramentary *Hucusque*, which we formerly thought was the work of Alcuin but is attributed by the latest scholarship to Benedict of Aniane, carries this provision one step further. It directs:

> If the bishop is present, it is fitting that he at once be confirmed with chrism, and afterward communicated. And if the bishop is absent, let him be communicated by the presbyter.[18]

Ordo Romanus XV similarly provides:

> The baptized children, if they can have the bishop present, ought to be confirmed with chrism. Which, if they are not able to obtain the bishop on the day itself, they shall do without delay, as quickly as they can obtain him.[19]

The point of all this is that where the Roman rite was followed, which soon became almost everywhere in Western Europe after Charlemagne, a new independent rite of episcopal confirmation was developing. This was not the situation in those portions of Europe where the various Gallican rites were followed. There the entire rite was performed by the celebrating priest, whether he was a bishop or presbyter.

It is somewhat ironic that the reservation of confirmation to the bishop, which is the sole reason for its separation from baptism in the Roman rite has been abandoned in the new Roman Rite for the Christian Initiation of Adults, and in the absence of the bishop the officiating presbyter is now directed to omit the customary post-baptismal anointing of the head with chrism and to substitute the *consignatio frontis,* the anointing of confirmation.[20] Thus, in one stroke the two distinctive features of Roman baptismal practice are abandoned: the double anointing by presbyter and bishop which goes back to the *Apostolic Tradition,* and the restriction of confirmation to the bishop.

The second important change in baptismal practice that we begin to observe in the medieval documents is the breakdown of the restriction of baptism to the solemn feasts of Pascha and Pentecost, and the resulting increase of baptism *quolibet tempore,* or as we say, at any old time. Although canon law still required all but emergency baptisms to be performed at Easter and Pentecost till the twelfth century, we find that, as is often the case, the regulations lagged somewhat behind the practice.[21] In 693, for example, the ecclesiastical laws of the king of Wessex decreed that children should be baptized within thirty days of their birth and provided stiff fines for parents who failed to comply.[22] We need not trace the history of this change. Suffice it to say that by the fourteenth century canon law had reversed its field and held that children must be baptized within a week of their birth.[23] This naturally resulted in the virtual elimination of the solemn baptisms of Easter and Pentecost.

The two changes combined to alter decisively Western initiatory practice. The ancient writers assumed that the bishops would personally preside at the solemn baptisms of Easter and Pentecost. So does the Gelasian Sacramentary. The Roman

Pontifical of the twelfth century, in fact, describes the pope, while proceeding to bless the font at the Lateran at the Easter Vigil, being met by the cardinals. They receive the papal blessing and are sent back to their *tituli*, or parishes as we would call them, with the admonition:

> Go, baptize your people in the Name of the Father, and of the Son, and of the Holy Spirit.[24]

The ceremony clearly expresses the bishops' presidency over the act of initiation. Since the majority of the cardinals were themselves bishops, the Roman tradition of the restriction of confirmation to bishops was preserved, but when the same tradition was reproduced in other dioceses, the effect was different. Where the Ambrosian, Visigothic, or Gallican rite prevailed, bishops did exactly what is here ritualized. They authorized parish priests to celebrate the entire rite of Christian initiation, using chrism consecrated by them for the signing of the forehead. When presbyters of the Roman rite baptized, on the other hand, they omitted the consignation, which was to be later supplied by the bishop.

When the Roman rite replaced the Gallican liturgies in the Carolingian empire, the Gallican clergy apparently did not know what to make of the new Roman practice of confirmation. They identified the traditional post-baptismal chrismation in the Roman rite with the consignation with chrism in the old Gallican rites, and were at a loss to understand the meaning of this second and later anointing. As more and more people came to be baptized by presbyters outside of the solemn Easter and Pentecost baptisms, it became increasingly important to distinguish between the now separated sacraments of baptism and confirmation. This is a process which still continues:

Rabanus Maurus in the ninth century suggested:

> Finally the Holy Ghost, the Comforter, is transmitted to him by the chief priest through the laying on of the hand, that he may be fortified through the Holy Ghost to preach to others the gift which he has himself gained in baptism.[25]

Another famous attempt is that of Faustus of Riez, whom Gregory Dix considers the source of all the later confusion about the meaning of confirmation:

The Holy Spirit bestows at the font absolutely all that is necessary to restore innocence, in confirmation he provides an increase of grace . . . In baptism we are born to new life, after baptism we are confirmed for combat.[26]

This passage made its way into the False Decretals, was quoted from them by Peter Lombard, and used by Aquinas in the *Summa*.

THE REFORMERS

This was the situation which confronted the Reformers in the sixteenth century, and to which they responded.

Calvin and Luther retained infant baptism as they knew it, reforming the rite in accordance with their principles, but of confirmation they had little kind to say. Luther, for example, says:

I allow that confirmation be administered provided that it is known that God has said nothing about it, and knows nothing of it, and what the bishops say about it is false.[27]

Calvin contributes:

This pretended sacrament is nowhere recommended in scripture, either under this name, or with this ritual, or this signification . . . And with this they joined detestable blasphemy, because they said that sins were only forgiven by baptism and that the Spirit of regeneration is given by that rotten oil which they presume to bring in without the word of God.[28]

In the face of these powerful attacks it is astounding that the rite of confirmation survived in any form in Protestantism. Both Luther and Calvin, however, believed that there had once been a "godly" form of confirmation in the church, apparently harking back to the apostolic impositions of hands in Acts. Calvin's reconstruction of this rite in the *Institutes* is this:

Those who had been baptized as infants, because they had not then made confession of faith before the Church, were at the end of their childhood or at the beginning of adolescence again presented by their parents, and were examined by the bishops according to the form of the catechism, which was then in definite form and in common use. But in order that this act, which ought by itself to have been weighty and holy, might have more reverence and dignity, the ceremony of the laying on of hands was also added. Thus the youth once his faith was approved, was dismissed with a solemn blessing.[29]

Calvin was not, of course, describing something which had actually happened in the early church, but his understanding of the meaning of confirmation became determinative for a Reformed understanding of confirmation. I believe, also, that this is the way in which Archbishop Cranmer understood the rite of confirmation which he included in the English Book of Common Prayer.[30]

What we find in the Western Churches after the sixteenth century, with the exception of those churches in the Anabaptist tradition which rejected infant baptism, is the late medieval Roman tradition. There is no catechumenate prior to baptism, except where it survived as a purely ceremonial opening rite in the baptismal liturgy. Infants are baptized soon after birth by the parish pastor. A rather serious effort is made, however, to catechize Christian young people, and the end of that formal process is normally the ministration of confirmation and admission to reception of the eucharist. The new pattern, then, is infant baptism, a post-baptismal catechumenate, followed by the confirmation of adolescents and their admission to the eucharist. Among Roman Catholics, the rites were the same ones used in the late Middle Ages. The Anglican Prayer Book in its various editions preserved water baptism, followed by the signing of the forehead with the cross (although the chrism was lost in 1552). The central act of confirmation became the "scriptural" laying on of hands by the bishop accompanied by the traditional Western prayer for the sevenfold gifts of the Spirit. Lutheran and Reformed practice is somewhat more diverse, but the same pattern persists. Confirmation becomes what the Reformers believed it should have been: a solemn blessing of children who have completed their catechesis accompanied by their admission to holy communion.

RECENT DEVELOPMENTS

The last twenty-five years have seen a great ferment in both the theology and practice of Christian initiation. Infant baptism, taken for granted by most traditions, has been called into question. Does it make any sense in our religiously pluralistic society to baptize those too young to request baptism for themselves? Would it not be better to dedicate them in some appropriate rite, and wait until they could make their own decisions about renouncing the world, the flesh, and the devil, and becoming Christ's faithful soldiers and servants in one or another of the competing regiments of his army? These questions are being asked not only by the spiritual heirs of the Anabaptists, but by Roman Catholics, Anglicans, Lutherans, Presbyterians, Methodists, and members of the United Church. The separation of baptism, confirmation, and first communion has also been called into question. The new Roman Catholic rite expects them to be reunited for adult candidates, raising the obvious question of why not for children also.[31]

I have been personally involved in the revision of the rites of initiation in the American Episcopal Church.[32] These have had three principal recensions. The first, *Prayer Book Studies 18*, dealt with the contemporary question head-on. The committee opted to retain at least the option of infant baptism, and defended the practice in their introduction.[33] They also produced an integral rite of the celebration of Christian initiation entitled "Holy Baptism, with the Laying-on-of-Hands," in which the consignation, optionally performed with chrism and accompanied by the traditional Western prayer for the seven gifts of the Spirit, immediately followed baptism in the context of the eucharist. The bishops were somewhat wary of this rite, and, although it was printed in *Services for Trial Use*, permission was given for its trial only in modified form. The rite as printed could be used only by bishops when baptizing persons who had reached the normal age for confirmation. The bishops did, nonetheless, approve the admission of unconfirmed children to reception of the eucharist.[34]

The version, which after an intermediate state in *Authorized Services 1973*[35] appeared in The Book of Common Prayer,[36] does not substantially alter the baptismal liturgy, although it does not refer to the consignation after baptism as confimation. At the theological level it identifies the consignation with the proper baptismal action. I am happy to be able to point out that this is precisely the point I made in 1966 in *Baptismal Anointing*.[37] The formula in the Prayer Book is "N., you are sealed by the Holy Spirit in Baptism and marked as Christ's own forever."[38] It immediately follows the prayer for the seven gifts of the Spirit.

Confirmation, as it appears in The Book of Common Prayer, is not the *spiritale signaculum* of the Middle Ages, which is clearly a part of the baptismal rite, but is a renewal of the baptismal covenant, accompanied by the imposition of the hand of a bishop. It is in no sense a completion of baptism.[39]

The Lutheran Book of Worship[40] seems to me to take much the same stand. The 1976 *A Service of Baptism, Confirmation, and Renewal* and the 1984 Book of Services[41] of the United Methodist Church appear to be an adaptation of these ideas to Methodist practice.

The first two numbers of the Canadian Anglican Liturgical Series[42] seem to me to carry through logically on one side of this process, uniting the laying on of hands with baptism, and providing a service of reaffirmation and commitment which is not called confirmation and does not include the imposition of hands.

The new Roman Catholic provisions raise different questions. The Rite of Christian Initiation of Adults,[43] with the restoration of the catechumenate and unified initiatory rite, raises sharply the question of who the proper candidates for initiation are, but by maintaining a pattern of baptism, first communion, and later confirmation for children, it fails to deal seriously with the question of the meaning of confirmation. Pope Paul, in the apostolic constitution on the sacrament of confirmation, calls "the seal of the Holy Spirit" the form of confirmation, but there does not seem to be general agreement about the meaning of confirmation as a rite separate from baptism. Some would make it a "rite of Christian maturity," whereas others see it as a delayed completion of baptism.[44]

I believe that we can say that there is a new pattern emerging in the Western Churches today. The question of infant and adult baptism is mooted. Both will apparently coexist. There is no doubt that adult initiation should follow the classical pattern, which is substantially that of the new Roman Catholic rite. Where children are to be baptized, the emerging consensus is that they will be initiated with a sacramental rite which includes all that the early church considered necessary for complete initiation. This is followed, either immediately or at an early age, by first communion. There is no consensus about infant communion, but there is wide agreement that young children should communicate.[45] There is also agreement that some form of "reaffirmation of vows" is necessary for those baptized in infancy, although there is none as to whether this or the post-baptismal consignation should be called confirmation.

I do not believe that we are in a position to give final answers to the questions which confront us regarding confirmation and its place in the sacramental process of initiation. We are breaking down a late medieval synthesis and developing a new one, at varying rates of speed. We need time to allow it to develop. I believe the same is true regarding the issue of infant and adult baptism. It is not nearly as clear-cut as it is sometimes thought to be. We need to allow the Holy Spirit to lead us into truth, and the Spirit does not work on our timetable. We may have to be content with a common core of *praxis* for the present, as we turn our theological and pastoral attention to theoretical answers.

Notes

1. *De Resurrectione Carnis* 8 (trans. LLM).

2. *The Roman Pontifical: Rite of Confirmation, Ordination and the Blessing of Oils*, Provisional Text (Washington, D.C.: National Conference of Catholic Bishops, 1972) 7.

3. *La Tradition apostolique de Saint Hippolyte*, ed., Bernard Botte, Liturgiewissenschaftliche Quellen und Forschungen, vol. 39 (Münster: Aschendorff, 1963) par. 21.

4. Tertullian, *De Baptismo* 8.

5. Tertullian, *De Corona* 3.

6. *Apostolic Tradition* par. 21.

7. Gregory Dix, *The Treatise on the Apostolic Tradition of St. Hippolytus of Rome*, reissued by Henry Chadwick (London: SPCK, 1968) 33-40.

8. Tertullian, *De Baptismo* 6, 8. Tr. Ernest Evans, *Tertullian's Homily on Baptism* (London: SPCK, 1964).

9. *De Baptismo* 8.

10. Ibid. 7.

11. Gregory Dix, *The Theology of Confirmation in Relation to Baptism* (Westminster: Dacre, 1946); L.S. Thornton, *Confirmation: Its Place in the Baptismal Mystery* (Westminster: Dacre, 1954).

12. *De Baptismo* 18.

13. St. Ambrose, *De Sacramentis*; St. Cyril of Jerusalem, *Mystagogical Catecheses*.

14. *Le Sacramentaire Grégorien*, ed., J. Deshusses, Specilegium Friburgensis, vol. 16 (Fribourg: Editions Universitaires, 1971) par. 356-376; *Liber Sacramentorum Romanae Aeclesiae Ordinis Anni Circuli*, ed., L.C. Mohlberg, Rerum Ecclesiasticarum Documenta, Series Maior, Fontes IV (Rome: Herder, 1960) par. 193-199, 225-228, 254-257, 283-328, 419-424, 444-462.

15. Ibid. par. 450.

16. Ibid. par. 609-615.

17. Eusebius, *Historia Ecclesiastica* 6.43.15.

18. Sac. Greg. par 1088.

19. *Ordo Romanus XV* 113-114, ed., M. Andrieu, *Les Ordines Romani du Haut Moyen Age*, vol. 2 (Louvain: Specilegium Sacrum Lovaniense, 1948) 119.

20. *Rite of Christian Initiation of Adults* (Washington, D.C.: United States Catholic Conference, 1988) par. 215-216, 231-235.

21. A. Friedberg, *Decreta Magistri Gratiani*, vol. 1 (Leipzig, 1899) 1367-1368.

22. J.D.C. Fisher, *Christian Initiation: Baptism in the Medieval West*, Alcuin Club Collections, vol. 47 (London: SPCK, 1965) 82.

23. Ibid. 109-112.

24. Michel Andrieu, ed., *Le Pontifical Romain au Moyen Age*, vol. 1, Studi e Testi (Vatican City: Bibloteca Apostolica Vaticana, 1938) par. 20, pp. 242f.

25. *De Clericorum Institutione* (PL 107:314) quoted in English from Fisher, *Medieval West* 21.

26. Dix, *Theology of Confirmation* 21.

27. *Von ehelichen Leben*, quoted from J.D.C. Fisher, *Christian Inititation: The Medieval Period*, Alcuin Club Collections, vol. 51 (London: SPCK, 1970) 172.

28. *Tracts Containing Antidote to the Council of Trent: Antidote to the Canons on Confirmation; Commentary in Acts 8.16*, both quoted from Fisher, *Reformation* 254.

29. J. Calvin, *Institutes of the Christian Religion* 4.19.4. Ed,. J.T. McNeill, trans., F.L. Battles, Library of the Christian Classics, vol. 21 (Philadelphia: Westminster, 1960) 1451f.

30. See L.L. Mitchell, "What Is Confirmation?" *Anglican Theological Review* 55 (1973) 210-212; Marion J. Hatchett, "The Rite of 'Confirmation' in The Book of Common Prayer and in *Authorized Services 1973*," *Anglican Theological Review* 56 (1974) 292-310.

31. Aidan Kavanagh, "Christian Initiation of Adults: The Rites," in *Made, Not Born* (Notre Dame: University of Notre Dame Press, 1976) 128.

32. See L.L. Mitchell, "Revision of the Rites of Christian Initiation in the American Episcopal Church," *Studia Liturgica* 10 (1974) 25-34. Reprinted as Chapter 8 in this book.

33. *Holy Baptism with the Laying-on-of-Hands: Prayer Book Studies 18 on Baptism and Confirmation* (New York: Church Pension Fund, 1970).

34. *Services for Trial Use* (New York: Church Pension Fund, 1971) v-vi.

35. *Authorized Services 1973* (New York: Church Hymnal Corporation, 1973) 1-23. A further intermediate form was published as *Holy Baptism and A Form for Confirmation for Reception and for the Reaffirmation of Baptismal Vows* (New York: Church Hymnal Corporation, 1975).

36. *The Proposed Book of Common Prayer* (New York: Church Hymnal Corporation and Seabury, 1977) 297-314, 413-421. The "Proposed" is omitted in editions after 1979 when the book was finally adopted.

37. L.L. Mitchell, *Baptismal Anointing*, Alcuin Club Collections, vol. 48 (London: SPCK, 1966) 190.

38. Ibid. 308.

39. See note 30 above.

40. *Lutheran Book of Worship* (Minneapolis: Augsburg, 1978) 121-125, 198-201. The preliminary studies were: Inter-Lutheran Commission of Worship, *Contemporary Worship 7: Holy Baptism; Contemporary Worship 8, Affirmation of the Baptismal Covenant* (Minneapolis: Augsburg, 1974, 1975).

41. United Methodist Church, *A Service of Baptism, Confirmation and Renewal* (Nashville: United Methodist Publishing House, 1976); *The Book of Services* (Nashville: United Methodist Publishing House, 1985) 52-61.

42. *Christian Initiation*, Canadian Anglican Liturgical Series, vol. 1 (Toronto: Anglican Book Centre, 1974); *Membership: Its Meaning and Expression*, Canadian Anglican Liturgical Series, vol. 2 (Toronto: Anglican Book Centre, 1975).

43. *Rite of Christian Initiation of Adults* (Washington, D.C.: United States Catholic Conference, 1988).

44. See Urban T. Holmes, *Confirmation* (New York: Seabury, n.d.).

45. Urban T. Holmes, *Young Children and the Eucharist* (New York: Seabury, 1972).

12

Sunday
as a Baptismal Day

SUNDAY IS NOT ONLY THE DAY OF THE LORD'S RESURECTION, IT IS THE first day of creation and the day of the pentecostal outpouring of the Holy Spirit on the apostolic church. Sunday is therefore the day of the Trinity with specific biblical reference to each of the three persons of the godhead.

Sunday is also the day of the church. It is the day of the eucharistic assembly and the traditional day for celebrating the other great sacrament of our participation in the paschal mystery, holy baptism. Clearly the great vigil of Easter is the primary traditional baptismal day, but the weekly Pascha too is an appropriate and traditional occasion for baptism. Tertullian wrote:

> The Passover provides the day of most solemnity for baptism, for then was accomplished our Lord's passion, and into it we are baptized . . . After that, Pentecost is a most auspicious period for arranging baptisms, for during it our Lord's resurrection was several times made known among the disciples, and the grace of the Holy Spirit first given.[1]

It is this tradition to which the first Anglican Book of Common Prayer in 1549 referred when it began its baptismal rite with this extended rubric:

It appeareth by ancient writers, that the Sacrament of Baptism, in the old time was not commonly administered but at two times in the year, at Easter and Whitsuntide, at which time it was openly ministered in the presence of the congregation: Which custom (now being grown out of use) although it cannot for many considerations be well restored, yet it is thought good to follow the same as near as conveniently may be: Wherefore the people are to be admonished, that it is most convenient that Baptism should not be ministered but upon Sundays and other holy days, when the most number of people may come together. As for that the congregation there present may testify the receiving of them that be newly Baptized, into the number of Christ's Church, as also because in the Baptism of infants, every man present may be put in remembrance of his own profession made to God in his baptism.[2]

The Anglican tradition is not alone in its desire to celebrate baptism on Sundays. The Roman Catholic Rite of Baptism for Children includes the statement:

To bring out the paschal character of baptism, it is recommended that the sacrament be celebrated during the Easter vigil or on Sunday, when the Church commemorates the Lord's resurrection. On Sunday, baptism may be celebrated even during Mass, so that the entire community may be present and the necessary relationship between baptism and eucharist may be clearly seen.[3]

This rubric is retained in most traditions for theological and practical reasons. Since baptism is a sacrament of our participation in the dying and rising again of Jesus Christ, celebrating it on the weekly day of resurrection is appropriate theologically. Since it is the sacrament of our incorporation into the church, celebrating it when the church assembles to perform its characteristic action, the Sunday eucharist, is appropriate. Since baptism has traditionally been described as "enlightenment," celebrating it on the day of the creation of light is appropriate; since it is the sacrament in which we receive the Holy Spirit, celebrating it on the day of the Spirit's outpouring is appropriate; and since baptism is the action of the Father, Son, and Holy Spirit, what better occasion to celebrate it than the day that focuses on the action of the holy Trinity?

A second theological reason derives from the intrinsic connection between baptism and eucharist. Baptism and eucharist have a common content: our participation in the mystery of Christ's death and resurrection. Once for all in baptism and week by week in the eucharist, we enter into union with Jesus Christ in the power of his redemptive acts of dying and rising for us and for our salvation. Baptism is most properly celebrated in close association with the eucharist, so that the incorporation of the new members into the Body of Christ is sealed by their participation as members of that Body in its most distinctive act, the eucharistic feast, and by their reception, as the Body of Christ, of the body of Christ.

The second-century account of baptism in the First Apology of Justin Martyr concludes with the newly baptized being led into the eucharistic assembly of the faithful where they participate in the prayers of the faithful, the exchange of the kiss of peace, the offering of the gifts, and the reception of communion.[4] A similar conclusion to baptism is found in the early third-century description in the *Apostolic Tradition* of Hippolytus.[5] The same connection is found today in the Rite of Christian Initiation of Adults, The Book of Common Prayer, and The Lutheran Book of Worship,[6] all of which assume that the baptismal rite will be concluded by a eucharistic celebration.

RENEWAL OF THE BAPTISMAL COVENANT

When considered from the viewpoint of Christian initiation, the eucharist is the final repeatable act of the rite of initiation. What is renewed whenever we celebrate the holy eucharist and receive the body and blood of Christ is our indissoluble baptismal covenant. Since Sunday is the eucharistic day par excellence, it is also the baptismal day par excellence.

Baptism then is not only associated with Sunday in all its symbolic meanings, but it is placed in the center of the worshiping life of the Christian congregation, so that, as the 1549 Book of Common Prayer reminded us, our participation in the baptism of others may be the occasion for the renewal of our own baptismal commitment. The life of the entire Body is renewed by the incorporation of new members, and it is symbolically most significant that the congregation be present in more than token form for its celebration. It is typical of the privatization of worship, so characteristic not only in the late Middle Ages and the Reformation but also much of our own contemporary culture, that the congregation's participation in baptism is seen in individual rather than corporate terms. If baptism truly is the sacrament of Christian initiation, then it is the concern not only of the candidates and their family and friends but of the entire congregation. The event is more than a spiritual opportunity for individuals to renew the covenant that binds its members to the head and to one another. The individuals in the congregation are renewed because the Body of which they are the members is renewed, and the Body is renewed because its members are renewed not only on the occasion of, but also by the addition of, new members.

In most membership organizations the initiation of new members is a major event in their annual calendars. All existing members ordinarily attempt to participate in the initiation rite. What is so abundantly clear to volunteer firefighters, the American Legion, the Odd Fellows, and the Knights of Columbus does not always seem to be that clear to Christians; baptism has sometimes been celebrated as a quasi-private ceremony for the candidate's family and friends.

THE MOVEMENT TO PUBLIC BAPTISM

The restoration of public baptism has been a significant goal of the liturgical movement, and in this area the movement has had a high degree of success. The present Prayer Book of the Episcopal Church, for example, provides: "Holy Baptism is appropriately administered within the Eucharist as the chief service on a Sunday or other feast.[7] Similarly, the Lutheran Book of Worship says: "Baptism should be celebrated within the chief service of the congregation.[8]

The celebration of baptism as a private, or quasi-private, service, even on Sunday, misses one of the major points of Sunday baptism and saps the strength of the symbolism. As Alexander Schmemann so eloquently reminded us:

> From an act of the whole Church, involving the whole cosmos, [baptism] became a perfectly private ceremony, performed in a dark corner of the church, by "private appointment," and in which the Church was reduced to "minister of the sacraments"

and the cosmos to the three symbolic drops of water, considered as "necessary and sufficient" for the "validity" of the sacrament.[9]

The celebration of baptism as part of the Sunday eucharist, with the participation of the assembly, is the most obvious way not only of avoiding this particular difficulty but also of positively affirming baptism as the action of the whole church and as integral to its life.

These two ideas, Sunday baptism and baptism at the eucharist can, of course, be separated and frequently have been in practice. Baptism is celebrated on Sunday, but not as part of the eucharistic celebration, and baptism is celebrated in conjunction with the eucharist, but not on Sunday. The Reformed tradition has generally celebrated baptism at its noneucharistic Sunday services, and for three hundred years the Anglican tradition associated baptism with Sunday evensong. This practice, of course, makes evident the connection of baptism with the life of the congregation, but it does not manifest its close connection to the eucharist.

Roman Catholics, although insistent that the baptism of adults should normally take place at the eucharist at which the neophytes receive their first communion, seem to consider this practice unnecessary, or even undesirable, for the baptism of children; the baptismal rite permits it but warns: "This should not be done too often."[10] The Roman Catholic baptismal liturgy for children, as it appears in the official text, clearly expects that children will be baptized on Sunday and presumes some sort of liturgical assembly. One wonders how often in practice the assembly is simply the baptismal parties, with baptism again playing no part in the ongoing liturgical life of the congregation.

Sometimes baptism is celebrated at the eucharist on a day other than Sunday. Epiphany in many parts of the church has been a day for a public baptism, although it has generally been replaced in the Western Churches today by the feast of the Baptism of Christ on the following Sunday. Certainly the public celebration of baptism may be appropriate on occasions other than Sunday. Such occasions include the principal holy days, such as Epiphany or All Saints, which have baptismal themes and are celebrated as if they were Sundays. Here the active participation of a large congregation and a clearly suitable occasion outweigh the more theoretical reasons for preferring a Sunday. A holy-day celebration of baptism is certainly preferable to Sunday baptisms celebrated apart from any public service.

Occasionally a baptismal eucharist is celebrated on a weekday for purely practical reasons, such as the availability of specific persons—presiding ministers or godparents. The Episcopal Prayer Book, for example, suggests the bishop's visitation, often on a weekday evening, as an appropriate occasion for the celebration of baptisms.[11] This will, of course, be a well-attended service, often better prepared and more festively celebrated than the Sunday eucharist. Sometimes the inability of parents or sponsors to be present on Sunday morning suggests another time. A reasonable pastoral criterion for deciding the appropriateness of this decision may be to consider whether the baptism will be truly an assembly of the church or merely an excuse for a private celebration.

There are, of course, practical problems involved in having baptisms as part of the Sunday liturgy. In a congregation with many baptisms, the baptismal liturgy could easily become a weekly event. The Roman Catholic rite for children expressly warns against having baptisms at Sunday Mass too frequently, and Anglican and Lutheran service books suggest that baptism be regularly scheduled on specific occasions. The Lutheran Book of Worship recommends:

> It is appropriate to designate such occasions as the Vigil of Easter, All Saints Day, and The Baptism of Our Lord for the celebration of Holy Baptism. Baptismal celebrations on these occasions keep Baptism integrated into the unfolding of the story of salvation provided by the church year. Such baptismal celebrations allow full attention to be focused on the matter of initiation in a way which is impossible when baptism is celebrated every few Sundays.[12]

A similar recommendation and list of baptismal feasts is in the Anglican Prayer Book.[13] By and large, people have responded positively to baptism as part of their regular Sunday worship, when it is so restricted. For many small congregations, five or six baptismal feasts each year will be sufficient, and initiation can, as the Lutheran Book of Worship suggests, become the focus of the congregation's worship on that day. Larger congregations need to be more careful in their planning.

One large Roman Catholic parish schedules baptisms at the Saturday evening Mass once a month. This makes it possible for children to be baptized within a month of their birth and prevents over-using the baptismal liturgy. Other large congregations with multiple Sunday services schedule monthly baptisms at different services, so that the baptism may take place at the service the family usually attends, without having too many baptisms at any one service.

Other practical problems, such as the increased length of the service when baptism is celebrated, can often be met by careful advance planning. Sometimes rearrangement of the schedule is helpful. What is necessary is a conviction of the importance of celebrating baptism as part of the regular Sunday worship of the congregation and not as a private service scheduled for the convenience of friends and relatives. If the celebration of baptism at a principal Sunday liturgy is important to the community, ways will soon be found to overcome practical difficulties.

INITIATING CHANGE

My own experience, and that of many parish clergy who worked hard to introduce their congregations to public Sunday baptism, has been that the congregation's liturgical life has been enriched by the practice. Baptism takes its proper place as the sacrament of entrance into the church and becomes real in people's lives. Once they experience baptism as part of the ongoing round of liturgical celebration of the mystery of salvation, they are no longer willing to settle for baptism apart from the parish liturgy, even at the cost of inconvenience.

More rarely, parents feel that their children are being cheated by being baptized with other children and not having "their own" baptism. But if the baptism is well done, and followed by a congregational celebration of the event in the parish house with coffee and cake, the objections often vanish. For the many congregations that regularly follow their Sunday eucharist with a coffee hour, the baptism provides a focus for a gathering already scheduled. For those that do not do this every Sunday, baptismal Sundays become occasions.

Many clergy and parish liturgists will express their intellectual assent to these observations but when planning baptismal liturgies will do "what we have always done." I continue to be astounded by the number of congregations that have thoroughly reformed and renewed the Sunday eucharist and left baptism in its privatized medieval state. Others have completely renewed their practice of adult baptism, following the Roman Catholic Rite of Christian Initiation of Adults or their own church's version thereof, and left their practice of infant baptism unchanged.

A number of reasons are put forward for this reluctance to change baptismal practice; the most common is the supposed conservatism of the laity and their unwillingness to alter longstanding habits. Considering the waves of liturgical change that have broken over most congregations since 1964, it seems more likely that it is the clergy who are unwilling to make one more change.

It is, in fact, easier to explain to adult candidates that their baptism will be at the Easter Vigil or on Pentecost and to give them solid reasons for it than it is to deal with parents and godparents who have not been part of a program of baptismal preparation. Perhaps we should devote attention to parental and congregational preparation for infant baptism comparable to the effort expended on adult baptismal preparation. The existence in the same congregation of two distinct baptismal practices, one for adults and one for children, creates the real danger that the theologies of infant and adult baptism will become as different as their praxis: the "one baptism" will divide into two separate and unequal rites supported by different theologies—but that is another problem.

Tertullian, in the passage quoted earlier, concludes his discussion of the proper occasion for baptism by saying: "For all that, every day is a Lord's day: any hour, any season, is suitable for baptism. If there is a difference of solemnity, it makes no difference to the grace."[14] I suspect that his belief is shared by many "practical" liturgists. Baptism is valid and efficacious whenever it is celebrated, so what is all the fuss about? Certainly this is true, if we are talking about real necessity. Our concern today, however, focuses on the fullness of the sacramental sign. We want tasty, chewable bread, red wine, aromatic chrism, and lots of splashing water. Good, but certainly the Body of Christ is a primary sacramental sign. When the Body gathers to celebrate the Lord's service on the Lord's Day, it most clearly symbolizes and ritualizes what is being done if on that occasion it grafts new members into Christ and into itself.

Notes

1. Tertullian, *De Baptismo* 19; cited from E.C. Whitaker, *Documents of the Baptismal Liturgy* (London: SPCK, 1970) 9.

2. F.E. Brightman, *The English Rite* 724 (spelling modernized).

3. "Rite of Baptism for Children" 9, in *The Rites of the Catholic Church* (New York: Pueblo Publishing Co., 1976) 191.

4. *I Apology* 65.

5. *Apostolic Tradition* 21.

6. In the Lutheran Book of Worship it is provided that: "Older children and adults should commune for the first time during the service in which they are baptized. Infants may be brought to the altar and receive a blessing." It also expects baptism to be celebrated "within the chief service of the congregation." Although this does not require that baptisms be celebrated at the eucharist, it implies that it is normative, and extensive directions are given for so doing. See *Lutheran Book of Worship*, Ministers Desk Edition (Minneapolis: Augsburg Publishing House, 1978) 30.

7. *The Book of Common Prayer* (New York: Church Hymnal Corporation., 1979) 298.

8. *Lutheran Book of Worship*, Ministers Desk Edition 30.

9. Alexander Schmemann, *For the Life of the World* (New York: National Christian Student Federation, 1963) 47.

10. "The Rite of Baptism for Children," *The Rites* 191.

11. *The Book of Common Prayer* 312.

12. *Lutheran Book of Worship*, Ministers Desk Edition 30.

13. *The Book of Common Prayer* 312.

14. Tertullian, *De Baptismo* 9.